Also by Karen Kingsbury:

MISSY'S MURDER

QUANTITY SALES

Most Dell books are available at special quantity discounts when purchased in bulk by corporations, organizations, or groups. Special imprints, messages, and excerpts can be produced to meet your needs. For more information, write to: Dell Publishing, 666 Fifth Avenue, New York, NY 10103. Attention: Director, Diversified Sales.

Please specify how you intend to use the books (e.g., promotion, resale, etc.).

INDIVIDUAL SALES

Are there any Dell books you want but cannot find in your local stores? If so, you can order them directly from us. You can get any Dell book currently in print. For a complete up-to-date listing of our books and information on how to order, write to: Dell Readers Service, Box DR, 666 Fifth Avenue, New York, NY 10103.

Carol Montecalvo—Eight years of marriage to Dan had left her estranged from her family, seventy pounds overweight, but still deeply in love.

Dan Montecalvo—His drinking had gotten worse, his gambling debts were piling up, and his wife, Carol, was insured for a half-million dollars.

Suzan Brown—She knew something about the night Carol died, but could she be trusted?

Brian Arnspiger—A cop's cop with his instincts screaming that Dan had killed his wife—all Brian had to do was get the evidence.

Ben Bernard—He was a smooth, incredibly good prosecutor, and he knew how to make every innuendo, every damning fact count to convict Dan.

Lorn Aiken—He was a red-hot defense attorney who never took on a client who lied to him; he was prepared to bring up the forgotten footprints, the rifled cash box, the missing guns, the slit screen door to prove Dan's innocence.

Maree Flores—She never thought she'd fall in love again, and this soft, sweet woman had . . . with a man on trial for murder.

FINAL VOWS

VOWS

MURDER, MADNESS
AND TWISTED JUSTICE
IN CALIFORNIA

•

KAREN KINGSBURY

A DELL BOOK

Published by
Dell Publishing
a division of
Bantam Doubleday Dell Publishing Group, Inc.
666 Fifth Avenue
New York, New York 10103

The trademark Dell® is registered in the U.S. Patent and Trademark Office.

ISBN: 0-440-21198-0

Printed in the United States of America

Published simultaneously in Canada

October 1992

10 9 8 7 6 5 4 3 2 1

OPM

Dedicated
to

Donald,
for your unending love and support.
My love for you is stronger
than I thought possible.

Little Norm,
my inspiration.
I love you so much, Norm.

Dad, Mom, Sue, David, Tricia, and Lynne,
for your love and encouragement.

Don and Betty, Phyllis and Sonny,
my second family.

Jo Ann,
for making me laugh,
and always saving me a spade when I go nil.
Even when we're not playing cards.

And especially to the Good Lord,
who has always given me life abundantly.

ACKNOWLEDGMENTS

I would like to thank the people who helped make this book possible. First, a special thanks to Brian Arnspiger, whose energy and abilities as a detective are unequalled; and to Ben Bernard, who is without a doubt one of the most brilliant prosecutors ever. Thank you for helping me decipher 8,600 pages of evidence.

Also, thanks to Lorn Aiken, Chuck Lefler, and Gene Brisco. Your dedication in standing behind a man you believe to be innocent is admirable and makes you a credit to your occupations. Thank you for everything.

I would also like to thank my husband for having a limitless amount of patience while this project pulled me away from home time and again. Donald, without you I could never have pulled this off. I love you.

Thanks also go to my father, Ted Kingsbury, for acting as my primary sounding-board throughout the writing of this book. And to my mom, Anne Kingsbury, for being my West Coast publicity specialist. You've helped me more than you know. I love you, both.

A special thanks to Pam, Sue, and the preschool staff as well as to Carrie Foster.

Finally, I would like to thank Leslie Schnur for believing in my work; Mitch Horowitz and Mercer Warriner for their editorial brilliance; and Arthur Pine for pushing me forward. I consider myself privileged to be working with all of you.

AUTHOR'S EXPLANATORY NOTE

The events described in this book are taken directly from court transcripts and other public records and documents, as well as from numerous interviews with the many people involved. However, in many instances, to better communicate the story and the atmosphere surrounding the events, incidents and dialogue were dramatically recreated based on court testimony and other public records, and interviews with various participants or other knowledgeable individuals.

May Atwater, Ralph Atwater, Kevin Bennington, Ben Bernard, Laura Bernard, Joe Gamboda, Ron Hardy, Cathy Hines, Dan Hines, Tricia Lynn, Jack McKenzie, Donald S. Meine, Raj Rakia, Vic Santinni, Carmelo Tronconi, Jon Tronconi, Maria Tronconi, Roseanna Tronconi, and Annette Wilder, and the names of a few other minor characters, are all pseudonyms. The author has chosen to change these names and disguise the identities of certain of the people involved in this story. This has been done to preserve privacy. Any similarity between the fictitious names used and those of living persons is, of course, entirely coincidental.

1

On the evening of March 31, 1988, just after 10:30, Carol Montecalvo reached into her dresser drawer for a pair of lightweight blue shorts, folded them neatly in half, and placed them inside her brown vinyl suitcase. Hawaii would be warmer than Burbank, California, where spring temperatures often dropped to the low 50s at night, and Carol had packed several pairs of big, baggy shorts. She sorted through her nearly full suitcase. A few more items and she would be finished.

Easing herself slowly onto the bed, she drew in a deep breath and ran her fingers through her short, dark brown hair. It was hard to believe that in less than twelve hours she and Dan would be on an airplane leaving the hectic pace of Los Angeles County for the peaceful Hawaiian Islands. Carol closed her eyes and silently began to pray.

Her expectations for this trip were high. Lately she had grown more and more concerned about her husband's drinking. The problem had not yet affected their marriage, which Carol believed was still better than most even after nearly eight years. As far as she knew, Dan didn't cheat, didn't complain about the weight she'd gained in recent years, and for most of their marriage hadn't let alcohol cross his lips.

The problems had started in 1986 when a bleeding

ulcer had forced Dan to quit work. Not long afterward he began drinking to ease his frustration and boredom. At first he took only a few mixed drinks in the evenings but after a year of unemployment, drinking had become part of his daily routine. Sometimes he was so drunk Carol would wonder how he drove home from the bars without killing someone.

Carol began to think up ways she could rescue him and improve their marriage—before the alcohol could do permanent damage to both. She believed Dan needed only some time away, a place where he could regain the faith in God he'd had early in their marriage. There had been just one problem. Because of Dan's disability they had barely enough money to buy groceries. Carol tried to imagine ways they might scrape together the money for a trip, but the demands of day-to-day living were always too costly. A getaway vacation would be financially impossible.

At about that time, Carol began to pray that God would somehow provide them with the means.

Answered prayer came in the form of a sales contest sponsored by her employer—Pacific Bell Yellow Pages. First prize: An all-expenses-paid trip to Hawaii. The couple had visited Hawaii early in their marriage and during their stay had fallen even deeper in love with each other. Hawaii, she decided, would be the perfect place for Dan to rediscover that love, abandon alcohol, and come home a changed man.

Carol knew the changes would need to be drastic. By late 1987, Dan had turned fifty. He had slid even deeper into depression and alcohol abuse, perhaps because he realized he was no longer a young man and would have fewer opportunities to turn his life around. Carol, who at forty-two was no less in love with her husband than she had been the day she'd married him, knew this trip might be Dan's only chance.

The more Carol thought about the vacation the harder she worked. Through the end of 1987 and into 1988 there were evenings she wouldn't come home until eight or nine o'clock when she was certain she couldn't sell one more ad. In January when the company named Carol the Southern California winner, no one was less surprised than her supervisor. In fifteen years with the telephone company, Laura Annetelli had never seen a sales representative sell ads like Carol Montecalvo.

Carol could hardly wait to tell Dan the good news.

If Dan had been thrilled later that night when he came home from the bars and heard about the trip, he was most likely too drunk to remember. Carol patiently repeated the story the next morning, refusing to allow Dan's increasing reliance on alcohol to dampen her excitement.

The hopes and dreams of her entire lifetime took shape as Carol began planning the vacation. The Montecalvos scheduled it for April and even saved enough money to lengthen their trip by two days. More than a week in Hawaii and surely Dan would be more relaxed, his ulcer might get better, and they could make plans for their future. Best of all, Carol believed with all her heart that Dan would stop drinking during this vacation. In fact, she believed the trip could quite possibly change their entire lives.

"Want to take a walk?" Dan sauntered into their bedroom combing his hair as he glanced at the open suitcase on the bed. He had been packing in the next room and taking care of last-minute necessities before the trip. "I could use a break."

Carol smiled and held out her hand. She was a short woman of Italian ancestry who kept her dark hair attractively cut close to her plump face. Those who knew her agreed that Carol's eyes were by far her best feature —sparkling brown eyes that were every bit as full of compassion as they were full of life. In fact, she would have been quite pretty if not for the extra seventy pounds she carried.

Carol took great pains to hide her weight by wearing fashionably loose black and navy clothing and by always adding matching stockings, shoes, and accessories to her outfit. Makeup was also important to Carol, and she rarely left for a day at the office without painstakingly applying the subtle peach and brown hues that brought her soft face to life. She took pride in her appearance, and perhaps she wanted to imagine herself as she had been the day she married Dan—a much slimmer 130 pounds.

If Dan minded Carol's excess weight, he never said so. Carol had even commented to friends that Dan had always been patient and understanding about the weight she had gained over the years. In fact, outsiders tended to notice Carol's weight far more quickly than her husband did. Although several inches taller than Carol, Dan was a rather small man; therefore, when the two of them stood together, Carol's weight tended to be more obvious to others. In addition, Dan seemed to shrink in comparison, appearing even smaller than he actually was.

Carol, however, saw Dan as larger than life. He had the inexplicable ability to charm her and the shy, humble way he spoke to her still made her weak at the knees. Although she was aware of Dan's troubled past, she thought him a handsome misunderstood gentleman with charming black-brown eyes, black hair, and a dashing mustache.

In truth, Dan was born and raised in Boston, and his accent, one associated with the poorer sections of that city, reflected his lack of education. But that did not change Carol's opinion of Dan. No matter that he looked like the gangsters in B-rated films, she thought he bore many similarities to James Dean in *Rebel Without a Cause*.

Carol's friends smiled politely when she talked about Dan that way, lending further credence to the notion that love really was blind. Not that they found Dan unattractive. He simply was not the prince charming Carol made him out to be. Dan stood five-eight, 170 pounds, and wore his thin black hair short and slicked back toward the right side of his head. His voice had a hard edge from years of cigarette smoking.

There had been a time when women had enjoyed Dan's dark looks, but that time had long since expired. What had once been a pleasant, baby face was now spoiled by a slightly ruddy complexion from excessive alcohol consumption, and troubled, beady dark eyes. And while not overweight, he was beginning to soften around the middle and no longer possessed the type of physique that most women admired. Either way, their friends at Overcomers' Faith Center Christian Church believed that physical shortcomings mattered little to the Montecalvos, who always seemed so happy and in love with each other.

That night appearances were the last thing on their minds. Dan clasped Carol's outstretched hand and helped her up, waiting for her response. She shook her head and yawned. "Not tonight. I still have a lot of packing to do."

Dan pulled her into a hug, and began stroking her hair. "I just wanted to start this vacation a day early. Come on, it'll be quick. Just a walk around the block."

Carol laughed at his persistence. "Okay, okay. You win." She kissed him on the cheek. "I'll walk. But let's make it a short one. What time is it anyway?"

Carol slipped her flip-flop sandals on as Dan glanced at his watch. "Quarter to eleven. Think you'll be warm enough?"

Carol nodded. Although her office dress was impeccable, at home she was most comfortable wearing flip-flops, sweatpants, and casual blouses. Occasionally, like that evening, she would even go without a bra. Carol didn't care what anyone thought of her need to be casual after work. In her opinion, home was all about feeling safe and comfortable.

She followed Dan down the hallway of their three-bedroom home and out the front door. "If it gets a little cold we'll just walk faster."

Dan shut the door, testing it to be sure it was locked. "Same way?" he asked, nodding his head in a northerly direction up South Myers Street.

"Same way," she answered.

Four or five times a week the Montecalvos walked in that direction, past several neighbors' houses, around the block, and back home to the house they had shared since Christmas 1985. Dan took Carol's hand in his and the couple started walking.

Fifty yards down the street they passed Suzan Brown's house. Earlier that March evening, like most evenings, Suzan had been busy building Popsicle-stick lampshades in her garage. This habit was not the only indication of the forty-two-year-old woman's oddities. She was also in a wheelchair, seemingly without reason. Her neighbors routinely saw Suzan romping about her backyard playing with her three dogs and appearing perfectly able-bodied—the chair nowhere to be seen.

If that wasn't enough, Suzan's appearance raised more than a few eyebrows around the neighborhood. She was heavyset and wore her brown hair short and straight, cropped close to her head. On her arms were tattoos of anchors and hearts and whenever she dressed up she'd wear men's trousers and dress shirts. In fact, if a person didn't know her, he or she might easily have mistaken her for a middle-aged man.

Most of the time Suzan's sexual preference tended toward women—many of whom she had met while serving time in jail for various charges. But occasionally she would date men—especially those who looked like her.

Although Suzan sometimes sold Avon products and once in a while received five dollars for one of her Popsicle-stick lampshades, her primary means of support came from a monthly military pension for her role as a nurse in Vietnam and from a monthly government disability check. Even with that money, she could not afford to lease her one-thousand-dollar-per-month home in Dan and Carol's stable neighborhood without her roommates. It seemed to Suzan's neighbors—none of whom were fond of her—that the woman was always taking in new boarders. Word around the neighborhood was that some of these boarders contributed by paying a portion of the rent and providing drugs for Suzan's weekly parties.

South Myers Street was lined with fruitless pear trees that in the summer fanned out to form a green archway over the road. Set back twenty feet from the sidewalk, the single-story homes were quaintly small with adequate front and backyards separated by beige cement block walls. This was the kind of neighborhood that typified Burbank.

For the most part, these rather plain homes were built in the 1950s and still housed the original owners. A majority of the residents along South Myers were getting on in years, their houses paid off and their children moved away. They could sometimes be seen sitting on their front porches in the middle of the afternoon sipping lemonade and discussing the virtues of being Republican.

But occasionally, as with the Montecalvo home, the houses had been sold to new families. As is often the case when this sort of turnover begins, some of the homes had been sold to people whom neighbors saw at odds with Burbank's quiet image. Worse, some of the houses had been rented to unstable low-income people whom longtime Burbank residents found quite distasteful.

This was how neighbors viewed Suzan Brown. Although her rent included a weekly gardening service which maintained the property, Suzan often kept her garage door open allowing anyone who passed by to see the disarray inside. This was not an acceptable practice along South Myers Street. Also, shady characters frequently drove by Suzan's home, stopping for only a moment, and returning to their cars counting what appeared to be currency. Drugs had never been a problem on the quiet street, but neighbors felt certain Suzan Brown was buying and selling something more than Avon.

Many of the neighbors had long since agreed that Suzan was a crazy woman. They even suspected her and some of her transient boarders of performing a handful of burglaries that had been happening in the neighborhood in recent years.

Because of that, they kept a close eye on the woman. Almost every night, often dressed in the same shorts and tank top, she would roll her wheelchair out the front door and into the garage at exactly 8 o'clock. Then she would spend nearly three hours making Popsicle-stick lampshades before going back into the house for the 11 o'clock news. Many nights her routine included looking for Dan and Carol sometime between 10 and 10:30. The couple walked nearly every evening, and watching them pass was one way Suzan gauged the time. After 10:30 Suzan stopped looking. By her assessment, the couple never walked later than that.

So when the Montecalvos strolled past her house that evening at 10:50, Dan did not notice whether Suzan was sitting in her garage. Perhaps, in keeping with her schedule, she had already gone in for the night, or maybe the couple had been too wrapped up in their conversation to notice her. Or perhaps, as defense attorneys and investigators would later contend, Suzan had been so busy orchestrating a neighborhood burglary that night that she had spent only an hour or so making her lampshades. Unaware of any of those possibilities or the importance they would have in later years, Dan and Carol continued their walk without any discussion of their quirky neighbor.

As the Montecalvos made their way around the block and back up South Myers Street toward home they did not cross the street until they had passed the house of their next-door neighbor, Ralph Atwater. The Montecalvos did this on purpose to avoid Ralph's German shepherds. The dogs barked whenever anyone walked near Ralph's property.

At 10:56 that evening, Ralph was caught up in a routine of his own as he prepared for bed and the 11 o'clock news. His wife had been asleep for some time, but he rarely went to bed before the news.

He pulled his striped pajama top over his head and turned back the covers on his side of the bed. Ralph's wife, May, thought it odd that her husband liked to end his day watching the news. After all, there was nothing good in the news. Natural disasters. Crooked politicians. Senseless murders. Innocent people getting the raw end of the stick. Most people had enough real-life problems without getting tangled up in the sorry affairs of perfect strangers.

Ralph only laughed at his wife's assessment. He thought the news was exciting. Amazing and terrible things happening to real people. Drama at its best. Never did he feel more in tune with the world around him than after watching the 11 o'clock news. He picked up the remote control, turned the television on, and hit the mute button. Fixing his eyes straight ahead at the small color set, Ralph waited.

At exactly 11 o'clock, the familiar faces of ABC's news anchors flashed across the screen. Ralph hit the mute button again, allowing sound to accompany the pictures. The introductions rolled on in typical upbeat news fashion. Ralph rather liked the opening theme song of the network news. He turned the volume up a level, glancing over to be sure the sound wasn't disturbing his wife.

But at 11:01, when the song was almost finished, a different sound caught his attention. It was frantic—a scream or cry perhaps, and it seemed to be coming from next door. Quickly Ralph hit the mute button again and turned toward the noise. For nearly ten seconds Ralph tried to make out the voices, but he could tell only that someone was very frightened and upset. For a split second the voices stopped and Ralph listened, perfectly still in the silent room. At that moment the quiet was broken by two sudden blasts of what seemed to be a car backfiring. Before Ralph had time to analyze the sounds, another single crack rang out.

Next to him, May sat straight up in bed.

"What happened?" she asked, her eyes filled with panic. "What was that?"

Ralph knew instinctively the sounds had nothing to do with a car's exhaust system.

"Gunfire," he whispered. "Sounded like three shots."

May reached for her husband's arm and he could feel her hands shaking. "What should we do?"

Ralph climbed out of bed and walked to the window that directly faced the Montecalvo's home. The two families did not socialize together, but they were casual acquaintances and Dan had asked Ralph to water their lawn while they were in Hawaii.

"They don't leave until tomorrow, do they?" he asked.

"No. Why, what do you see over there?"

"Nothing, nothing. But it sounded like the shots came from next door."

"Oh, my God, Ralph. What if something happened to them?"

Slowly, he walked over and sat down on the bed. His mind raced with ideas of what he might do if Dan and Carol really were in trouble. But before he could form a plan, he heard sirens in the distance. In seconds, they were closer and Ralph was certain they were headed toward 315 South Myers, where the Montecalvos lived.

At that same moment, five houses down the street, the 11 o'clock news was four minutes old when Suzan Brown thought she heard something in her backyard. She, too, muted her television set and listened intently. It sounded like her woodpile had come crashing down, but now there was only silence. Suddenly she remembered the three loud sounds she'd heard a few minutes earlier. She began considering possible connections between those sounds and the noise she had just heard in her backyard when in the distance she heard sirens getting closer.

Back at the Atwater home Ralph went to the window again and watched as the first police car arrived. A uniformed officer with his gun drawn carefully climbed out, using the car door as a shield. Keeping his head low, the officer darted silently across the street. Ralph was glued to the scene, horrified and unable to believe that a crime, maybe even a murder, had just occurred in his neighborhood.

At 11:06, with Ralph intent on the scene unfolding next door, the Atwaters' dogs began barking. They were so loud he was sure they would ruin the officer's cover.

"Darn dogs," Ralph whispered as May joined him at the window. "Bark at anything."

More than once Ralph had vowed to get rid of the dogs. The slightest thing could set them off and once they got started they could bark for an hour or more without letting up. They barked whenever anyone walked near the property.

Now something terrible had happened next door and his dogs were barking so loudly they were going to give the officer away. Ralph believed the gunmen were still inside the Montecalvo house. Unless of course they had fled the other way—northbound toward Suzan Brown's house and away from his dogs.

After all, until the officer arrived, his dogs hadn't barked once all evening.

2

The call came through to the Burbank Police Department that evening at 11:03 and 40 seconds. Telecommunications operator Janet Brown answered the call and immediately the computerized 911 emergency system displayed the caller's address and telephone number on Janet's terminal screen. At the same time, the system's reel-to-reel recording device clicked into action.

"Emergency nine one one, what's your message please?" The young operator spoke quickly and calmly as she had been trained to do.

"Please help me, hurry up!" The man was hysterical, screaming and sobbing as he spoke, and Janet could not understand him.

"Sir, you can't breathe? Is that what you're saying?"

"We've been shot!"

"What?" Janet was straining to understand the man.

"Shot! My wife's bleeding, she's dying. Hurry!"

For a moment the man continued to sob into the telephone while Janet and her coworker, Faye Malcolm, began sending emergency calls to police in the area.

"Please. Please hurry," the man pleaded.

"They're on the way, sir, they're on the way."

Then, at 11:04 and 20 seconds, the caller hung up, apparently convinced that help would soon arrive.

Instantly, Janet redialed the telephone number that appeared on the screen while Faye informed police and paramedics that someone at 315 South Myers Street had just been shot.

At 11:05 the phone rang in Dan and Carol Montecalvos' house. Dan answered it on the second ring.

"Hello?"

For a split second, Janet Brown thought she had the wrong number. Either she had caught the man between sobs or this was not the same hysterical caller she'd spoken with a minute earlier. Then, before Janet had a chance to identify herself, the man again began crying loudly.

"Hello?" he shouted. When the man recognized the voice of the emergency operator, he became furious. "Somebody help! My wife's been shot and I've been shot!"

"Okay, stop crying now, okay?" Janet spoke as she would to a distraught child. "Stop—"

At that point the man began sobbing even harder, interrupting the operator. "My wife is dying here!"

"Okay, I need to know where your wife's been shot, I need to know for the paramedics."

"I don't know," the man sobbed. "It's hard to tell. There's blood everywhere. We walked into the house and somebody tried to kill us. They started shooting. There was two people . . ." The man paused a moment, sobbing loudly into the telephone. "Oh, my God. My wife is dying, lady, if you don't get somebody here."

"We are on the way, we are on the way. Did the people who were shooting get out of the house?"

"Yes."

"Which way did they go?"

"I don't know."

"Did they leave out the front door?" Janet strained to understand the caller's end of the conversation.

"Yeah, I guess. Out the front door."

"How many were there?"

"Two." The man was breathless, sobbing and gasping for air. "Hurry!"

"Units are on the way, sir. We've got paramedics coming to help you out. Okay? Sir?"

Janet turned to Faye, who had been monitoring the conversation and feeding information to officers en route to the scene. "He hung up."

Faye announced over police radio, "Confirming your response. All units call is at three fifteen, three-one-five South Myers Street, 187 in progress. A man stated he'd been shot. They walked into the house and some subject started shooting. Possibly two subjects. Subjects left out the front door. Nothing further."

With that statement, every available Burbank police officer immediately began responding. A 187 in progress meant someone was being murdered. Burbank is a town where police might go through an entire year with no more than one or two murders. In fact, police personnel liked to say that when an officer had an occasion to draw a gun in Burbank the incident became the talk of the station for several weeks.

At 11:05, when Janet was still talking with the caller, Faye Malcolm got word that the first officer had arrived at the scene just fifty-seven seconds after the call had come in. But it would be another seven minutes before police would enter the Montecalvo home.

Later, doctors would disagree about whether an earlier entry might have made a difference in Carol's survival. Officers would contend that they were worried the suspects might still be inside, despite Faye's police radio announcement that suspects had already fled. Regardless, by 11:05—while precious blood drained from Carol Montecalvo's body—officers began arriving and placing themselves at various points in front of the Montecalvo house where they would wait a full seven minutes before making entry.

When the man hung up on Janet the second time, she leaned back in her chair and frowned at Faye. "There was something strange about that call," Janet said.

"What?"

"It's probably nothing," Janet said. "He hung up on me a couple times."

Faye was filling out paperwork on the call and still monitoring the officers' progress at the scene. "Happens all the time. People are upset, someone's hurt, they hang up the phone."

"It wasn't the hang-up, but the way he answered the phone when I called him back," Janet said.

"What do you mean?"

"Well, it was like at first he wasn't even upset at all. Just kind of, you know, 'Hello?' as if nothing was wrong. Then after maybe a second he was all of a sudden hysterical again."

Faye shrugged. "Who knows. People get pretty weird in a situation like that. Don't worry about it."

Janet nodded and fell silent, listening to the police activity over the monitor. Later she decided she must have been overanalyzing the situation.

While Faye and Janet worked with the hysterical caller, Burbank police officers across the city had begun making their way to 315 South Myers Street. Officer Ron Caruso was heading the opposite direction less than a mile away from the location when dispatch announced a 187 in progress. Instantly he screeched into a U-turn, waiting until the car was completely under control before pushing the gas pedal to the floor. At that hour on a Thursday night, less than a mile from the crime scene, there was no need for sirens and lights. Caruso felt a wave of adrenaline rush through his body.

Fifty-seven seconds later he arrived in front of the house. With a response time of less than a minute, he thought it possible that the suspect or suspects might still be inside even if the victims believed they had gotten away. As he had driven up the street, he had seen no activity whatsoever. The entire neighborhood seemed asleep, with lights on at only a few houses—including the house where the shooting had occurred. In fact, as he parked across the street Ron noted that 315 South Myers was perhaps the only house on the block that was completely lit up, the way Dan and Carol had left it when they took their walk.

This was unusual. Burglars typically broke into dark homes that seemed empty. He made a mental note of this detail, pulled his gun out from his waistband and climbed out, shielding himself with his car door. Keeping his head low, he darted across the street and waited behind a tall bush for backup units. The sound of distant sirens was growing closer.

Officer Rick Medlin was at the busy corner of Victory Boulevard and Alameda Avenue about four miles from South Myers Street when he got the order to report to a murder in progress. Three minutes later he was at the scene and noticed that several police cars had already arrived. He parked five houses away, drew his gun, and climbed out of the car. Quickly, he made his way from one front yard to the next using the houses as a cover, finally stopping at the house just south of the crime scene.

At almost the same moment dogs in the backyard of that property began barking and Medlin considered moving to a different location. But he decided to wait, ducking behind a four-foot wall separating the two houses.

Several officers were already scattered about the lawn of the house next door, their guns drawn. Medlin turned and watched the house, looking and listening for any sign of life. He noticed that two cars were parked in the driveway, which was adjacent to the wall he was hiding behind. *Strange,* he thought, *breaking into a house with two cars sitting in the driveway.*

Suddenly he saw movement in the hallway. Medlin glanced at the other officers but because of his view-point he appeared to be the only one aware of the motion. He raised his head and watched as a man with dark hair, his eyes cast downward, began walking down the hallway toward the door. For a moment he stood in the doorway, taking in the police activity on his front lawn. At that instant the man grabbed his right side and began limping down the steps. An officer across the street notified dispatch that a man had exited the residence. It was 11:09.

By then a police helicopter unit had begun flying overhead looking for suspects. The whirring staccato of the copter's propeller combined with the barking dogs made it almost impossible to hear the man.

"Help me!" he shouted, stopping at the bottom of the steps and facing the officers hiding near the front of his property. "I've been shot! Can't you see that? Why won't someone get over here and help me?"

Medlin felt his body tense. At first, when the man had walked down the hallway without a limp, Medlin thought he was a suspect. He pushed the thought from his mind. Obviously this man was a victim.

Standard procedure at a crime scene mandated that the nearest officer take charge of the situation. Medlin looked around and saw he was closest. Even though the man was probably a victim, Medlin knew enough to treat him as a suspect until he was safely in police custody. The officer stood up quickly, giving away his cover and gaining the man's attention. Medlin aimed his gun at the man.

"Put your hands in the air and walk away from the house," Medlin shouted. Amid the commotion the man seemed not to hear the command. He remained frozen at the base of the steps, still holding his right side.

"Help me! I've been shot!" His voice rose a notch above the commotion.

"Listen, get your hands up where I can see them and come over here." Medlin motioned with his gun for the man to walk toward the garage.

The man winced and clutched his right side a bit tighter, putting his one free arm up in the air as he began limping toward the cars parked in his driveway. He stopped once to rest against the white Nissan, parked nearest him, and then slowly moved closer to Medlin, using the car as a crutch.

Across the street Officer Glen Sorkness moved in to assist Medlin.

"Medlin, get inside." Lieutenant Art Moody barked the order and Medlin and Sorkness exchanged a knowing glance.

"I'll take it from here," Sorkness said. Medlin nodded and turned to join three other officers for an initial check of the house. The front door had been open since they arrived on the scene. Medlin opened the front screen door and entered the residence with the other officers right behind him. The lieutenant made a note in his log: Officers entered home at 11:12 P.M.

Sorkness waved his flashlight toward the paramedics parked just down the street. Inside the ambulance Kelly Chulik and Jeff Williams had been waiting. These were the most difficult calls for paramedics. Murder in progress meant someone might be dying inside, but until they were given the all-clear sign they were forbidden to approach. That night as each minute passed Chulik and Williams grew more nervous. They were trained to save lives, not wait outside. When they finally saw Sorkness wave the flashlight, the paramedics snapped into action. They grabbed their medical kits and ran toward the house.

Sorkness was already questioning the wounded man. Expertly, Chulik and Williams began working to get his vital signs while Sorkness continued the interview. Chulik noticed that the man had been shot once in the back just above his right hip. Although the victim was complaining of severe abdominal pain, Chulik noted there was very little blood near the wound. At that moment, two other paramedics joined them with a stretcher.

"They're ready for you inside," one of them said, motioning Chulik and Williams toward the house. "We've got this one."

Chulik led the way, running up the front walk and into the house. The officers had taken just two minutes to assess the situation and determine that the suspect or suspects had already fled the scene.

Once inside, Chulik saw the woman lying motionless in the hallway. She was heavyset with dark brown or black hair and he could see she was lying in a thick pool of clotting blood. She didn't appear to be breathing.

"Doesn't look good," he muttered as he knelt near her and rolled her onto her left side.

The woman's eyes were open and lifeless and her face was covered with sticky, dark red blood. Chulik guessed she had been lying in a pool of her own blood for several minutes. Now the dark red fluid had coagulated into clots the size of cotton balls, which were stuck to her face and the carpet she had been lying on. A dark ring of dried blood circled the woman's face, showing how deep the puddle had been. Chulik noticed two large holes in the back of the woman's neck. The fleshy area just above the woman's chin had a dime-sized hole where one of the bullets had exited her body. Chulik guessed the other bullet was still inside her, possibly lodged in her spinal cord. Later the bullets would be examined by forensics experts to determine what caliber gun had fired them.

She wore sweatpants and a loose tank top which made it easy for the paramedics to work on her. She was also not wearing a bra. Clutched in her right palm was a wadded-up damp paper towel and automobile registration papers, and near her head was a set of keys. Chulik brushed the thick blood away from the woman's mouth and nose and listened for respiration. There was none. Next he felt the pulse on the right side of her neck. Again there was no response.

"Paddles," Chulik said and instantly Williams handed the electric heart-starter equipment to his partner. Chulik placed them over the woman's heart and pushed a button, sending an electric shock into her body. This time when he felt for a pulse he tried not to think about the woman's skin. It was cold and had the stiffness of a cadaver.

3

The longer the paramedics worked on Dan Montecalvo, the more hysterical he became. At first he seemed interested only in his gunshot wound, but as the minutes slipped by he began screaming that his wife needed help inside.

"What's taking so long?" he sobbed. "Someone help her! My wife is dying in there!"

Officer Glen Sorkness tried to pacify him. Sorkness was tall with blond hair and a physique some men work all their lives to attain. In his single days, his fellow officers had dubbed him "Snake" for his wily way with women. The name had stuck, despite the fact that he was now a happily married family man.

Despite Sorkness's efforts to calm the hysterical man beside him, it was obvious he was not going to go willingly with the paramedics until he found out about his wife.

By then, a buzz had spread through the neighborhood and residents had begun to gather in front of their homes. So far, Suzan Brown was not among them. A few teenage boys on bicycles had ridden as close to the scene as police would allow. As the paramedics began to wheel the stretcher toward the ambulance, Dan jumped off and began running toward the house without any sign of the limp he'd had when he first appeared in the doorway.

"I have to see my wife," he shouted as he ran. "Why won't someone help her?"

"Listen, Mr. Montecalvo," Sorkness said as he caught up with and grabbed the man. "They're working on your wife right now and we can't have you getting in the way. Now, let's take you to the hospital."

He helped the paramedics strap the man down and wheel him into the ambulance before he had a chance to free himself again. Sorkness climbed into his police car and followed closely behind the ambulance. The drive to St. Joseph's Medical Center in Burbank took just five minutes but it gave the officer a chance to think about the man's behavior.

At first he hadn't seemed to remember that his wife was dying inside, so busy was he limping and complaining about his own injury. But when they tried to take him away from the scene, he became intent on knowing her condition and, despite his gunshot wound, was suddenly able to jump off the stretcher and run. Of course, at that time Sorkness knew nothing about Medlin's earlier observation that the man had appeared to manufacture the limp only upon seeing police in his yard. Sorkness figured the man's reaction probably had something to do with a panic-induced adrenaline burst.

Sorkness was accompanying the man to the hospital for one reason: to gather information about the shooting. The police would eventually have to solve this case based largely on the details Mr. Montecalvo could remember. If his wife lived, she would also be a valuable source of evidence. Time was of the essence.

Back at the house Sorkness had asked the victim several questions about what happened, but he had been too distraught to give intelligent answers. Sorkness had gotten the man's name—Dan Montecalvo. Sorkness wondered whether Dan's wife would live. He had left before any report on her condition had been given.

The ambulance swung into the hospital parking lot and Sorkness followed closely behind. He waited until they were inside the emergency room before beginning the interview. He had decided against taking notes. After nearly twenty years with the police force, Sorkness felt confident relying on memory. Later in the evening he would include the man's comments in his report. Sorkness watched as the nurses worked to stabilize him. He decided to start with the easy questions.

"You feeling okay?" he asked softly, watching for the man's reaction. Although the nurses had not yet administered any drugs, the man seemed considerably calmer than he had been earlier at the house.

"I'm in a lot of pain," Dan answered, wincing as the nurse drew a blood sample from his right arm. "How's my wife? She here somewhere? Where is she?"

"Sorry, Mr. Montecalvo, I have no information about your wife right now. I'm sure you'll hear something soon." Sorkness paused a moment and moved a bit closer to the bed. "What happened tonight?"

"Burglars," Dan answered, shaking his head and putting his left arm over his eyes. "Damn burglars."

Sorkness tried to be patient. "Mr. Montecalvo, I know this is going to be difficult for you but I need you to take it from the beginning. What exactly happened tonight?"

Dan took a deep breath and nodded, moving his arm from his face and Sorkness wondered if he was going to become hysterical again. Instead the man sighed and began to talk.

"Me and the wife were on vacation, supposed to go to Hawaii tomorrow morning, had the trip all planned out and everything," he said. "Tonight, well, you know, we packed and went out to eat at the pancake house here in Burbank. After that, went by the May Company. You know, bought some stuff for the trip. Then we came home."

Sorkness interrupted. "What time was that, Mr. Montecalvo?"

"Oh, I don't know. Might have been sometime around nine-thirty, ten o'clock. Something like that."

Sorkness nodded. "What happened after you got home?"

"Well, nothing at first. I mean, you know, we packed a few more things and then we took a walk. We take a lot of walks at night, you know. Later in the evening."

"What time was the walk?"

"Must have been maybe ten-thirty, ten-forty-five." Dan winced as he struggled to find a more comfortable position.

"You lock the house up before you left?"

"Yeah, we always lock the house up, locked it up good and then we took a walk around the neighborhood."

Sorkness made a mental note of those details. "What happened next?"

Dan rubbed his eyes and again Sorkness wondered if he'd be able to make it through the entire story. "We finished the walk, got back to the house, and we noticed the tags on my wife's car were set to expire tomorrow."

Sorkness looked puzzled. "You mean the registration tags?"

Dan nodded. "Yeah, we was gonna take her car to the airport tomorrow and we didn't want any delay with the police, you know, getting pulled over for expired plates or nothing. So I told the wife to go on inside the house, get a wet paper towel so we could clean it off and everything."

"You both went inside then?"

Dan shook his head. "No. The tags were in my car, the other car, inside the glove box. That's where they'd been for a long time and we just remembered about them because of the trip and because they were about to expire the next day and all."

"Then what?" Sorkness said, picturing the events as Dan described them.

"Well, so I went toward my car to get the tags from the glove box and my wife went inside the house for the paper towel."

"She had the house keys?"

Dan nodded. "Yeah. She opened the house up, went inside, and that's when it happened."

Sorkness waited as Dan buried his head in his hands and began breathing very fast. He wondered if these questions were too much for the man. But Sorkness knew if he could get the man past this point in the story he'd have enough details to start an investigation.

"Mr. Montecalvo, I'm sorry. I need to know what happened next."

"Okay." Dan slowed down his breathing and continued to talk with his head facedown in his hands. "She walked inside and I heard her shout, 'What are you doing here?' and then all of a sudden there were two loud shotgun blasts."

"You were still outside at this time?"

"Right, out by my car looking for the registration tags. Soon as I heard her scream and then those shots . . ."

"Go ahead."

"I ran into the house to see what was going on, you know?"

Sorkness nodded.

"Well, I got inside the house and right away I was grabbed from behind, around the waist. I never had a chance to see what the guy looked like, just got grabbed soon as I walked inside."

"Was it a man?"

Dan shrugged. "I think so. I don't know."

"He say anything?"

"No, nothing. Before I could get free I heard a gun go off a third time and felt this deep pain in my right side. I knew I was shot, no doubt about it."

"Then what?" Sorkness watched Dan's expression but the man seemed to be holding up better than he'd hoped.

"Well, you know, I fell to the floor and all, just lay there for a few seconds. While I was down there, seemed like I felt someone moving near my head and I heard someone say, 'Come on, let's get out of here.' "

"Was it a man's voice you heard?"

"Well, now that you mention it, I think it was a man's voice. He didn't talk real loud or nothing. Couldn't really tell what his voice was like. But I'm almost positive it was a man."

"Okay, so what happened next?"

"Well, I was just lying there trying to get up but I was in a lot of pain. Then I remembered my wife. I had to help her out, so I got up and walked into the hallway."

Dan began rubbing his eyes again, looking like he was about to break down. Sorkness thought the man was holding up very well considering he had just found his wife shot in their family home. Sorkness figured the man must have still been in serious shock because otherwise he would probably have sobbed through the entire story.

"I found her and she was just lying there, bleeding," Dan said quietly. "So I checked her and I knew she was still alive." He paused.

"What then?"

"I began praying. I just asked the Lord to please help my wife, please let her live. Then I ran into the bedroom to call for help but I couldn't get the phone to work. So I ran into the den and called from there. That's when I saw the cash box pried open, lying empty on the floor."

"How much money was in the cash box?"

"Somewhere around eight hundred dollars in bills and maybe another twenty dollars in change."

Upon hearing that detail Sorkness was almost certain the shootings had taken place as the result of an interrupted burglary. Over the past year police had been dealing with a rash of break-ins, especially in the older part of Burbank where South Myers Street was located.

"Okay, what happened next?"

Dan nodded. "I told the lady we was hurt, we needed help. Then I hung up and went back to help my wife. At that time, she was still holding on. Then the phone rang and I had to leave her again to answer it. The nine-one-one lady wanted to know about the burglars, what happened and all."

Sorkness nodded.

"Don't remember exactly what I told the lady. Told her the burglars had already gone, told her we'd been shot and we needed help. Then I hung up again and left the phone off the hook."

"Why'd you do that?" Sorkness watched the man's reaction, hoping he wasn't pushing him too far.

"Again, my wife was bleeding in the other room, in the hallway. She'd been shot twice and I wanted to help her. The operator was wasting time on the phone when she should have been getting someone in there to help us," Dan said, clearly irritated.

Sorkness nodded. "All right, what happened next?"

"I went back to my wife and she was still alive. I kept thinking to myself, where are the police, where's the paramedics. She was dying in there and no one was coming to help. I looked down at her and I said, 'Honey, hold on. Don't give up. Help's coming,' things like that. And I kept praying."

"You give her mouth-to-mouth or any other first aid?" Sorkness asked softly. He didn't want to upset the man any further. But it might be helpful later to know what had been done to help the woman before paramedics arrived on the scene.

"No mouth-to-mouth or nothing. But I took her pulse, just to make sure she was still hanging in there."

"You felt a pulse?"

"Yeah, she was alive all right, definitely hanging in there at that time."

"You take it from her wrist or where?"

Dan began rubbing his eyes again and when he answered Sorkness heard his voice crack. "Took it from her neck, right side of her neck. Knelt right there beside her and checked it to make sure she was still with me. Then I stayed right there and prayed."

"What then, Mr. Montecalvo?"

"Well, nothing happened. Nothing at all. Kept waiting and she was alive but no one showed up. Then I thought I heard something outside, helicopters or something. That's when I got up and walked outside and saw all the police waiting around."

Sorkness heard an edge in the man's voice. He seemed very upset that police had taken several minutes before sending someone in to help his wife. "Anything else you can remember?"

"Yeah, the cops pulled a gun on me. Treated me like some kind of criminal while they waited around and refused to let those paramedics inside. Why wouldn't they let someone help her? She was bleeding everywhere and still they wouldn't let the paramedics inside."

Suddenly both men heard someone approaching and they watched as a kind-looking middle-aged man entered the room. He was conservatively dressed and reached out to take Dan's hand.

"Hello, Pastor." Dan's chin began to quiver. "You hear what happened?"

As soon as he had arrived at the hospital, Dan had asked the emergency room nurse to call the Reverend Wil Strong. Now, less than an hour later, the pastor had come to offer whatever support he could give.

"Dan, we're praying for you both. How is she?"

Dan shook his head and again began breathing very fast. "She's been shot pretty bad."

Pastor Strong turned to Sorkness. "Have you heard anything, sir?" he asked politely.

Sorkness shook his head. "Not yet. I'm sure they're doing all they can for her."

For a moment an uncomfortable silence filled the room and the three men each seemed lost in his own thoughts. The nurses had long since stabilized Dan and left him alone with the officer. X rays had determined he would need emergency surgery to remove a bullet lodged near his intestines. While the surgical team prepared for the operation the two men had been able to talk without interruption. Now, with the pastor in the room and the questioning finished, there seemed to be nothing to say.

At 12:33 in the morning, ninety minutes after Dan's call to the 911 emergency operator, a doctor walked into the room and motioned Sorkness toward him. Dan watched with interest as the two men talked in hushed tones for several seconds. When they finished, the doctor turned and left.

Sorkness cleared his throat.

"Mr. Montecalvo, I have some bad news." He paused a moment realizing there was no tactful way to deliver the blow. "Your wife is dead. She died at the scene. There was nothing they could do—"

Sorkness was interrupted by Dan's scream. "No! No! Not my wife! No!"

The officer hung his head for a moment, giving Dan some privacy as his screams gradually changed to gut-wrenching sobs. Pastor Strong moved closer to Dan, taking his hand and bowing his head, moving his lips in prayer. In a few seconds Dan was more hysterical than he had been back at the house. Instantly, the nurses rushed into the room and began trying to calm him. Sorkness looked up and saw that Dan was wiping his eyes and holding onto the pastor's hand. Then, for a moment, Dan's eyes met Sorkness's and the officer was struck by a disturbing observation. Dan's eyes were completely dry.

4

Two houses north on the same side of the street as the Montecalvo home, Suzan Brown stood motionless in front of her living room window as the paramedics shut the double doors on the ambulance and pulled away. Finally, when the ambulance had disappeared and the sirens faded into the distance, she turned away from the window. Gunfire, swarms of police, paramedics, helicopters with blazing spotlights, hordes of media reporters and cameramen. Nothing like this had ever happened on South Myers Street.

Suzan looked down at herself, smoothing out the wrinkles in her faded shorts and tank top, and began walking quickly toward the front door. Her wheelchair remained folded in the corner of her messy living room.

"Where you going?" Suzan turned to see one of her short-term guests, Ron Hardy, walking toward her. Suzan looked angrily at Ron, a stern brown-haired man with a burly, unkempt appearance. He worked odd jobs and lately he had been occupying a space in her bed. For that privilege, Suzan would say he paid a small amount toward rent and indulged her in large quantities of speed. Until that evening, Suzan had had no complaints.

"Stupid jerk, Ron!" Suzan bellowed at him, not intimidated in any way by his approach. "This is all your fault!"

Ron said nothing, only shrugged his shoulders and turned back toward the kitchen.

"Did you hear me, you stupid jerk?"

"Shut up, woman," Ron shouted as he walked to the sink and washed his hands. Suzan thought it must have been the eighth time he'd washed his hands in the past thirty minutes. To her they still looked bloodstained.

Suzan glared at him a moment longer before turning her attention again to the scene down the street. More members of the media were arriving now. She could no longer stand to stay on the sidelines.

With no sign of whatever physical handicap usually confined her to a wheelchair, Suzan walked down the sidewalk to the Montecalvo house. For the next hour she made herself available to every television and newspaper reporter at the scene.

Later, three newscasts and one newspaper would carry interviews or statements from Suzan Brown. *The Burbank Leader* ran a story about Carol's murder with comments from her. "I was already planning to move, but I'm calling my realtor tomorrow morning. I want to get out of here right now," Suzan told the paper. "You bet I'm scared. We usually leave our garage door open, but after all the excitement I made sure it was closed."

It was only later that detectives would learn from Suzan's friends that she'd never had any intention of leaving South Myers Street before Carol Montecalvo was murdered.

Sometime around one o'clock that morning when much of the commotion that had surrounded the Montecalvo house for two hours had died down, Suzan returned home. By then, nearly everyone in the neigh-

borhood knew what had happened. Burglars had bro
ken into the Montecalvo home, thinking the couple wa:
gone for the night. But they had only been walking
around the block. When they returned to the house
Carol walked in first and surprised them. The burglars
had made her pay for the mistake with her life. Dan had
been luckier. He had been shot in the waist, but he was
going to live.

Back inside her home again Suzan found Ron sitting
at the kitchen table. She joined him for a cup of coffee
while she filled him in on everything the reporters had
told her. She was no longer angry with him, and could
not decide whether she was afraid or excited about
what had happened.

"How do you feel?" She looked at Ron.

"Look. Stop with the questions." Ron stood up and
slammed his coffee cup down on the scratched surface
of the table. "Drop it."

Ron walked into the den and flopped onto the worn
sofa. Within minutes, he was snoring. An hour later
when Suzan could no longer stand to think about the
events of the evening, she walked back to their bedroom
and tried to fall asleep. Instead, she lay awake, wide-
eyed, the effects of adrenaline and caffeine causing her
entire body to tremble and her mind to rush.

As she lay in bed during those early-morning hours
after Carol Montecalvo's murder, Suzan began to patch
together bits and pieces about the evening that she
hadn't remembered at first. New details began to fill in
around those that had already been there and she
slowly decided that she and Ron had been at home
when they heard the three shots ring out. Not at the
Montecalvo home as she'd first thought.

In fact, she told herself, what had really happened

was that she had heard someone running alongside her house shortly after hearing the sound of gunfire. She thought about this for some time and slowly another bit of description began to emerge. After hearing the footsteps alongside the house, she was almost certain she had heard the woodpile come crashing down. Yes, she was sure about it. First there had been gunfire, then about a minute later there had been the sound of someone running beside the house and a few seconds after that the woodpile had come crashing down. The problem was, she could no longer distinguish whether this new information came from the cobwebbed corners of her memory or from the boundless recesses of her imagination.

When she woke the next morning, Suzan lay perfectly still for several minutes. In her mind, she replayed the sound of someone running through her yard and then knocking down her woodpile. At that instant, she became convinced that the sounds had been real and not part of some unusual dream.

But before she gave the matter further thought, Suzan found herself thinking about breakfast. It was not until late that evening, after she'd spent several hours adding to her collection of lampshades, that she again began thinking about the murder and the strange noises she had heard. By then, she had long since forgotten about the bloodstains she was convinced she had seen on Ron Hardy's hands.

At the same time that evening, Burbank police officers Mike Gough and Ronald Cervenka were parking their car along South Myers Street. They had waited until after 9 o'clock—nearly twenty-four hours after the murder—to begin door-to-door interviews with neighbors.

From inside her home, Suzan Brown watched the plainclothes officers begin their rounds. She quickly turned from the window, grabbed a flashlight, and walked into her backyard toward the woodpile.

Sure enough. The pile had collapsed and small logs lay scattered on the ground. Suzan shone her flashlight around the area and she saw a tennis-shoe print. It was a deep indentation adjacent to the woodpile in the dirt space between the pile and the cement wall closest to the Montecalvo house.

She bent over to get a better look at the footprint. *Must be Reebok,* Suzan thought, looking at the multisided design on the heel. Suzan often wore Reeboks and knew the design well, and she quickly deduced that whoever had been in her backyard must have been wearing Reeboks.

Suddenly Suzan knew she had to tell the officers about her discovery. She unlocked the gate that led to her front yard and went out in search of the police.

Gough and Cervenka had already spoken with neighbors at two houses and were walking back to their car to compare notes when they saw a heavyset woman bounding down her driveway in their direction. She was dressed in rumpled-looking shorts and a tank top. The sun had set hours earlier and by then a cool wind had begun to blow through the streets of Burbank. Silently both men wondered why the woman wasn't dressed more warmly.

"Hey, wait a minute," she yelled as she got closer to them. "You policemen?"

Cervenka stepped forward and waited until the woman stopped just a few feet from them. She was out of breath and as she gulped in huge amounts of air both officers noticed tattoos on her shoulders.

"Yes, we're talking to neighbors about Mrs. Monte-calvo's murder," Cervenka said politely. "Trying to find out whatever we can."

Suzan Brown nodded excitedly. "I've got something for you," she said, turning back toward her house and motioning for the officers to follow her.

Gough and Cervenka glanced at each other and shrugged. Cervenka led the way as they followed Suzan Brown into her backyard. She picked up a flashlight and shone it on what appeared to be a partially col-lapsed woodpile.

"See, I heard something last night, you know. Some-thing like a loud backfire sound, only come to find out it's gunshots." Suzan was talking quickly and the of-ficers struggled to understand her. Cervenka lifted his hand to slow her down.

"We'd like to take a report of whatever you heard, ma'am, but first we need your name."

"I'm Suzan Brown, that's Suzan with a z not an s. S-u-z-a-n," she said, shifting her weight back and forth from one leg to the other. "Lived here about ten years, off and on."

Cervenka wrote the information in his notebook and exchanged a glance with his partner. Neighbors had warned them about a crazy woman named Suzan.

"Okay, now what did you hear last night?"

"Well, it's like I said. Sounded like a backfire, but come to find out it was bullets, you know? Two shots real quick and then a third one." Cervenka began scrib-bling down notes while Gough glanced around the backyard. The woman had not yet said anything help-ful.

"So, that's when I remembered there was sort of like a sound of wood falling down right after the shots.

Then I could swear there was a sound like someone was running away, maybe even right in my own backyard."

With this statement, Suzan captured the officers' attention.

"After you heard someone running through your yard, did you check for intruders?" Cervenka asked.

Suzan shook her head. "No. I forgot about it, actually. You know, what with the excitement and all over at the Montecalvo house. Too much going on. But then I came out here tonight to see my dogs and I find this." She turned on the flashlight she'd been holding and aimed it toward the fallen woodpile.

"Not just the woodpile, but then there's this Reebok footprint, too." Suzan pointed the light toward a strip of soft dirt adjacent to a brick wall.

Cervenka knelt down and carefully checked the footprint. After a few seconds he stood up and cast a puzzled expression toward the woman. "How do you know it's a Reebok?"

"All I ever wear," she answered, noticing as she spoke that she did not have tennis shoes on. "Well, you know what I mean," she said, chuckling softly. "I only wear Reebok tennis shoes. Whenever I wear them kind. Of course, back in Vietnam they didn't have Reeboks, so I didn't wear them back in Vietnam. In fact, this kind of reminded me of Vietnam and the time I was . . ."

Cervenka nodded solemnly as Suzan launched into a meandering story and motioned to Gough, who interrupted her. "Thank you very much for the information, Ms. Brown." They'd had enough of this strange woman and her story. By then they were convinced that she was indeed the crazy woman neighbors had warned them about. She seemed harmless enough, but they made a note to keep an eye on her.

"I'd advise you to stay away from the footprint for a few days in case we send someone over to make a plaster cast impression of it. Might be important for evidence."

That evening Suzan never mentioned that she might know who killed Carol. Neither did she mention that she and her friends were heavy drug users who had been partying the night before and had run out of money an hour before the murder. And she said nothing about one of her guests and how many times she believed she had seen him wash his hands the night before.

As the officers left her yard that night, Suzan Brown was certain they would be back to make a plaster impression of the footprint. Just like she was certain she had heard someone running through her yard.

Because of that, Suzan was very surprised when the Burbank police did not return the next day with a bucket of ready-to-pour plaster. In fact, not until the trial did anyone ever speak to her again about her conversation with police officers that night. And no one ever made a plaster impression of the footprint.

As the days of the murder investigation wore on, the forgotten footprint grew more and more difficult to see until finally the image disappeared completely from the soft brown dirt in the backyard of Suzan Brown's home.

5

In some ways, the events and circumstances that crossed Carol Tronconi's path with that of Dan Montecalvo were neither surprising nor unforeseen. Although Carmelo and Maria Tronconi's daughter was highly educated, she was desperately naive in her dealings with men. Worse, Carol was interested only in men who represented a challenge, whose problems might be solved only with her help.

Nevertheless, neither Carol's parents nor her brother and sister ever thought she would marry a man like Dan Montecalvo—a man who had never held a steady job, never been able to stay clear of trouble, and never mastered the art of commitment. A man who was everything her father was not.

Carol's father, Carmelo Tronconi, met his petite, dark-haired bride during the Great Depression when they were both in their late twenties. Carmelo, or Mel as his friends called him, had grown up the youngest in an Italian farming family that made its living off an adequate piece of land in Buffalo, New York. The Depression was especially hard on farmers who lived in Mel's neighborhood. Long after his older siblings had left the farm, Mel stayed on, helping his parents with the chores.

He was a handsome young man with a nearly six-foot-tall strapping frame that was perfect for the hard physical work of farming. Years earlier, Mel had dreamed of having a farm of his own one day. But by the time he and Maria married in 1939, the Depression had made the dream impossible. His parents had been forced to sell their farm and Mel had no money to buy land of his own.

Because he had been farming while his friends attended school, Mel suddenly found himself job hunting without the assistance of even a high school diploma. Maria, meanwhile, had earned her college teaching degree while she was still single. But like other educated women in the 1930s, she gave up any thought of a career the moment she became Mel's wife. Throughout the 1930s, Mel struggled to provide for them by working long hours as a machinist and a floor sander. For a few years he and his brother even tried to get their own hardware business off the ground, until they succumbed to the pressures of the fickle economy. Time and again Mel found himself frustrated in his job search by his lack of education.

His persistence finally paid off in 1940 when he was hired by their local telephone company as a maintenance worker. The job carried union benefits and a high-paying salary. Long after he'd found the job, Mel refused to forget how many he had missed out on because he wasn't an educated man. He promised himself that his children would have every opportunity to attend college, regardless of the sacrifices he might need to make.

"Doesn't matter if I have to work round the clock, Maria," Mel would say, determination ringing sharply in his voice. "Someday our kids are going to be college graduates."

Maria would smile sweetly. So far they had no children and she thought it a bit premature to be thinking of college educations. But if Maria ever thought her husband was a bit extreme in his fierce resolution, she never said so. She was a docile wife, easily allowing Mel to be ruler of the household.

Early in their marriage, the Tronconi family lived in a working-class neighborhood on the ethnic Italian west side of Buffalo, where in 1941 they were blessed with a daughter, Roseanna. Mel was not happy bringing his tiny baby girl home to a neighborhood of working-class people. He believed his children deserved better than that.

During the next several years he often worked overtime, scrimping and saving enough money so that in 1945, shortly after the birth of their second daughter, Carol, the family could finally afford to move. By then, Mel's salary with the telephone company was better than many professionals made and Mel saw to it that their new home was situated in an upper-class area where their neighbors were doctors and lawyers and corporate executives. Mel had already convinced his family that they were a class above the people in their previous neighborhood, so the Tronconis had no trouble adjusting to their new setting.

At that time Buffalo was made up of nearly one million people spread throughout various suburbs and communities. Those were the days when even the heart of the city was a safe place, before crime became such a problem that people were afraid to ride the bus downtown at night. When his children were growing up, Mel was proudly aware that he had provided them with one of the best possible places to live.

What Mel did not realize was that his attempt to provide a superior lifestyle for his children had left them sheltered and completely unaware of the uglier side of life. In all their years growing up, the Tronconi sisters never saw drug addicts or gang members or prostitutes loitering on their sidewalks. None of their friends came from single-parent homes or had parents on welfare. And they grew up innocently believing that all people were essentially good, contributing members of society.

Even people like Dan Montecalvo, whose upbringing had been everything theirs was not.

During the next eight years there were times when Maria marveled at the difference between her two daughters. Roseanna was calmer, often content to read or play quietly in her room. Not so with Carol. The Tronconi home was situated on a city bus line and from an early age Carol would scare her mother by disappearing outside to watch an occasional bus speed down her street.

At age four Carol disappeared from her family's front lawn and wasn't found until Maria walked to the end of the street where a group of older neighborhood children were playing hockey. There stood Carol, playing goalie with children twice her age. As Maria watched her daughter, she realized she was getting a glimpse of the handful Carol would become. She was not a disobedient child, she simply had a voracious appetite for life and enjoyed living it to the limit.

The summer between kindergarten and first grade, Carol became the first Tronconi girl to bring home a boy. Standing together hand in hand, Carol proudly introduced the child beside her as her "boyfriend." Roseanna, four years older, recognized the innocence in Carol's statement but she was silently mortified at the thought of holding a boy's hand. Later that year—when

Roseanna was still afraid of escalators and wary of venturing too far from home—Carol began drawing pictures of faraway places where she would travel when she grew up.

Carol was eight when her brother, Jon, was born in 1953. The two girls helped their mother with the newborn baby and the three siblings grew close despite their age differences. That year, Carol's neighborhood peers began noticing the vivacious dark-haired girl in their midst and she became extremely popular. Eventually she and her friends formed a club that held after-school meetings and played games at various homes.

Carol was equally popular among her peers at Public School No. 56 in Buffalo. As soon as the other children would see Carol walking along West Delavan Avenue, they would rush out to meet her. At age thirteen, she was voted class queen for the annual eighth grade dance.

Carmelo and Maria were proud of their daughter's popularity. Carol was a princess growing up in the secure kingdom of a safe neighborhood and a good school system, unaware of the harsh realities outside the castle walls. By the time Carol entered Lafayette High School on the west side of Buffalo, she was bright and beautiful and had come to expect things to go her way.

This positive outlook produced in Carol a cool self-confidence that made her a natural at nearly everything she tried. During her high school years she became a wiz at ice skating, downhill skiing, and tennis. She was equally adept with her studies, her role in student government, and as a flutist in the area's All-City High School Band.

What made Carol even more attractive was that her confidence never became conceit. Sometimes on weekends Carol would transform from the constant blur of motion into a quiet, serene young lady. She attended Sunday mass each week and also made time for her family. Many of those afternoons were spent at their Aunt Florence's lakeside home, where Carol would set up an easel and paint nature scenes. The quietness of those times seemed to recharge whatever inner energy fueled Carol.

When she was fifteen, Carol became interested in an Italian boy who lived just two houses down the street. At first, Carol figured the romance would be short-lived because the boy was merely an average student and an average athlete. Life was meant to be challenging and she found very little to challenge her in such an average boy. But her opinion of him changed overnight when her father pulled her aside one evening and expressed his disapproval of the situation.

"It's simply too easy to get into trouble dating a boy who lives so close." He sounded stern. Carol could feel the boy's worth rising with each word her father spoke. "I don't want you to see him anymore. Is that clear, young lady?"

Because Roseanna had been easygoing and willing to comply with her parents' wishes, Mel was completely unprepared for Carol's rebellious attitude. The relationship continued for months, with Carol sneaking out at night to meet the boy and share an occasional kiss. Carol was sixteen when her father found something else to complain about and stopped talking about the boy down the street. With the challenge gone, Carol broke off the relationship.

Two events helped shape Carol when she turned eighteen. First, her best friend, Cindy, was killed in an automobile accident. Almost overnight, Carol began paying attention to her father's speeches about higher education. It was as if she suddenly saw how precarious life could be and wanted to make the most of hers while she still had time.

In a matter of weeks, she enrolled at the State University of New York at Buffalo and began taking psychology courses. It was 1963 and the country was just beginning to accept the fact that women might want careers, even after they got married. For the next few years, Carol pursued her dream of becoming a psychologist, immersing herself in her studies. In college Carol again found herself surrounded by people who were ambitious and came from good homes. The safe, secure kingdom had merely been transformed from her neighborhood to the ivy tower of academia.

Occasionally Carol would read about people in her psychology books who had not fully bonded to their parents, or who lacked the ability to love or be loved. But always a textbook solution was presented and those people would wind up cured. Once in a while Carol would find herself attracted to the problem-riddled people in her textbooks. She could think of no greater satisfaction than to use her knowledge of the human psyche to straighten out such a person.

In 1967 Carol graduated with a bachelor of science degree in psychology, but after a summer of unsuccessful job hunting she became disillusioned with the field. For all its textbook appeal Carol was disappointed with the working world of psychology. She thought the therapists were too clinical and unfeeling and eventually she decided she could change more lives by becoming a teacher. She reenrolled at the university and two years later earned a master's degree in education.

By that time Roseanna had also graduated with a

master's degree in education and promptly married her college sweetheart. Mel was disappointed. He had expected his children to repay him, in a manner of speaking, for providing them with an education. He believed in children living at home for several years after their college graduation and helping with expenses the way he had on his father's farm.

Disappointed with Roseanna, Mel began to hope that Carol would move home once her education was completed. Of course that was the farthest thing from his younger daughter's mind. Although still rather naive, she had become a liberated, independent-minded woman who was looking forward to living on her own and starting her career as an educator.

When Carol's intentions became clear, her relationship with her father grew strained. But while Mel was distant and unable to relate to Carol, her mother found ways to bridge the gap. She and Carol had become very close friends and in the early 1970s they even took a trip to California together.

Just before graduating with her master's degree, Carol met Raj Rakia, a man from India who was also earning his master's degree at the university. The son of a doctor, Raj came from a highly educated family and had traveled throughout the world. He was the first man who had challenged and excited Carol in years. Long after their relationship had grown serious, Carol brought him home to meet her family. Later that night, Carmelo exploded in an angry display of temper.

"I will not have any daughter of mine dating some foreigner," he told Carol angrily after Raj had left. "I forbid you to see him again."

Carol was sorry her father felt the way he did, but his tirade did nothing to change her mind about Raj. Twice more she brought him by her family home. On these occasions, Carol and Raj would hold hands and sit close together on the family sofa. Mel was obviously displeased with the couple's displays of affection. The resulting tension was worsened by Raj's silence despite Carol's attempts to include him in family activities and conversations. Even Roseanna had a bad feeling about him and told Carol as much.

"How would you act?" Carol insisted defensively. "Dad sits there breathing down his neck, what would you do? When he's alone with me, he's a wonderful man."

No one in her family was shocked when Carol disregarded their opinions and got engaged to Raj shortly after graduation. Upon hearing the couple's announcement, Mel declared that no one from the family would attend the wedding. Still, Roseanna planned to be by her sister's side during the ceremony until her son fell ill with pneumonia and she was forced to stay home. So, in a private ceremony not attended by anyone from her family, the two were married.

Although Carol had always been a pretty girl with sweet, clear-skinned features and flashing brown eyes, she constantly battled her weight, especially when she was upset. But she dropped to a mere 110 pounds for her wedding. Later Roseanna received photographs from the ceremony and was forced to admit that Carol looked happier than ever. Clearly, Carol truly was in love with her mysterious, dark husband.

After the wedding, Carmelo maintained his distance from Raj. Because of the resulting conflict, no one in the family was surprised when Raj and Carol moved to Madison, Wisconsin, later that year. Carol immediately took a job in the counseling department of the University of Wisconsin. But the accounting job Raj had lined up fell through and after a month of unemployment he accepted a job at a large firm nearly two hundred miles away. Carol was shocked that her husband would agree to work so far from home. But he told her that in his culture men did what they needed to do and tried to keep their emotions from interfering with their decisions. And, as he told her, the job would only be temporary until he could find something closer.

At first Raj commuted but eventually the strain began to wear on their relationship. Finally, he decided to take a small apartment a few miles from his office. Carol wanted to quit her job and move in with him, but he dismissed the idea.

"This is only a temporary arrangement, my dear," Raj told her, kissing her on the forehead. "Do not worry. We will be together again soon."

Disappointed and confused by her inability to influence her husband, Carol kept the news about Raj's move to herself. Although she was still close to her mother, the chasm that was developing between Carol and her father had widened when she moved to Wisconsin. Sometimes her mother would even talk to her in hushed tones so that Mel would not find out the two were talking. During that time, Carol confided in her mother the truth about the separate living arrangements she and her husband now shared and no one knew better than Maria the loneliness her daughter was battling.

After Raj's move, at first the couple visited each other on the weekends, and then sometimes only once a month. As was customary when she was unhappy, Carol gained twenty pounds during this period and reached her heaviest weight ever. She also realized that she had tragically married a man who was either incapable of expressing emotions or simply without emotions to express.

Sometimes Carol would call Raj and spend hours pleading with him to come home and work on their marriage. After all, Italian Catholic families did not get divorced. Worse, a failed marriage would give the appearance that her father had been right about Raj all along.

Finally, as the couple's relationship deteriorated to the point that they had become little more than strangers, Carol agreed to a divorce. Several months passed before she mustered enough courage to call her mother with news of the failed marriage.

For the next five years, Carol remained single, living alone in Madison. In search of a cure for her broken heart, Carol turned from Catholicism to nondenominational Christianity. She read the Bible and began to develop a relationship with Christ that was unlike any she'd had with a human being. One year after divorcing Raj she decided that if Christ had died for her, it was time to start living for Him.

Roseanna and Maria often shared their belief that despite Carol's increased devotion to God, she must have been very lonely after divorcing Raj. When Carmelo learned of Carol's divorce he gloated about being right. He also told Carol he expected her to return home. When she remained in Wisconsin instead, Carmelo became even more frustrated with his younger daughter. Involved with her own life, Carol prayed for her father's forgiveness and tried to avoid dwelling on the rift. Occasionally she would call her father and try to mend bridges. But Carmelo was a man who not only held a grudge, he nurtured it. Each time Carol called, she thought his reaction was cold and unfeeling.

Over the years the strain between father and daughter caused her friendship with her mother to fracture. Maria loved her daughter deeply, but her lengthy conversations with Carol caused conflict with her husband. Gradually the two began eliminating those conversations.

But if Carol's real family was unable to show her the love and forgiveness she craved, her church family was more than willing. By the late 1970s Carol's ties to the church had grown even stronger and she participated in Bible studies and support groups that took the edge off her loneliness.

In 1978, because of Carol's compassion and desire to help people change, a friend named John involved her in a prison ministry program. At this time, Carol was thirty-three years old, still single, and with time on her hands. Eventually, John later asked her to write to an inmate who was interested in God but had stubbornly refused to become a Christian. Intrigued by the possibility of changing a hardened criminal, Carol readily agreed. Not long after, the man—serving time at the Federal Correctional Institution in nearby Oxford for bank robbery—became her regular pen pal.

His name was Dan Montecalvo.

Almost immediately, Carol was taken by Dan's plight. He seemed to her a quiet and sincere man who had been unjustly dealt a dreadful hand in life. In her opinion, his life was the classic textbook example of what happens when a person does not properly bond with his parents during the early childhood years. His letters told her how no one had given him a chance and how he had stolen money only because he'd been desperate.

The more she learned about Dan, the more she began to fantasize about meeting him in person and helping him become a happy, functioning member of society.

When that finally occurred, just before Christmas 1978, Carol was not prepared for the impact Dan made. His brown eyes seemed to be crying out for help. He spoke in a shy, quiet manner and seemed as vulnerable as a homeless puppy. But there was something more than the challenge of deciphering Dan's psychological makeup, although Carol was intrigued by the prospect. She also felt an overwhelming rush at the thought of being needed. From the beginning Dan made it very clear to Carol that he desperately needed her.

They spent that entire first day strolling about the visitors' courtyard, talking. Carol asked him one question after another, trying to analyze the history that had shaped the man. Dan, in turn, seemed to be fascinated by her sophistication. He also told her he hadn't expected anyone as pretty as she was. Carol blushed and found herself feeling better than she had in years. During their three-hour visit, Dan grew more talkative and seemed to be happy for what Carol decided must have been the first time in his life. By the visit's end, he had begun thinking of Carol as his personal savior.

In truth, all Carol's textbook knowledge was no match for the years of street-smart behavior Dan had picked up. What Carol never realized was that sometimes a person cannot be changed, sometimes there are people for whom the textbooks simply have no answers. But she was confident beyond any doubt that his troubled psyche—once explored and analyzed—was able to be helped. A month later, when Dan agreed to become a Christian, Carol believed she was seeing this process in action.

So confident was Carol in Dan's potential that three months later she was thrilled when Dan brought up the subject of marriage. At first their conversations had only hinted at how different their lives might have been had they met in other circumstances. But then Dan began getting serious.

"I want to marry you, Carol," he told her, taking her hands in his during one of her visits. "But I could never ask you to give your life to me. Not when I might be in prison another ten years."

By late 1979 they began searching for ways to make the dream a reality. Carol no longer cared whether Dan was in prison or out. She had fallen in love with the man whom she had worked so hard to change. She knew everything about him and was convinced they couldn't live without each other. They agreed to wait at least a year, praying all the while that God would allow them to be together. More than a year later, prison officials granted the couple permission to marry. When the marriage looked as if it would finally take place, Carol telephoned her mother.

"He's in prison now, Mom," Carol explained matter-of-factly. "But he's had a terrible childhood. Now that we're exploring his past, he's becoming a completely different person. He's really a wonderful man."

Images of Raj flashed through Maria's mind and she resisted the urge to cry out to her daughter, to stop her before she could ruin her life by making such a terrible mistake. But Maria knew her husband would say enough about Carol's plans for both of them and the warning went unspoken. Later, when she shared the news with Mel, he shook his head angrily.

"She is no longer the girl we raised, Maria," he said. "She has a mind of her own. I love that girl, but if that's how she wants to live, if that's the thanks we get for putting her through college, I wash my hands of her."

Less than two years later Dan and Carol were married in the prison courtyard. Carol had searched carefully for an off-white cotton dress that hung gracefully to just above her ankles. Carol was still about ten pounds overweight but she thought the dress did a good job of hiding the fact. She held a bouquet of yellow and orange summer flowers and on the sunny morning of July 14, 1980, promised to love and honor Dan Montecalvo as long as they both should live.

Carol would later comment that tears had welled up in Dan's eyes when he repeated the promise. In her eyes, Dan looked more handsome than ever, dressed in the brand-new navy blue suit that Carol had purchased for him. Armed guards watched curiously from their posts as the brief ceremony took place, but other than two of Carol's church friends there were no attendants to witness the couple's vows. Regardless, Carol later commented that the wedding was beautiful. This time, she would say, she had no doubts she was marrying the right man. Dan had completely changed from the deviant, self-destructive person he had been in his younger days. Carol was certain that Dan was now ready to love her the way no man had loved her before.

But while Carol and Dan seemed to be developing an inseparable bond despite his confinement, her relationship with her family was fading into childhood memories. Maria still talked with Carol as often as she dared without angering her husband, but whenever she suggested that Mel forgive her he would raise his hand angrily.

"She's made her bed, Maria," he would bark. And the subject would be closed. In all her life, Maria wanted only for her husband to forgive Carol and again include her in family activities and conversations. When he refused, the resulting tension nearly broke Maria Tronconi's heart. Her dream of a happy family reunion never materialized and in 1982 Maria died of a heart attack. When Carol attended her funeral, she and her father barely spoke to each other.

With Dan still in prison, Carol was often lonely and her only contact with her family was an occasional letter to Roseanna, who had settled in West Amherst, a suburb of northeastern New York. Once in a while she would write to Jon, who was still living at home while working toward his master's degree. Carol would sometimes wonder sadly if her father found solace in the fact that his three children had done as he'd wished and graduated from college. Was it enough now that his wife had died with a broken heart and he had all but disowned his younger daughter?

But there was no mention of those feelings in the letters she wrote to Roseanna, especially after Dan was released from prison in January 1981, and the couple moved to California. Carol's letters from California were so upbeat and filled with surface observations that Roseanna never had any idea whether her sister was truly happy in her marriage to Dan.

Although Roseanna had always intended to visit Carol and Dan in Burbank, her busy schedule kept her from making the trip. Then, on April 1, 1988, Roseanna received a call from her father. In all her life Roseanna had only seen her father cry once—when her mother had died. Even then his tears had been controlled. But now he was sobbing, and Roseanna had to strain to understand him.

"Dad? What is it? What happened?" She motioned for her husband to keep their two children quiet.

"Carol," he said. There was pain in his voice that scared Roseanna. "Oh, Lord. My precious baby. Carol."

"What is it, Dad? What happened?"

"She's dead."

Roseanna felt sick to her stomach. "Dad, are you sure?"

"Yes." He was still sobbing. "She was shot and killed. Some crazy man, some burglar, broke into the house and killed her. Oh, God, Roseanna. My baby is gone."

Tears began to fill Roseanna's eyes. None of the family had been able to tell her good-bye. They had run out of time and now Carol had died without knowing how much they all loved her.

"Dad, what'll we do?"

"We need to go there, to Burbank. There's a memorial service at her church next week." Mel began to cry even harder. "I can't believe she's gone. My baby is gone."

A lump had risen in Roseanna's throat, making it impossible for her to respond.

"Roseanna? Do you think Carol knew how much I loved her?"

"Yes, Dad. Of course she did."

"But I never got to tell her I was sorry." He sounded so distraught Roseanna worried he might pass out. "I was sorry, you know. I didn't mean to let things go like they did! Oh, my God. My baby, my Carol."

From his hospital bed, Dan had arranged for Carol's body to be flown back to New York, and in the following week Mel Tronconi buried his youngest daughter next to her mother. When that was done, he and his two remaining adult children flew to Burbank to attend a brief ceremony in memory of Carol. It was the first time Carol's family had met Dan Montecalvo.

"She loved you all very much, sir," Dan told Carmelo as the two men shook hands.

Mel nodded and tried to choke back the sobs lodged in his throat. "I think you can understand the circumstances, why there has been so little contact. But that's in the past. Let's keep in touch."

Carmelo had decided that if he had run out of time with Carol, he would make it up to her memory by maintaining a friendship with the man she had loved. For Roseanna, the service taught her something of her sister's life as it had been before her death. She was deeply loved by the friends she had made at church and at work. Roseanna returned home grieving that she had not visited Carol in the years before her murder. What Roseanna found strange was the fact that none of Carol's close friends seemed to know Dan very well. She wondered if Carol had been as happy in her marriage as she had clearly been in her friendships.

In fact, even months after their sister's death, Roseanna and Jon had just one way of knowing whether Carol had indeed been happily married. The answer was reflected in her weight.

As a young girl, Carol's problem with her weight was only evident when she was troubled. She might gain ten or fifteen pounds or—when she was very upset as she had been prior to divorcing Raj—even twenty pounds.

At the time of Carol's murder, Roseanna and Jon had not seen their sister for several years, and they anxiously awaited photographs sent to them by the Burbank Police Department. Looking at those pictures months after Carol's murder, they were convinced beyond a doubt that Carol had been more than unhappy. She had been miserable. The pictures indicated that Carol had gained more than seventy pounds since marrying Dan.

6

On April 1, 1988, sometime after one o'clock in the morning, Cathy Hines was woken out of a deep sleep by the sound of her ringing telephone. Instinctively, she checked to see that her husband was asleep by her side. Cathy Hines was a homicide evidence technician for Glendale, a city adjacent to Burbank but with more people and more crime. In fourteen years of analyzing evidence, Hines had come to understand late-night telephone calls. In her line of work they meant just one thing. She picked up the phone on the second ring.

"Hello," she said quickly, her voice sounding uneasy as she struggled to wake up.

"Cathy? This is Pastor Wil." The man's voice was calm and reassuring, but Cathy detected an undercurrent of seriousness. Her pulse quickened as she glanced at her watch and noticed it was April first. April Fool's day. For a brief instant she hoped this was someone's idea of a bad joke.

"What is it, Wil?"

"I'm afraid I have some bad news. I'm at the hospital. Dan and Carol Montecalvo have been shot; burglars broke into their house." He paused, his breath sounding shaky as he inhaled, another indication that something awful had happened. "They don't know if Carol's going to make it."

"My God, Wil." Cathy's voice was merely a whisper and she felt the blood draining from her face.

"Dan's asking for someone from Women's Aglow. You're the only one I could think of. Can you get here right away?"

Cathy ran her hand through her shoulder-length, dark brown hair and began shaking her husband awake. "Yeah. Tell him I'll be there as soon as I can."

By then her husband had caught the urgency in Cathy's voice and sat up in bed. Before he had time to ask her what had happened, she began sobbing, collapsing into his arms.

Cathy Hines and Carol Montecalvo met in July 1984, when Cathy first joined Women's Aglow in Burbank. The group was diverse—made up of nondenominational Christian businesswomen and homemakers who met on the first Saturday of the month to sing worship songs, pray for each other, build friendships, and hear one or more guest speakers. The organization also raised money for charitable causes and gave its members a place to share their personal victories and needs. Cathy had been thrilled to join Women's Aglow, hungry for the friendship of other churchgoing women.

Even in this setting, where the women were known for their kindness, there was something special about Carol, and through Carol, Cathy could finally understand the scripture that described the eyes as windows to the soul. Carol's brown eyes were loving and full of life. At that first meeting, Cathy found Carol treating her more like a sister than an acquaintance. Of course at that time, Cathy was unaware of Carol's particular need to find close relationships among her friends owing to her estrangement from her family.

Over the years Cathy marveled at how Carol persisted when others gave up; she loved when most people turned their backs, and most importantly she never stopped hoping. Especially when it came to her husband, Dan. Almost unanimously, the congregation at Overcomers' Faith Center Church thought of Dan as a kind and loving husband. He did not often attend Sunday services with Carol, but, as Carol was quick to explain, this was because Dan had to work on Sundays. When he did attend, he proudly held Carol's hand and stayed attentively by her side. Those who knew Carol had the impression that Dan was very much in love with his wife.

But once in a while Cathy would visit Carol at home and get glimpses of something else. There were also times when she would prod Carol with questions about Dan. More than anyone else at church, Cathy was aware that Dan drank too much and that he often missed Sunday service because he had a hangover, not because he had to work.

Cathy saw other signs that the Montecalvos' marriage was not completely blissful. The most obvious was the number of times Carol attended social functions by herself. She had even been unable to talk Dan into coming to Cathy's wedding in 1986. Cathy was also aware that nearly everyone else in the congregation knew nothing of Dan's drinking or of Carol's concern for him, because Carol could not bear to paint such a dismal picture for the people who truly loved and cared for her. Cathy marveled at Carol's consideration for Dan as well as for her friends. Not in all her life had Cathy ever known someone like Carol Montecalvo.

* * *

Now Carol was fighting for her life. That April morning, as Cathy dressed while praying for her friend's survival, she remembered a discussion they'd had three weeks earlier at church. Carol had taught kindergarten Sunday School that day and although she had been just as kind and sympathetic as usual, Cathy had sensed something was wrong. Dan hadn't been to church in several weeks, and Cathy figured his absence was beginning to wear on Carol. When the service was over, she approached Carol and asked her where Dan had been. Carol lowered her head as her eyes filled with tears.

"I'm sorry," Cathy said, pulling Carol into a hug as her heart went out to the woman who had been such an inspiration to her. "He's having a hard time?"

Carol nodded, wiping her wet cheeks with the back of her manicured hand. "Please pray for Dan. He's been drinking a lot." She swallowed a sob and lowered her head again. "I'm really worried about him."

In the days after that conversation, Cathy thought Carol seemed to grow happier, excited about the vacation she and Dan were planning to Hawaii. There was never again mention of Dan's drinking or of any other problems the couple might have been having. Still, the image of Carol crying that afternoon stayed with her for weeks after their discussion.

Thirty minutes after the telephone call with Pastor Strong, Cathy and Dan Hines walked briskly into the emergency room at St. Joseph's hospital red eyed and still in shock. The pastor and his wife, Sandra, were waiting for them. Cathy turned toward the minister, who embraced her. "She's gone, isn't she?" Cathy cried, pulling away again and looking intently into his eyes.

Strong nodded. "There was nothing they could do for her, Cathy. She's with the Lord now."

Cathy nodded, shutting her eyes tight, sobbing convulsively. For the first time in her life, she was angry with God. Angry that he would allow Carol to be killed, angry that despite her goodness Carol could fall victim to a burglar's bullets. Cathy's husband moved next to her, putting his arms around her shoulders and drawing her close.

Pastor Strong said nothing, aware that Cathy needed this time to grieve. He had questioned the wisdom in calling Cathy so late at night with the news. But they were all Christians—family as far as he was concerned. His Bible-believing congregation of 250 people was a mixture of young and middle-aged couples, many of whom had children. Most of them were blue-collar, working-class people, but a few were highly paid, educated professionals. For the most part, although they talked about the virtues of higher education, they primarily wanted their children to grow up relying on God as they did. Above all, the people at Overcomers' Faith Center believed in overcoming the trials of this world while they waited for the blessings of the next. But never had Pastor Strong been dealt a trial such as this one.

Members of his church were neither extremists nor fundamentalists, but they believed in the teachings of Christ, especially when it came to helping one another. Strong knew they would certainly need each other now; so much had happened so quickly. During his years as a minister, Wil Strong had personally helped many of his church members deal with death. In his late forties, Strong had the build of a college quarterback and the friendly eyes of a family pediatrician. He was a man who both physically and spiritually brought comfort to those who were grieving. But tonight—after Carol's violent murder—he felt incapable of comforting anyone.

The pastor looked at Cathy, fresh tears streaming down her face as she and his wife, Sandra, held hands and prayed silently. All that Wil Strong had ever learned in Bible college and in fifteen years of working with various Christian congregations taught him everything that happened was God's plan. Even this. He silently recited Romans 8:28. "All things work to the good for those that love God." Carol certainly loved God. Yet, for all his knowledge and experience, something in the corner of Wil Strong's heart struggled with the human questions surrounding her death. Why would God allow it? What good could possibly come from such a tragedy?

The pastor closed his eyes and tried to draw an extra breath of strength. Finally, when Cathy's sobs subsided, he quietly suggested the one thing he knew would bring comfort.

"Let's pray." Strong looked at the others and bowed his head. "Father, we come to you now in need of your great comfort and compassion. Our sister, Carol, has gone into your loving arms and we are left behind. Please restore to us your peace and grant us understanding as we grieve over her loss. Lord, we also lift up to you our brother Dan. The months ahead will be very hard on him as he learns to live his life without Carol. Please help him recover from his injuries and help us all see your plan in what has happened. We love you, Father. In Jesus' name we pray, Amen."

While Carol's friends prayed for him in the waiting room, Dan was being wheeled into surgery. X rays had shown that the single, .25 caliber bullet that had entered the right side of Dan's back just above his hipbone was now lodged in the left front of Dan's body near his small intestines. Emergency surgery was necessary to remove the bullet and stitch up the holes in Dan's insides. The operation would also give doctors a chance to clean out the wound, thereby preventing peritonitis—a serious illness that often occurs when material from the intestines or appendix spills into the body.

Although doctors wanted to perform surgery as quickly as possible, Dan's situation was not a matter of life or death. Doctors would later say that left untreated, Dan probably would have fallen victim to peritonitis, and possibly even died from the illness. But, unlike Carol's, Dan's gunshot wound was never life threatening.

As Dan lay strapped to the operating table in the early hours that April morning, a technician prepared to perform a gunshot residue test on his hands moments before surgery began. The technician took a Q-tip, dipped it into a solution, and wiped it across his palms and fingers. Then she took a small, disclike piece of paper, peeled off its protective seal, and pressed it on the same parts of his hand.

"Hey, what's all that for?" Dan asked.

"Policy," came her tight-lipped response. "You're involved in a shooting, we test for residue."

After that, Dan refrained from asking questions about the test. But those in the room with him remember that as the woman finished collecting the samples and then sealed the items in an evidence jar, Dan's face seemed to grow several shades paler.

Because of his surgery Dan was not able to talk to Cathy Hines until that afternoon. The hours that had passed since Cathy had learned about Carol's murder had done little to ease the paralyzing pain and grief that at times threatened to overcome her. She had spoken to Pastor Strong. Dan was still asking to speak to someone from Women's Aglow, someone who had known Carol. After that, Cathy had contacted two other women from the Aglow group and at 5:30 that afternoon they gathered in the hospital lobby. They made their way to the third floor and as they approached Dan's room, Cathy saw that he was sitting in a comfortable chair, staring calmly at a television set suspended from a spot near the room's ceiling. For an instant, Cathy thought Dan might be in shock. He looked like he was enjoying a leisurely afternoon, not suffering from a gunshot wound received only hours earlier during a burglary in which his wife had been killed.

Before Cathy could give Dan's appearance further thought, he turned toward them and suddenly, as if he'd been given some private cue from an unseen director, began bawling. The women looked at one another, each having noticed the man's dramatic onset of emotion. As they moved closer, they could see that the man was not just crying, he was also beginning to sweat.

Must be some sort of side effect from the surgery, Cathy thought to herself as she watched tiny droplets of sweat begin racing down Dan's forehead and neck. Dan's loud crying and profuse sweating continued for five minutes while the women stood uncomfortably about the small room. Then, as suddenly as the emotional outburst had started, Dan stopped crying and looked pointedly at Cathy.

"I wanna know something, Cathy," Dan said, his voice devoid of the grief he'd shown only moments earlier. "You work for the cops. Why would they do a gunshot residue test on me?"

The question startled Cathy, who had been expecting to comfort Dan about Carol's death, not talk about the procedures of a homicide investigation. "Well, Dan," she said slowly, "Carol was murdered. Any trained detective knows enough to check people who were with the victim at the time of her death."

Dan shook his head impatiently. His eyes were dry but sweat drops still rolled down his forehead. This time he sounded angry when he spoke. "Why me? They think I had something to do with this? They think I killed her?"

For reasons Cathy couldn't explain, she had a sudden urge to turn and run far away from this man who was drilling her with questions. Her experience with Dan Montecalvo had been limited, but during the few conversations they'd had, Cathy had always thought him to be a reasonable man, despite his drinking problem. But the man in front of her no longer fit that image. In fact, he was irrational, unusually anxious about standard police procedures.

Cathy realized she'd taken too long answering his question because suddenly Dan looked as if he were ready to jump out of his chair and scream at her.

As the other women stood nervously behind her, Cathy cleared her throat and forced a smile, praying that her voice would not betray the strange nervous feeling growing in the pit of her stomach. "Like I said, Dan, it's standard procedure. They eliminate you as a suspect so they can move on and catch the person who's responsible," she said quickly. "Understand?"

Dan dropped his forehead into his hand and began massaging his eyebrows with his thumb and forefinger. Ten long seconds later, he looked up so suddenly, so ferociously, that a gasp caught in Cathy's throat and she unconsciously took a small step backward. "Tell me this then," he snapped, narrowing his eyes. "The police are still in the house. Why? It's been nearly twenty-four hours. What would the police still be looking for?"

Again Cathy felt a strange urge to run from the room. This was not the conversation she had imagined having with Dan about his wife's murder.

"Sometimes it takes a few days to go over everything at a crime scene, Dan," she said softly.

"What?" Dan sat up straighter in the chair and began nervously running his hand through his greasy dark hair. "A few days? I've gotta get out of here. What are they doing there?"

"Dan, you need to be thankful that they're doing a thorough search. They have to dust for fingerprints, check for weapons, collect hair samples. It takes time."

Dan shook his head again, his face contorted in frustration. "They've been there long enough." Then he looked pointedly at Cathy. "Cathy, can you ladies ask one of those doctors to let me out?" Dan smiled, glancing at each of the three women in the room. When he spoke again he sounded calmer, more controlled. "Tell 'em I have some business to take care of. I mean, I gotta get home. The police could be tearing the place up."

Cathy was sure the doctors would laugh at the request. Dan had just come out of major surgery. He'd just lost his wife in a homicide. No doctor would allow him to leave the hospital and return to the scene of the crime so soon. Still, because she was beginning to feel like she would suffocate if she didn't leave his room, she agreed to the request.

Cathy motioned to the others. "Sure, Dan. We'll ask them. We have to get going anyway. Just wanted to stop in." She paused. For a moment, Cathy had to struggle to choke back the sob lodged in her throat. Tears began trickling down her cheeks. "We're so sorry about Carol. We're praying for you, Dan."

Dan nodded impatiently. "Yes. Please ask the doctors about that, will you? I've really gotta get out of here."

As the other women mumbled their quiet good-byes and turned to leave, Cathy was struck by a strange thought. She and her husband had recently bought their house from a man whose wife was killed in a traffic accident. The man was so devastated by her loss that he could no longer live in the house they had shared. In fact, he had no interest whatsoever in even setting foot in the house after she had died.

As Cathy left Dan's hospital room that evening she realized that this was how she had expected Dan to feel, too. After all, Carol had been shot and killed in their home. Cathy knew from her years of investigating murders that when a bullet enters a body near the head or neck, it sprays the victim's blood several feet and in all directions. She was almost certain that Carol's blood would still be on the floor and walls of their home. What reason could Dan possibly have for wanting to return to that kind of scene so soon after the murder?

Cathy tried not to imagine an answer to the question, but as she slipped into bed that night her thoughts made it very difficult to sleep.

7

At two o'clock in the morning, three hours after Carol Montecalvo's murder, field evidence technicians from the Burbank Police Department had begun performing a thorough search and investigation of the murder scene. At that time, based on the information they had received from Dan, the Officers were working under the assumption that a burglary had occurred. Evidence technicians looked for specific details concerning point of entry, signs of forced entry, missing valuables, fingerprints, and so on.

Inside the Montecalvo home the first clue as to how the burglars made entry into the home had been discovered when Officer Brian Cozakos, one of the first to arrive at the scene, walked through the house and observed the back door. Hours later he would write this in his report: "I walked out through the *open* rear den sliding window and checked the rear back yard."

Since Cozakos was the first officer to approach the rear of the house, it became clear that the sliding glass door that led to the backyard had been open before the police arrived. The deduction, then, was quite simple. Point of entry must have been through the back door.

Next there was a question of whether or not the entry had been forced. When Dan told police that his house had been locked up as he and Carol took their walk, what he really meant was that the front door and the back screen door had been locked. Dan smoked cigarettes; Carol did not. On a typical night, their rear sliding glass door was open to allow the cigarette smoke out and fresh air in. Therefore, if burglars had entered the Montecalvo home through the back of the house, they would not have had to do anything to that door because it was already open.

There were many ways of determining whether entry had been forced. Police looked for pry marks near or around door jambs, broken windows, missing lock mechanisms. Although many officers at the scene probably looked into whether there had been forced entry, the responsibility for making a judgment call on the issue rested on Detective Patrick Allen Lynch.

Lynch had received a call at home sometime after 11:30 that night advising him to report to a murder on South Myers Street and take charge of the investigation. As he drove to the scene, Lynch remembered that the city's last homicide had been months earlier. That was about par. There were usually just one or two murders each year in Burbank. He also wondered if this murder would be similar to that of either of the two murders that took place in 1987. Both were still unsolved and therefore a continuing source of frustration for the homicide detectives. Lynch knew that his department had the wherewithal to solve murders. He alone had more than ten years experience with the department, in addition to forty hours of special homicide education and another sixty hours of advanced homicide investigation training. But all of that preparation hadn't helped in the last two murders.

As Lynch began checking the back screen door for signs of forced entry, he felt a surge of hope that this murder would be solved. The screen had been slit just inches from the locking mechanism. In his official report of the crime scene, Lynch wrote this about that detail: "The rear sliding screen had a cut or tear slightly above the lock assembly, which would allow someone to unlock the screen door." They had proof of forced entry.

There was something else the police noticed. Just off the main hallway, a safe had been left open and in front of it, a metal cash box lay empty on the floor. Since the box was empty, police recorded another telltale sign that the house had been burglarized—missing money. Later, Dan Montecalvo would confirm this by telling Officer Sorkness that the box had held eight hundred dollars in bills and as much as twenty dollars in coins.

With evidence as to point of entry, forced entry, and missing property, Burbank police began to suspect that this murder was related to the unsolved homicide that had occurred a year earlier and only a few blocks away. That case involved an off-duty sheriff's deputy, Charles Anderson, who was shot and killed when he surprised burglars in his home. Because the two cases appeared similar, Burbank police notified the Los Angeles County Sheriff's Department. Although Burbank police had jurisdiction in murders that occurred within city limits, county sheriff's investigators were still working with Burbank police to solve the Anderson murder because the victim had been one of their men. So when they heard about the newest case, several sheriff's deputies and evidence experts rushed to the scene.

One of those experts was fingerprint specialist deputy Linda Arthur, who prior to investigating the Montecalvo murder had dusted for fingerprints at more than three hundred murder scenes. She had thirteen years experience and had attended the FBI Academy at Quantico, Virginia, for the best basic and advanced latent print courses available. When she arrived at the home on South Myers, she used a powdery black chemical called Ninhydrin to dust the rear door, front door, telephones, open safe, and empty cash box. Another technician dusted for prints in the bedrooms and living room. The sootlike powder highlighted the curves and ridges of the freshest fingerprints and palm prints. Immediately, Linda Arthur realized that there were several fresh prints on both the rear door and the cash box. Fresh prints were another detail that suggested a burglary had occurred.

Deputy Arthur was also in charge of lifting three shoe prints from the kitchen floor. A report listing evidence collected that night stated that two Kodak boxes containing three electrostatic shoe prints were officially tagged as evidence on April 20, 1988. Detective Lynch was apparently concerned enough about the shoe prints that he requested fellow detective Kevin Krafft to get inked impressions of the shoes worn by all police or sheriff's personnel for the purpose of elimination.

While sheriff's and police investigators pieced together proof that the house had indeed been burglarized, Burbank police officer Ronald Caruso was finishing initial interviews with the Montecalvos' immediate neighbors. He and two other officers had learned that one neighbor had heard his ladder fall off his backyard brick fence while another neighbor, immediately next door to the Montecalvos, had noticed his window screen lying on the ground. Caruso found that information particularly interesting. Perhaps the burglars had tried the neighbor's house first and been frightened away. At three o'clock that morning, Caruso wrote a note about the screen and gave it to Detective Krafft.

Certainly by then, those working the scene had what appeared to be plenty of evidence that there had indeed been a burglary at 315 South Myers Street. There was the point of entry, proof of forced entry, missing money, fresh fingerprints and shoe prints, and signs that a burglar had been in the neighborhood. With this in mind, at 5:55 that morning, Detective Krafft wrote a report containing this synopsis of the case: "Evidence has been located appearing to indicate that this is in fact a confirmed 459 PC attempt." In other words, at that point, the Burbank Police Department believed it had evidence enough to prove a burglary had occurred.

Not until one o'clock that afternoon would anyone consider that Carol's death might not have been caused by a burglar. That occurred when Detective Lynch did a computer check of Dan Montecalvo's background. As a list of criminal charges, a number of which took place while he was still a minor, appeared on the screen, Lynch's eyes widened. Multiple bank robberies, concealed weapons, impersonating an officer, breaking and entering. Lynch took a moment to absorb this new information. Then, putting aside his earlier convictions that a burglary had occurred at the Montecalvo home, he leaned out into the hallway.

"Hey, Krafft, come here," Lynch said, his voice loud enough to be heard by many of the Burbank police officers who had been at the scene the night before. "I think we've got our burglar."

8

Despite being the occasional butt of former *Tonight Show* host Johnny Carson's one-liners, Burbank, California, is not only beautiful, but it is also statistically the safest place to live in the Los Angeles area. As far as its residents are concerned, Burbank's quaint beauty and safety make up for the fact that it is getting on in years, lacking the glamour of Beverly Hills and the fast pace of Los Angeles. Even as violent crimes increased in Los Angeles at the beginning of the 1990s, Burbank, with its nearly 100,000 people, continued to be a seventeen-square-mile haven.

In July 1991 the Burbank Chamber of Commerce ran a banner headline across its newsletter that read, "Burbank: The Safe Place to Live and Work." The accompanying story supported the statement with facts and data. Not surprisingly, people in Burbank were very pleased with their police force and the safe environment they had seemingly provided.

On the average, Los Angeles residents were not as fond of their police force. This sentiment was particularly apparent in early 1991 when a black man driving a speeding car was stopped and beaten by four Los Angeles police officers. The incident sent public opinion of the big city's police force to an all-time low. But in nearby Burbank, police were still considered the good guys.

In fact, months after the beating, which received nationwide attention and brought police forces of other major cities under scrutiny as well, a survey was performed by an impartial pollster asking Burbank residents what they thought of their local law enforcement. A tremendous 92 percent said they were "extremely pleased" with the department and the performance of its officers.

This statistic might have been the result of Burbank's ethnic imbalance. Throughout the 1980s, nearly 85 percent of Burbank's citizens were white. In fact, in 1989, when a reporter contacted the Burbank Elks club to ask how many members were black, she drew this response from a white man who had lived there all his life: "We have no coloreds here, dear. Burbank is an all-white community. The coloreds have their own clubs over in Los Angeles."

So it was possible that Burbank residents were not deeply affected by the racial tension between citizens and police in nearby Los Angeles because they lived in a nearly minority-free community. But whether it was a result of ignorance or safety statistics, Burbank liked its police force.

Of course, in some ways the city's safety was only fitting, what with Disney Studios occupying a major portion of the business district. Crime had no place in a city that prided itself on having produced make-believe fantasies such as *Cinderella* and *Sleeping Beauty*.

The lack of crime in Burbank had a way of throwing off statistics. For instance, in 1990 Burbank experienced a 100 percent increase in homicides. This happened because instead of the one murder that took place the year before, there were two in 1990. If, in that same year, Los Angeles had suffered a 100 percent increase in homicides, an additional 983 people would have died.

The difference between Burbank and Los Angeles was so vast that to step across the invisible boundaries separating the cities was to more than double the chance of being a crime victim. This was also true back in 1911 when Dr. David Burbank sold 9,200 acres east of Los Angeles to developers who then made it into a city and named it Burbank. The picturesque city, wedged between what is today the Hollywood Hills and Verdugo Canyon, was a flat, lush oasis surrounded by a protective semicircle of mountains.

In fact, throughout the 1920s the only crime in Burbank was being manufactured on movie sets throughout the city. Over the next thirty years, Burbank with its green meadows and warm climate became the national headquarters for film and communications giants such as Warner Brothers, Disney, and NBC. By then, Burbank had also become home to Lockheed Aircraft Corporation. As Burbank grew, so did the feeling that life was better and safer there.

But that notion dissolved in the 1950s when organized crime invaded the area. Almost overnight, many of the country's best-known crime families made Burbank their headquarters. Organized crime became so entrenched in Burbank that on April 21, 1952, the California Crime Commission jolted the city out of its complacency by charging that "the people of Burbank are virtually without protection against the inroads of organized crime."

Among the infamous gangsters who made their homes in Burbank that year was mobster Mickey Cohen, who had been released from prison after serving a partial sentence for evading income taxes. Cohen and others operated illegal gambling joints on farms in full view of local authorities.

Within a few years it was clear to most Burbank businesspeople that many of the city's police officials were not terribly concerned with the presence of mobsters. For instance, once when two aggressive rookie policemen raided Cohen's casino, they were promptly transferred to another beat. After further review, the Burbank Police Department brass decided there hadn't been any gambling going on during the raid, but rather the rookie officers had only interrupted a fund-raiser led by a Jewish rabbi. The case against Cohen was dropped.

While residents of Burbank remained, for the most part, ignorant of the extent of organized crime and police corruption in their community, a small group of businesspeople formed a committee to clean up their city. The group hired a chief investigator who eventually turned up evidence that resulted in the resignation of the chief of police. One by one a majority of the city council members also resigned. Just like in the movies, the investigation had a happy ending. By 1954, with the help of a new police chief and new procedural rules, Burbank was once again a safe place in which to live.

After that, Burbank's brief bout with organized crime was always mentioned in a positive vein, commending the city and its citizens for banding together to make their community safe. One article about the episode written by Andrew Hamilton in the August, 1970, *Coronet* magazine, quoted John Canaday, a Lockheed executive and one of the founders of the citizens' group as saying, "It took major surgery to restore Burbank's reputation. . . . Now the job of the crime committee is to remind the patient occasionally that he might need a medical checkup."

Apparently the committee provided regular checkups and Burbank did its part by continuing to have a clean bill of health because the city's crime rate remained nearly nonexistent from that point on.

Most Burbank residents lived in neighborhoods much like the one Dan and Carol Montecalvo lived in. Quiet streets lined with stately trees, older homes that housed conservative, working-class people very near the age of retirement. Burbank was older than most neighboring communities in Los Angeles County and by the late 1980s it was showing signs of wear. Although South Myers Street had an air of respect and dignity, certain parts of Burbank contained homes and storefronts that were run-down. As property values skyrocketed in nearby Los Angeles and elsewhere in the San Fernando Valley, homes in Burbank were older and smaller and therefore cost several thousand dollars less. As a result, parts of the city had become home to low-income, working-class people. During the late 1980s many of these neighborhoods were affected by a higher-than-usual number of burglaries. Even with the increase, though, statistics clearly proved that a break-in was less likely to occur in Burbank than in most cities in Southern California.

For most people, living in a city with one of the lowest crime rates in the state is a priceless advantage. But for officers at the Burbank Police Department the crime-free atmosphere was sometimes bittersweet. Although the department was often credited for keeping Burbank safe, there were many days when its officers were given nothing more challenging to investigate than a parking dispute or a smelly neighborhood pig.

Throughout 1991 only eighteen articles had been written about crimes in the city. One was a story about two men arrested for stealing coins from a convenience store's muscular dystrophy jar; another told of actor Clint Eastwood's decision to use his truck to forcibly move a car parked in his studio parking space. A third article detailed a neighborhood fight to force a man to remove "Arnold," a miniature potbellied Vietnamese pig, from his backyard. Police officials were quoted in that story saying, "It isn't a matter of the pig's smell, it's simply against the law, and if the law is violated there will be jail time to serve."

The idea of serving time for housing a miniature pig meant one thing to residents of the city—Burbank police were not going to let any kind of wrongdoing go unchecked. The Burbank police force enlisted highly trained officers who in a larger city would have been quite good at solving crimes. With crime rates raging in Los Angeles, most of the officers in Burbank were frustrated at the thought of spending their afternoons and evenings at the local doughnut shop. They wanted a piece of the action, and were therefore apt to be particularly vigilant. People who had lived in Burbank longer than a year knew that as far as their city's police officers were concerned it really was a crime to jaywalk.

Despite its lack of murders, Burbank had a number of detectives, all of whom worked on a rotating schedule placing them in a different felony crime division each year. At any given time two detectives were usually assigned to the homicide division and even then there was rarely enough homicide work available to keep them busy.

Often, since they were needed on just one or two cases each year, Burbank homicide investigators spent many hours taking training courses and special classes in investigative work. There were classes on perfecting the technique of fingerprinting, seminars on the science of blood back-splatter, and courses on collecting evidence. Because of this extra training, Burbank police officers ranked among the most highly educated detectives in the state.

But despite the education and vigilance, when a homicide did occur within the city limits, the department seemed to have trouble solving it. At least this was true during the late 1980s. In a city as large as Los Angeles, this kind of thing might go unnoticed. Dozens of murder investigations are suspended in Los Angeles each year and few complaints are made about it. But in Burbank, people began cracking well-meaning jokes about the inability of Burbank police to solve anything but the kinds of crimes that might involve potbellied pigs or stolen coins. Of course, all the training in the world doesn't make up for hands-on experience. So the Burbank police were perhaps trapped in a vicious circle in which there weren't enough homicides to give the detectives the necessary experience to solve them.

Criminal defense attorneys in the area also began cracking jokes, only theirs were a bit more macabre and unfair. One attorney in particular liked to say, "The best advice I could give my clients is this: If you're going to kill someone, dump the body in Burbank. That way they'll never catch you."

Three unsolved murders in the late 1980s are legend in Burbank. In 1987, Sheriff's Deputy Charles Anderson was shot and killed in February when he interrupted burglars ransacking his Burbank home. Despite involving the Los Angeles County Sheriff's Department, Burbank police had still not solved the case four years later. The second happened when a local jeweler was gunned down in his store five months after Anderson was killed. No suspects were arrested and four years later the case was also still unsolved.

Then, on May 13, 1988, police found an exotic dancer dead in her Burbank apartment. The young woman's death came just six weeks after Carol's murder, which although similar to that of the off-duty sheriff's deputy had given police no real leads and no quick solution. The case interested citizens because although the dead dancer's neighbors said they had heard the young woman screaming and gagging, police ruled her death a suicide. Not until three years later—after a lawsuit by the woman's family—did police admit she had been a homicide victim and formally suspend the case for lack of evidence.

Still frustrated over the lack of suspects involving the two 1987 murders, and with no obvious suspects in their newest case, the hours after Carol Montecalvo's murder were something of a low point for Burbank police. By then, many of them were perhaps desperate to solve a homicide. So when police ran the rap sheet on Dan Montecalvo the day after Carol's murder and discovered a printout that could paper a wall, they believed to a person that they had solved the crime.

9

While the police began to focus their investigation on Dan Montecalvo in the days after Carol's murder, Suzan Brown remembered being secluded with three of her friends, staying indoors day and night. Tension hung heavy throughout the cluttered, poorly furnished rooms. None of them talked about what happened the night of March 31, but Suzan found herself doing more drugs than usual and arguing most of the time.

The Monday after Carol's murder, Suzan contacted her landlord and informed him that she planned to break her lease by moving immediately. No, she didn't mind losing her deposit. No, she didn't care if breaking her lease meant losing him as a reference. She was moving. If burglars were breaking into homes in the area and killing innocent residents, then she would have to find somewhere else to live.

Of course, the irony in all this was that by Suzan's assessment no one was more capable of burglarizing a home than Suzan and her friends. Especially thanks to Ron Hardy's influence. By Suzan's recollection he had helped her with several neighborhood break-ins.

This very subject was often the topic of conversation in those days after Carol's murder. In between taking large hits of speed and dangerously reversing the effects with massive amounts of alcohol, Suzan spent many hours trying to talk about their past escapades. Ron Hardy, however, had no interest in such conversations.

"Hey, remember that time we got the television, VCR, and a wad of cash from that home around the block?" Suzan would say, taking a drag from her cigarette. She was sprawled out on a torn sofa, the bulk of her legs hiding spots where foam rubber poked through worn places in the upholstery. "What a night!"

Ron glared at her. "Shut up, will ya?" he'd shout. "What's wrong with you?"

Suzan would look at him, a strange expression contorting her features. She was glad to be leaving in three days. Ron was beginning to get on her nerves and she had long since lost interest in him as a sex partner. "Just the truth, man," she muttered.

"Shut up!"

Ron stormed out of the room and Suzan shrugged. Why was he afraid of the truth? She remembered him having helped orchestrate several burglaries. As far as she could remember, there had only been two times when someone had come home while they were busy taking the goods. Of course, by her recollection they had taken care of that problem. The first time no one had lived to tell about the story.

Moving restlessly on the sofa, she was alone with her thoughts. Suzan remembered the last time she'd seen Carol Montecalvo alive. She had brought an order of Avon to the Montecalvo house and followed Carol into the den. There, she had watched hungrily as Carol had opened a safe and then a cash box, from which she had retrieved enough money for the Avon order.

As Carol had ushered her neighbor to the door that March afternoon Suzan hadn't been able to get the image of the cash box out of her head. *Must be hundreds in that thing,* she thought. Then suddenly Carol said something that caught her attention. ". . . lotions and other makeup so I'll be all set for Hawaii." Suzan had turned to stare at her.

"Going away, huh?" Suzan had said, raising one eyebrow.

Carol had patiently repeated herself. She had always felt Suzan Brown was in dire need of God's help. As always, she was willing to be kind to the woman in hopes of showing her what Christian love was all about. "Yes. We're going to Hawaii at the end of the month."

On March 31, when Suzan hadn't seen the couple walk past her house, she figured they had already left for their vacation.

Now Suzan sat trancelike on her dingy living room sofa recalling the conversation. "How did everything go so wrong?" she whispered to herself.

At that moment, Suzan stood up, walked to her wheelchair, and wheeled herself into the kitchen. Suddenly, she no longer remembered what she had been thinking only a moment earlier. Something about Dan, about eliminating witnesses. Something about a cash box and being gone to Hawaii at the end of the month. The details had vanished. Suzan shook her head, trying to clear the cobwebs.

Why had she been thinking such a strange thought? They hadn't burglarized the Montecalvo home. In fact, they hadn't ever burglarized anyone's home. Why on earth would they have to do away with witnesses? Suzan dismissed her thoughts, reached inside the refrigerator, and poured herself a glass of milk.

As she sat there, drinking her milk while her obese body overflowed from her wheelchair, Ron walked into the kitchen. He looked at her disapprovingly as he moved to the cupboard and began searching for something to eat.

"You done flapping your jaws?" He spat out the question angrily.

A blank look filled Suzan's face. "What?"

Ron turned to stare at her. "You done talking about all those break-ins? You finally gonna shut up?"

Suzan seemed genuinely confused by Ron's comment. "What break-ins?"

Ron rolled his eyes and shook his head in disgust. He had realized in the past year that she was not just one woman, as he had first believed. She seemed to be two and possibly three women. Depending on her mood, Suzan seemed to have at least that many personalities.

10

Once Burbank police knew about Dan's criminal background, it was just a matter of time before they discovered other similarly interesting bits of information about him. This process began in earnest four days after Carol's murder, when Burbank Police Sergeant Don Goldberg paid Dan a visit in the hospital.

On occasion, the two men ran into each other at Genios, an Italian restaurant in downtown Burbank. During the year before Carol's murder, Dan had started buying Goldberg a drink during these occasions. The two men would chat a while and eventually they developed something of a camaraderie. The difference was that Goldberg went there to eat; Dan went there to satisfy his unquenchable thirst for alcohol.

The idea of Goldberg visiting Dan in the hospital was the direct result of a meeting Detective Lynch held with several of his officers and other department personnel. Lynch, who at that time was in charge of the investigation, had briefed them about Carol's murder, strongly suggesting that Dan's history of bank robberies and other charges made him a worthy suspect.

As Lynch told the officers how badly they were in need of evidence to be sure of Dan's involvement, Sergeant Goldberg was struck by a bothersome memory. He waited until Lynch was finished before speaking.

"Lynch, got a minute? In private?"

Lynch caught the seriousness in Goldberg's voice. He nodded toward the others. "The rest of you are dismissed. We'll let you know how it goes." He motioned for Goldberg to follow him into his small office.

"What's up?"

Goldberg's eyes narrowed as he stared out the office window. Usually he didn't involve himself in this early level of an investigation. But Goldberg liked Lynch. He was one of the best detectives the department had ever had. If anyone could make good use of the information Goldberg was about to disclose, Lynch could.

Finally the sergeant drew in a deep breath. "Might be nothing," he said, still looking out the window. "That guy, Dan Montecalvo. I know him; talked to him a few times over at Genios. Asked me a lot of questions—always about the same thing." Goldberg paused again. "I don't know, maybe it's nothing."

"What'd he say?" Lynch asked, leaning back against the edge of his desk. Even though Goldberg was his superior, the two men had worked together on several cases and had never been affected by the difference in their ranks.

"The Anderson murder. He wanted to know how access was made, what was taken, how many shots were fired, whether we had any leads." Goldberg turned away from the window and stared directly into Lynch's eyes. "Now, why would a common guy on the street need to know so much about a burglary-homicide?"

A knowing look came across Lynch's face. The answer seemed obvious. The Anderson homicide had been just a few blocks away from the Montecalvo home and it was unsolved. If Dan had wanted to kill his wife, and if he knew enough information about the Anderson murder to make the details appear similar, he might have the perfect alibi.

Goldberg shook his head. "Like I said, maybe it's nothing. Maybe the guy was just paranoid, worried it could happen at his house."

"He was worried all right," Lynch said sarcastically as he grabbed a notebook and began scribbling. "He *knew* his house was next on the list."

Lynch finished writing and stared down at his notes. "Goldberg, I need a favor. Could make a big difference."

The sergeant nodded, turning away from the window and leaning against the office wall. "Whatever you need."

"Dan knows you, right?"

Goldberg nodded again and smiled. "Pretty well. The guy's kind of quiet until he's got a few Jim Beam's in him. After that Danny boy could talk up a storm."

"How 'bout visiting old Danny boy over at St. Joseph's. Ask him about Carol's murder." Lynch paused. "Oh, yeah. Something else. We found a few life insurance policies in Dan's briefcase. Might be nothing, but see if you can find out how much they were for. See if they were having trouble in the marriage, that kind of thing." Lynch thought a minute. "No uniform or anything, okay? Just a social call of sorts."

Goldberg chuckled and ran a hand over his bald head. "Hey, maybe I should bring flowers or candy; a sympathy card from all the boys at Burbank police."

Lynch shook his head, pulling a small electrical device from the top drawer of the desk and handing it to Goldberg. "I have a better idea. Wear a recorder. Who knows, we might all want to share in that conversation."

When Sergeant Don Goldberg knocked on Room 456

that April 4, the recording device Lynch had given him was strapped across his chest, completely out of sight. Goldberg had no problem with the procedure. As long as Dan had not yet been arrested, it was perfectly legal to record the conversation without his knowing about it.

Meanwhile, Dan had mixed feelings when he saw Goldberg walk into his room. Within the past seventy-two hours, Dan had grown increasingly certain that police were focusing their investigation on him. This bothered him so much that the day before he had withdrawn his permission for police to search his house.

Of course, that had neither surprised Lynch nor stopped the investigation at 315 South Myers. Ever since he'd interviewed Carol's friend, Cathy Hines, Lynch had known that Dan was angry about police searching his house. By the time Dan actually withdrew his consent, Lynch had long since had the paperwork for a search warrant drawn up. An hour after Dan demanded that police stop searching the house, the search warrant was approved and the investigation continued as it had before. Lynch decided that the only reason Dan withdrew his consent to have police search his house was that he was worried they might actually catch the responsible party.

To the church friends who stopped in and visited him at the hospital, Dan offered a different reason for his reluctance. He told them police were trying to find evidence that would connect him with Carol's murder. They were trying to frame him, he said. The solution was simple in Dan's opinion: He needed to do whatever he could to get the officers out of his home. That way they would be unable to fabricate evidence and look for clues that, according to Dan, just weren't there.

As one of his friends later observed, Dan was ripe for

such paranoid thinking. The recipe of his volatile personality, mixed with a heap of pressure and an alcohol dependency, made for a batch of paranoia the likes of which put people in mental hospitals.

Dan was so paranoid about police that with each passing day he became more convinced they were spying on him, tapping his phone conversations, and purposely ignoring, hiding, or even destroying information that might go against their newfound theory that Dan had killed his wife.

In the hours before Sergeant Goldberg's arrival, Dan began to feel the first stirrings of his unreasonable fear. During that time he had done little more than stare out his hospital window. *Why haven't they arrested anyone,* he had wondered. He had drummed his fingers nervously on the table next to his hospital bed. No one understood. Everyone seemed to be treating his situation as if it was just another common occurrence. Why weren't they listening to him?

How could they think I killed Carol, he had asked himself for the hundredth time. He remembered their last meal together and how happy Carol had been. Never, he told himself, could he hurt Carol. She was all he'd ever had, everything that had ever meant anything to him.

Why were the police looking at him? Dan had started to shake from the anxiety his thoughts were causing him. He knew that if they ever blamed him for Carol's murder, he would be unable to handle it. He had suffered enough trauma. The one person who had believed in him was gone forever.

Then he had pondered another line of thought. Why had God let this happen? What of Carol's strong faith? What had it given her? Dan's precarious faith in God was all but vanishing, as if now that Carol was dead, all bets with God were off. The way Dan saw it, God had let him down; therefore he would give up on God. After all, God had let him get into this situation. He would get himself out of it.

And so Dan was not entirely pleased when Sergeant Goldberg visited him that April afternoon. Still, even with his newfound paranoia, Dan never suspected that his buddy Goldberg was secretly tape-recording everything that was about to be said that afternoon.

"Hey, Dan," Goldberg said quietly, sitting down in the chair next to Dan's bed. "Sorry to hear about your wife."

Dan nodded uncertainly, casting a questioning look toward the sergeant beside him.

"How are you doing?" Goldberg leaned a little closer. The tape recorder he was wearing would do no good if it couldn't pick up Dan's side of the conversation.

"Not very good," Dan said. "Not good at all." He shook his head slowly. "They think I did it. I know they do."

"Did what?"

"Come on, Goldberg. I wasn't born yesterday. Your guys think I killed my wife. They did this gunshot residue test on me, they're still camping out at my house. By now they probably know about my background."

The conversation was getting interesting. Goldberg strained a bit closer to Dan. "So, you have a record. Lots of people have a record, Dan. That doesn't make you a killer."

"Look, Sarge, I've been through the system. I'm really scared they'll use that stuff against me." Dan wiped a few drops of sweat off his forehead.

"Hey, if you didn't have anything to do with Carol's death, don't worry about it."

"Of course I didn't have nothing to do with it." Dan began to raise his voice and Goldberg slid back in his seat. The recorder would have no trouble picking up this conversation. "Would I be in here with a hole in my side if I had anything to do with it?"

"You're worrying about nothing, Dan. It's not like you had a million in life insurance on her," Goldberg said. He was baiting the man lying in the hospital bed, looking for a diamond in a mine.

Dan released a shaky sigh and covered his face with his hands. "They probably know about that by now, too."

Goldberg moved closer again. "About what?"

"The insurance. Carol was a big believer in insurance."

"There was life insurance on Carol?"

"Four or five policies, I think," Dan said, his voice fading as he spoke.

"Must have been small policies," Goldberg said. "What were they, ten thousand each?"

Again Dan sighed, and a few seconds later when he looked up, Goldberg thought he looked much paler. "No. Might have been five hundred, six hundred thousand. Something like that."

Goldberg's eyes widened. Lynch was going to throw a party when he heard this. "That's more than half a million dollars, Dan."

"I know. That's why I'm worried."

"I can see why. That kind of insurance money makes a pretty strong case for motive."

Dan shook his head angrily. "That's not fair! Carol wanted that insurance because of my bad health. She was worried I would wind up on the streets if anything ever happened to her."

"Six hundred thousand dollars, Dan?" Goldberg asked, incredulously.

"Yes. Does that make me a killer? Because my wife was concerned about me?"

"Doesn't make you a killer, Dan. Doesn't look real good either."

"Look, she knew about my gambling and all. Carol was worried that if she wasn't around I might not be able to pay back my debts. She wanted to help me, even if she wasn't here." Dan began massaging his temples with his thumb and forefinger.

Goldberg's eyes grew still wider. "Gambling debts?"

Dan looked up in surprise. "You didn't know?" he said, rolling his eyes. "You would have soon enough. I gambled a bit. Used to do real well, brought in a pretty steady income that way. Then, I don't know, maybe a year ago I hit a bad spell. Lost a little and decided to quit for a while."

"How much is a little?"

"Twenty thousand, maybe a little more."

"Twenty thousand dollars?" This time Goldberg tried to hide the amazement in his voice.

"Yeah. Sounds like a lot. But in Vegas it's not so much. People run up that kind of debt all the time."

"You owe Vegas more than twenty thousand dollars?"

"Yeah, so?"

"Carol was insured for more than half a million dollars?"

Dan's shoulders slumped forward and he ran his fingers through his slicked-back hair. "See why I'm worried?" Dan turned toward Goldberg and suddenly his eyes looked less like those of a weasel and more like those of an abandoned puppy about to be hit by a car. "Listen, Sarge. I didn't kill my wife. Doesn't matter about the gambling and the insurance. I didn't do it. Carol was everything to me. Everything."

Goldberg nodded, standing up and extending his hand to shake Dan's. "Well, I don't blame you for being worried. I'd be worried, too."

"That's why I want to get out of here. I have to get home, straighten all this out before it's too late and they arrest me or something." There was an awkward moment of silence before Dan spoke again. "Hey, Sarge, I'm pretty scared. What should I do?"

"I'm no legal expert," Goldberg said before he left Dan's room that afternoon. "But I think if I were you I might be getting myself an attorney about now."

As he walked down the hallway, Goldberg had no doubts about whether Lynch and the others would find the conversation interesting. Of course the police already knew about Dan's criminal background. But Goldberg figured Carol's half million in life insurance and Dan's gambling debts would give investigators more than enough to begin building a case on. Goldberg waited until he was out of the hospital before reaching up under his shirt and switching the recorder off.

That same afternoon, while Sergeant Goldberg was chatting with Dan, Los Angeles County field evidence technician Phil Teramoto was busy in the crime laboratory. The day's work had been long and tedious and now, at nearly four o'clock, Teramoto had just one more test to complete—the gunshot residue swab test taken on Dan Montecalvo. The purpose of this test was to determine whether there were lead spiral particles on Dan's hands immediately after his wife's murder.

These particles typically appear on the hands of

someone who has fired a gun, providing the person did not wear gloves. After the bullet has been released by the firearm, a residue of lead particles sprays backward onto the hand. There are other reasons a person might have lead particles on his or her hands. A person who has been shot, for instance, might touch the gunshot wound and at the same time pick up lead particles. Or a person might pick up the particles working in a lead factory.

Two samples are always collected for gunshot residue tests. First, cotton swab sticks are swiped across the person's hands. Next, a second test is performed using the sticky surface of small disclike pieces of paper, which are also designed to pick up the particles.

Tests are usually only completed on the swab sticks. The process is inexpensive and less time consuming than the highly technical disc test. The drawback is that the swab test is also less accurate.

A negative result on a swab test means only that no lead particles have been detected during the chemical process. But if there were even one or two lone spirals of lead, this process might overlook them. This is not often a problem because the purpose of the test is to determine whether the person fired a gun, not whether they touched a gunshot wound or worked with lead. Gunshot residue usually contained hundreds of lead spirals, an amount that would certainly be discovered by a swab test.

There are occasions, albeit seldom, when an attorney or an investigating police officer requests the second test, which would determine absolutely the presence or absence of lead particles.

Detective Lynch had asked Teramoto to call him with the test results. Lynch had a strong suspicion that the test would be positive. If it was, they would have their first piece of physical evidence linking Dan to Carol's murder.

Teramoto checked his watch and began walking toward the testing room. The results would be readable by now. He picked up the test marked "Montecalvo—GSR swab test" and stared at the swabs under a microscope.

The process of reading the test took only a few seconds and when he was finished, Teramoto took a pen out of his lab coat pocket. He picked up the form attached to the test, filled in the section set aside for test results, and picked up the lab telephone.

"Detective Lynch?"

"Yeah, this is him," Lynch said absently. He was still waiting for Goldberg to return from his hospital visit with Dan.

"It's Teramoto over at the county crime lab."

Lynch sat up straighter in his chair. "What do we have?"

"Not much. The test was negative."

11

Dan Montecalvo officially became the primary suspect in the murder of his wife on April 6. This was the result not of what police found, but what they did not find during their five-day investigation at the Montecalvo home. After examining each piece of evidence and every police report, Lynch determined that there simply was not enough reason to believe a burglary had taken place.

This was his determination despite the slit screen door, the empty cash box, and the unidentified footprints found on the kitchen floor—all of which had been ample evidence of a burglary only a few days before. In light of learning about Dan's criminal past, Lynch figured the slit in the screen had probably been caused by normal wear and tear. For that matter, Dan had probably taken the missing cash, and perhaps a repairman had left the footprints in the kitchen. Simply put, by April 6 those details were no longer meaningful in the eyes of Detective Lynch. Once that was the case, the Burbank Police Department was able to focus its investigation entirely on Dan.

Had Dan known that his status had changed from being a possible suspect to being the only suspect he would not have been surprised. By then, Dan was frantic. For whatever reason, he felt that it was outrageous for the police to take five days searching his house.

That same morning, only hours after police had finished their investigation of his home, Dan was granted permission to temporarily check out of the hospital. Carol still had not been buried and Dan needed to make arrangements for her body to be sent back east for burial in the Tronconi family plot. The head nurse had agreed to allow Dan to leave on the condition that he return by that afternoon. Doctors wanted Dan to spend at least another two days in the hospital. As soon as he received permission to leave, Dan called Pastor Wil Strong.

"Wil, I need a favor," Dan said, his voice shaky and distressed.

"Whatever you need, Dan."

Several days earlier, Pastor Strong had learned that police were focusing their investigation on Dan. Strong had always thought of himself as a reasonable man, and that meant being open to the idea that anything was possible. He had long since stopped believing that because people were Christians they were incapable of evil —even something as evil as murder. Strong believed that as long as Satan was alive and well on planet Earth, he would try to worm his way into the hearts and souls of all people, including Christians.

Strong had spent many hours in the past few days considering the possibility that Dan might have killed Carol. But despite keeping an open mind, Strong was completely certain that Dan could never have done such a thing. Dan might have been a drunkard, he might have gambled too often and with too much money, but the pastor was positive about one thing— Dan worshipped his wife. Certainly there had been times when Strong wondered if Dan truly loved Carol. But in the pastor's experience, a person could worship someone without really loving them.

Carol had spent hours talking with Strong, sharing with him the problems she refused to mention in front of anyone but him and Cathy Hines. Yet even when Carol was distressed about Dan, she would constantly mention how much her husband needed her.

"I feel like I'm letting him down, like I can't do anything to reach him anymore," Carol would complain softly. "He needs my help, but the alcohol is killing him."

Pastor Strong would listen kindly, advising Carol to continue praying for Dan and to try to persuade him to enter an alcoholism treatment program.

From years of counseling Carol, and occasionally Dan, the pastor was convinced of certain things. First, Dan seemed to be dependent on his wife and to view their marriage as the single redeeming factor in his life. She had given him her time, her money, and her entire life by going against her family's wishes and marrying him. Then she had devoted herself to his rehabilitation and conversion. This may not have won her Dan's undying kindness. But he would forever be indebted to her. Strong believed that Dan kept Carol on a pedestal and even credited her with saving his life.

The more Pastor Strong thought about the situation, the more he believed that Dan was incapable of killing Carol. If Dan had been having financial difficulties, he would have known dozens of ways—most of them illegal—to put his hands on money. In fact, immediately after Carol's murder Strong had been given approval by the elders in their church congregation to loan Dan several thousand dollars until he could get back on his feet.

Strong believed Dan would sooner have robbed another bank, or hijacked an armored truck, before he could have aimed a gun at Carol and killed her.

And if those weren't enough reasons to believe in Dan's innocence, there were also the logistics of the crime. Strong did not believe that anyone with Dan's criminal knowledge would shoot himself in the side or back. There were too many lethal routes a bullet might take. No, Dan could not have killed Carol.

Regardless of what direction the investigation would take in the weeks and years to come, the pastor calmly and completely maintained his opinion. He was so convinced of Dan's innocence that when Dan called him that April morning from his hospital room, he did not hesitate to offer his assistance.

"How can I help?" Pastor Strong stood up from his desk and looked out his church office window, silently praying for Dan's healing, as he had done many times since Carol's murder.

"They gave me a temporary leave, gotta take care of a few things." Dan paused and Strong thought the man might be on the verge of breaking down. Dan drew in a deep breath. "Need to get Carol home, get her body sent back to New York so they can bury her."

"I understand." The pastor's voice was calm and reassuring. "How can we help?"

"I need someone to go by the house and get a couple of Carol's dresses. A green dress and a blue one, in the back bedroom, right side of the far closet. Could you do that for me, Wil?"

Strong could only imagine how difficult this ordeal must be for Dan—having to take care of his wife's funeral and burial plans from his hospital bed. "Sure, Dan. I'll have it taken care of."

"And could someone pick me up at eleven o'clock, take me by the funeral home?" Dan's voice broke and Strong could hear him crying as he struggled to speak. "I need to say good-bye, Wil. I haven't told my wife good-bye."

The pastor closed his eyes, feeling the man's pain as if it were his own. "Yes, Dan. Someone will be there to pick you up. They'll have Carol's dresses with them."

Dan was sobbing now, gulping back tears as he fought to finish the conversation. "Wil, there's just one more thing," Dan said as Strong strained to understand him.

"Whatever I can do, Dan."

"Pray for me, Wil. Please pray for me."

Minutes after their conversation ended, the Reverend Wil Strong summoned his associate, Keith Hershey, into the office and asked him to take care of Dan and whatever he might need that afternoon.

Hershey hadn't known Dan as long as Strong had, but in the summer of 1986 he had spent three days with the Montecalvos on a missionary trip to central Mexico. That trip had given Hershey a chance to get to know the couple in a way that made him feel as if he'd known them all his life. When they weren't preaching the gospel to Mexicans who gathered daily at the mission, they were working together passing food out to poverty-stricken families and homeless people. But what interested Hershey most about the Montecalvos was the way they worked together—laughing, casting the type of glances at each other that are usually reserved for newlyweds and love-stricken teenagers. In three days, Hershey decided that Dan and Carol had the kind of marriage most couples yearn for. There was no sign of bickering or harbored resentments. No boredom or disinterest.

When Hershey learned earlier in the week that police might be pointing a finger at Dan in the wake of what he considered a terrible tragedy, he decided immediately that the police were mistaken. Dan and Carol were best friends. He had seen that much with his own eyes.

Hershey drove up and parked in front of the Montecalvo house at 10:30 that morning. By then there was no sign of police. Dan had given a house key to Pastor Strong earlier in the week and Hershey now used it to open the door and let himself in. For a moment, the young pastor stood in the doorway stunned at the sight. The inside of the Montecalvo home had been completely taken apart. Books and papers were strewn about the floor, cupboards were open, their contents stacked haphazardly throughout the room. Slowly Hershey made his way around the piles of debris and belongings toward the back bedroom. As he passed the den on his right, Hershey looked inside. This room was even worse than the front room had been. File cabinets were open, piles of paper, receipts, and other records lay scattered about.

Hershey continued down the hallway and saw the dark circular bloodstain a few feet away, indicating the spot where Carol had bled to death. Darkened blood spots still covered the nearby walls. He shuddered as he gingerly stepped around the spot. Finally he opened the door to Dan and Carol's bedroom. This room, too, appeared to have been completely ransacked. The closets were emptied, clothes thrown across the bed and floor. The dresser drawers were open or pulled completely out and Hershey saw that their contents had been carelessly rifled.

As he found Carol's dresses, Hershey knew that burglars had not been responsible for leaving Dan's house this way. He wondered what Dan would think when he saw the place, and he hoped that by then someone would have put things back in order. Hershey left the house and climbed back into his car, making sure to hang Carol's dresses neatly in the back, then he drove to the hospital. Dan had already checked out and was waiting in the lobby. As the two men walked to the parking lot together, Hershey thought Dan looked gaunt and depressed.

"You okay, Dan?" Hershey quietly asked when they arrived at the car.

Dan nodded somberly. "I'll be all right. Carol would've wanted me to be strong."

"She was quite a woman," Hershey said with compassion.

"I know." Dan's eyes filled with tears and he looked away. "God knows I'm going to miss her; she was everything I had."

The men rode in silence to the funeral home. Years later, Hershey remained impressed by Dan's strength—being able to make funeral plans, arrange for transporting Carol's body back East and, finally, say good-bye to his wife. When they left nearly two hours later, Dan seemed paler, the circles under his eyes noticeably darker. But despite his recent surgery, he had held up under one the most emotional moments of his life.

They were driving back toward the hospital when Dan asked Hershey to go by the house on South Myers Street.

"I don't think that's a good idea, Dan."

"Keith, I said please go by my house. I have to see it

now." Dan was suddenly urgent, insisting that the pastor help him.

"I've been there, Dan. Trust me, you don't want to see it. Not yet."

"I can handle it. I need to see what they did to it." Dan was leaning forward in his seat now, turning toward Hershey and straining the stitched incision near his waist.

Hershey released a deep sigh. "Okay." He drove the two blocks to Dan's house and parked the car. "But let me come in with you. You've been through enough for one day."

"No." Dan was adamant, already moving to get out of the car. "I have to do this alone, have to see it and put this out of my mind once and for all."

"All right, Dan. I don't agree, but go ahead. Take five minutes. If you're not out in five, I'm coming in. Agreed?"

Dan nodded, then shut the car door behind him. Inside, Dan did not even recognize his house. He picked up loose photographs of himself and Carol and stared at them, tears rolling down his cheeks. How could they do this? How could they treat Carol's and his possessions like they were trash?

"They're going to be sorry for this," Dan muttered to himself. "They're wrong about me. Can't anyone see that?"

Dan began crying louder, angry, convinced that police had torn up his home looking for clues to prove he had killed his wife. Finally, when he could no longer stand being in the house another moment, he returned to the car.

"How could they do that?" he shouted, pounding his fist into the palm of his hand.

"I told you, Dan," Hershey said quietly. "It's a mess."

"No." Dan turned angrily toward the man who was helping him. "It ain't a mess, it's a disaster. Ruined. Looks like a hurricane came through and tore the place up."

"Was it like that when you and Carol were shot, did the burglars make some of the mess?"

Dan shook his head. "No. They only wanted one thing—money from the safe." He pointed at his house. "The police did that. They think I killed Carol, so they tore up the house looking for clues." Dan paused a moment and when he spoke again his voice was even louder. "It's their fault she's gone, not mine. They let her bleed to death. Took them fifteen minutes to get inside and help us. Fifteen minutes!"

Dan was shaking from the rage that was building as he thought about the time police had taken to respond to his emergency call and what he thought their motives were for dismantling his house.

"Drive me to the police station, Keith." It was a command, not a question, and this time Hershey responded without hesitation.

"What for?"

Dan's anger was focused now and he sounded calmer as he spoke. "I'm collecting my valuables and filing a report against the police for leaving my house in ruins. Then I'm going to do something else."

Hershey glanced at Dan, worried that the man might have gone over the edge. "What's that?"

"File a lawsuit."

"Why?" Hershey didn't like the tone in Dan's voice. It was as if he'd been terribly wronged and now he was going to get even. He didn't sound like a man who was thinking of God.

Dan answered Hershey without hesitation. "I'm suing the Burbank Police Department."

12

Eight days after Carol's murder, Detective Lynch learned that his police department was about to be sued by Dan Montecalvo. The suit—which was not officially filed until several months later—would accuse the Burbank Police Department of causing Carol's death because of its unacceptably long response time the night she was shot. According to Dan, he planned to seek one million dollars in damages for Carol's death and for subsequent police harassment.

By then, Lynch had talked with an assortment of people from Dan's past. In the process he had learned information about Dan's background that the mere sketch of his criminal record could not possibly have revealed. Based on this information, Lynch believed Dan had long since developed reasons to hate policemen. So he was not surprised to learn that Dan was now hurling accusations at the Burbank police. The way Lynch saw it, Dan probably hoped the lawsuit would take the heat off him.

Lynch was not worried about being able to defend the department's actions. His officers had merely followed procedure by waiting until they were certain no suspects remained in the house before entering. As for harassing Dan, he was their primary suspect. Questions had to be asked. Lynch smiled to himself as he sat at his desk. If Dan thought their questioning constituted harassment, he hadn't seen anything yet.

Lynch had no intention of letting Dan's impending lawsuit slow their investigation. Throughout the remainder of April, Lynch saw to it that the initial reports on Carol Montecalvo's murder were in order. Sometimes Lynch would read a report and be satisfied with the details they contained. Other times he would read a report such as those by officers Glen Sorkness and Rick Medlin and he would sense that somehow crucial information was missing.

For that reason, on April 16 Lynch asked Sorkness— "Snake"—into his office. When the door had shut behind him, Lynch presented Sorkness with a copy of the report he had written after interviewing Dan in the emergency room the night of the murder.

"Snake, read this thing over," Lynch said quietly, sliding the report across his desk.

Somewhat confused by the request, Sorkness did as he was told. When he was finished, he looked up. "Okay. Is there a problem with it?"

Lynch shook his head quickly. "No problem. Just seems a little shallow. Like there must have been more to it. You know, something else Dan might have said, something he might have done."

Sorkness glanced down at the report again, trying to grasp what the detective was saying. He paused. "It's all there. Everything he said, everything he did."

"You were with him when they told him his wife was dead, right?"

"Right."

"How'd he react?" Lynch reached for the report. "Says here he became hysterical. Does that mean he was screaming, shouting, crying, sobbing, what?"

A knowing look came across Sorkness's face. "I see."

"Think back, now." Lynch slid the report once more toward the officer. "Was there anything, even one or two important details, you might have left out?"

Sorkness thought a moment and then remembered Dan's eyes. "Now that you mention it, when they told him about Carol he seemed like he was sobbing and crying. But the whole time his eyes were completely dry."

Lynch smiled patiently. "Right. That's what I'm looking for. Details like that."

Sorkness nodded, scanning the report again and trying to remember other similar observations. "Want me to make a note of it somewhere on here?" he asked.

"No. Fill out a supplemental report form. Mention the bit about the dry eyes and anything else you can remember."

When Sorkness left the room, Lynch picked up the telephone and dialed Sergeant Bob Kight's four-digit extension. Although Lynch was the primary detective on the Montecalvo case, Kight was his supervisor and therefore officially in charge of the investigation. Kight had suggested that the officers might be able to remember more about what they'd seen the night of the murder. Now, listening to Lynch, he was thrilled to learn about the details Sorkness had been able to remember.

Throughout the spring and well into the summer, Lynch and Kight went over the police reports written after Carol's murder looking for areas where detail might be missing. On July 15, Kight called Officer Medlin into his office.

The original report Medlin had written about the night of Carol's murder included only the essential facts. For instance, he had not written about the barking dogs at the neighbor's house where he was crouched in the front yard. Neighbors had since been interviewed and none of them had heard dogs barking until the police arrived. That meant, in all likelihood, burglars had not escaped from the Montecalvo home after the shooting, unless they had gone north toward Suzan Brown's house.

Medlin had also not written in his original report that the house was well lit and that two cars were parked in the driveway—both reasons for police to question whether a burglary had actually taken place. He also had not mentioned that Dan had appeared to walk normally down the hall until he saw the police, at which time he had grabbed his side and begun limping. According to medical experts, Dan's injury was such that he might not have been forced to limp.

After an hour in the office with Kight, Medlin began to remember these details. They became so clear that when he and Kight had finished their discussion, Medlin was able to write a three-page supplemental report. In that report he coined Dan's behavior as something akin to "show time."

Finally satisfied with the initial and supplemental police reports, Kight and Lynch grew increasingly frustrated as the next several months slipped by. In their combined thirty years of police work they had come to trust their hunches. When their conversation focused on Dan Montecalvo's possible involvement in his wife's murder, they saw the puzzle pieces forming a picture that confirmed their suspicions. He was their man. He had to be. There were days when they rehashed each report, each piece of evidence taken at the scene. They spent hours telephoning Dan and Carol's friends. But still they had nothing concrete, no neatly tied package of evidence to present to the district attorney's office.

In the early stages of solving a murder, detectives like to use deductive logic. Therefore, if an animal looked like a skunk and walked like a skunk it probably was a skunk. But in Dan's case there was only the putrid smell of a skunk. And in the criminal justice system prosecuting attorneys needed to walk into court with something more than a bad smell.

So the months slipped by and the investigation continued, never really going anywhere. Not until January 16, 1989, nearly a year after Carol's murder, did the pattern of frustration change. That was the morning Kight handed the investigation over to Detective Brian Arnspiger.

13

A good number of homicide detectives grow up knowing they want to be police officers. They wear plastic badges as children, pretending to be cops and doing their best to catch the robbers. As teenagers, they watch police shows on television and imagine a day when they will be chasing the bad guys and making the arrests.

This was not the case with Brian Arnspiger.

The son of a machinist and a homemaker, Brian from birth had a way of taking over a situation and mastering it to his own benefit. In 1943, technology was such that Brian's mother had been unaware she was pregnant with twins. Twenty minutes after giving birth to a healthy baby boy, she began having more contractions. Soon afterward, Brian made his entrance into the world, instantly becoming the talk of the maternity ward and the unexpected miracle of the Arnspiger household.

The identical twins grew up in Norwood Park, Illinois, with their older brother, Gordon, and a younger brother, Gene. Norwood Park, an ethnic melting pot a few miles north of Chicago, was an idyllic place for children. During the summer, boys would congregate along Circle Avenue to play baseball and stickball. Groups of girls would huddle together on the steps of large brick home fronts, giggling and sharing secrets.

When winter came, everyone in the neighborhood gathered at the local park for ice-skating and hockey.

Brian began participating in the activities that brought life to his neighborhood as soon as he was able to walk. Before long, his father realized there was something different about his son. No matter what Brian did, it was never enough. If he found time to do well in sports, he still could get high marks in school. When he took extra time to study with his brothers after dinner, he would still find time to be the only one of his siblings to make his bed and clean his room.

Those were happy times for the Arnspigers. The boys' father had an average-paying job, their mother stayed home baking bread, making dinner, and providing her family with an atmosphere that was typical of the 1950s.

By the time Brian entered high school in 1957, he had sprouted to more than six feet tall with the lanky build of a wide receiver. While his twin brother found satisfaction in playing musical instruments, Brian played baseball and football and ran track.

On the field, the brown-haired athlete finally found an arena where he could express his intensely competitive, overachieving personality. His brothers were also athletically inclined, each excelling in baseball. No one in the family was surprised when Brian managed to earn honors not only in track but in baseball as well.

The only negative factor in their otherwise blissful life was the Puerto Rican gangs that sometimes hung out near William Howard Taft High School. Occasionally these gangs would intimidate students while they walked home by blocking off a street corner. More than once, Brian took the initiative and used his fist to lay flat the largest gang members until, eventually, they no longer were a problem.

The way Brian saw it, people had a right to live in a town and walk to their high school without feeling afraid. Having thrived since childhood in a strict though nurturing environment, Brian was fiercely protective of it. He could think of no better reason to fight than to preserve the sense of safety and morality that prevailed during the fifties and early sixties.

In 1961 the Arnspigers moved to Burbank, California, to escape the cold Illinois winters and so Brian's father could pursue work as a machinist in nearby Los Angeles. There was never a question about which of the Arnspiger sons would learn the trade, following in their father's footsteps. Brian had been watching his father since he was a little boy and after the move to Burbank he, too, became a machinist. He and his father grew even closer and although he was taking college courses Brian believed he would be happy to spend the rest of his life repairing, perfecting, and designing machinery.

At that time Brian's social life revolved around his family and his involvement at Burbank's Christ Lutheran Church of the Missouri Synod. Brian enjoyed attending church because its members still very much espoused the values of the 1950s: conservatism, good manners, decent morals.

It was after a weekly church meeting in late 1962 that Brian heard that President Kennedy had announced that a war with Cuba—and possibly even the Soviet Union—was imminent.

As Brian read the headlines that day, absorbing each detail about the Cuban missile crisis, he believed that his country was on the brink of another worldwide war. One article in the paper told the story of a nineteen-year-old East German youth who was killed trying to escape over the Berlin Wall. Brian was haunted by the picture of the dead young man sprawled across rolls of concertina barbed wire, a victim of the pursuit of freedom. For several long minutes tears filled Brian's eyes and he was unable to tear himself from the picture. Slowly and painstakingly, he ripped out the article, folded it, and put it in his pocket.

Not long afterward, remembering the price the young German had paid, Brian walked to the local recruiter's office in Burbank and enlisted with the United States Air Force. His job as a machinist would have to wait.

When the missile crisis was diffused a few days later, Brian was not sorry about his decision to join the Air Force. Like sports, the service provided Brian with an outlet and, not surprisingly, he excelled under the Air Force's strict discipline. Brian was assigned to the Bossier Base Atomic Energy Commission, which operated within the confines of Barksdale Air Force Base Strategic Air Command in Shreveport, Louisiana.

Shortly afterward two of Brian's brothers also became involved with the military, eventually ending up in Vietnam. Although Brian's assignment with the Atomic Energy Commission was prestigious and required top-secret clearance, he was frustrated that the position did not allow him to fight in the war against Vietnam. Three times Brian put in requests to leave the commission and join his brothers overseas, but his was a permanent duty assignment and his requests were consistently turned down.

When Brian became aware that he was going to stay in Louisiana he turned his attention to more personal matters. During the following months he married his first wife, Bobbi, and within a few years of living on base the couple had two children, David and Diana.

While in the Air Force Brian got his first taste of law enforcement, serving four years as a member of the Air Police. Still, when he left the service in September 1966, Sergeant Arnspiger brought his young family back to Burbank with no thought of becoming a police officer. Instead, he returned to work with his father, while Bobbi set up house in a small home near Brian's parents.

Then, in the late 1960s, the country seemed to have forsaken its values and morals overnight. College students staged public demonstrations, drugs and sex were encouraged as a means of expression, and women could be seen burning their bras in their quest for equality. Brian was disgusted by these changes and grew increasingly tired of the sudden crime and rampant drug use that seemed to be affecting even his community.

"Dad, maybe I ought to be a cop," he would occasionally confide to his father.

But the senior Arnspiger would only regard his son with disapproval and shake his head. "Why would you want to do a foolhardy thing like that, Brian?"

"Someone has to do it. Come on, Dad. Aren't you sick of the way things have changed?" Brian moved away from the workbench and looked intently into his father's eyes. "Who's going to make a difference if I don't?"

The older man laughed. "Don't take the world so seriously, son." He patted Brian on the shoulder. "Anyway, you wouldn't be happy as a public employee, working with people."

For the next four years, Brian believed his father was

right. But then in the early 1970s, something happened that changed his mind forever.

Brian's grandmother owned an apartment complex in Hollywood called the Romaine Gardens. Several times a week, the seventy-year-old woman would walk slowly down to Western Avenue where she would buy fruit and vegetables from the open air market. One afternoon, she did not return.

Brian and his father finally located her at a nearby hospital, beaten and bruised and scared to death. As the pieces of the story began to unravel, the Arnspigers learned that the woman had been coming home when she had been attacked by two purse snatchers. The men had not been satisfied with taking the elderly woman's purse. They had also knocked her to the ground, seriously injuring her. A passerby had found her and taken her to the hospital.

That afternoon as Brian gently stroked his grandmother's soft, wrinkled hand, he felt overwhelmingly angry and helpless. Afterward he took personal responsibility for her safety, visiting her several times a week and making sure the grounds of her apartment complex were free from the shady characters that lurked in the area.

Despite his actions the older woman was mugged a second time. This time Brian knew he would be unable to live with himself if he didn't do something to help people like her. He drove to the Burbank Police Department and, at age thirty, signed up as a reserve officer.

From the beginning, Brian loved the position. There was the physical training, the camaraderie of the other officers, and, in his opinion, the ultimate thrill of putting crooks in jail. A year later Brian tested for a full-time position with the department and out of nearly 150 people he finished with the second highest score.

After two years, Brian was promoted from rookie to field training officer, a position that usually took much more experience to attain. During that time, in a three-month span in 1976, Brian was involved in two events that opened his eyes to the roller coaster of emotions in police work.

The first happened in June, shortly after midnight, when he and his partner came across a car completely engulfed in flames. A circle of onlookers stood helplessly nearby pointing at the car. Brian understood what was wrong; someone was trapped inside. With no concern for his own safety, he raced toward the car, opened the door, and pulled a 300-pound man to safety. Seconds later, the car exploded. The man lived because Brian gave him artificial respiration until paramedics arrived. Brian was awarded the department's first ever Medal of Valor award for his efforts.

Ninety-six days later Brian was still feeling the heady effects of knowing he was responsible for saving a life, when he and his partner responded to a burglary in progress. Brian was inching along the back wall of the building when a man burst into the alley and began shooting at him. Brian returned the fire and dove for the ground as one of the burglar's bullets passed through his right bicep. The burglar turned and ran, collapsing out of Brian's sight. Not until later at the hospital did Brian learn that one of his bullets had pierced the burglar's chest. The man died that night in the hospital.

Brian now understood the high stakes with which he was playing. This was no athletic competition, no game for high achievers. It was life and death. He learned the next day that the man he had killed was an ex-convict, on parole for armed robbery. He had been released from prison just a few months before.

Brian did not regret what had happened to the man. Crooks were responsible for ruining society, making streets unsafe, and placing in jeopardy the lives of innocent citizens and officers like himself. After that incident Brian became very good at catching burglars and putting them in jail. He learned the special tricks of hunting them down and finding enough evidence to make a case against them. Brian rejoiced in the sound of a jail door slamming shut on a convicted burglar. It was a sound that kept Brian going during even the toughest cases.

Although Brian was more than satisfied with his newfound career, his personal life took a beating in the late 1970s. In 1976, his parents retired to the Southwest and only a few months later his father died of a massive heart attack. In the years after that, while Brian tried to deal with his grief, he and Bobbi began to realize that somewhere along the course of their marriage they had stopped sharing their ideas and dreams, fears and hopes. By then they had a third child, Bill, and by all appearances seemed to have the perfect family life. But Brian was dedicated first and foremost to his job, often working until the early hours of the morning before coming home. Finally, after eighteen years of marriage, Brian and Bobbi realized they barely knew each other anymore. His determination to keep the streets safe had left an uncrossable chasm between them, and although they were both sorry to see their marriage end, they divorced in 1981.

Brian dealt with the blow by throwing himself even more fully into his work. By late 1981, six years after he had joined the police force, Brian's superiors recognized that many of their burglaries were being solved by the careful documentation and investigative work of Officer Arnspiger. That year Brian was promoted to detective. Based on the department's rotating schedule, he was assigned to the burglary division.

Though few homicides occurred inside Burbank's city limits, burglary had always been a problem—especially in the late 1980s. Brian loved his new position. There was a rush that came with tracking down burglars—slimy creeps like the guys who used to beat up his grandmother—and finding out where they were stashing the goods. The climax came the moment he and his partner burst through the front door, guns drawn, and made an arrest. Finally, after months of going after burglars with almost reckless abandon, Brian began to believe that the pain of his broken personal life would one day fade.

After his divorce Brian treasured his weekends, when he coached his children's Little League teams. Even as a youth coach, Brian could not tolerate people being treated unfairly. When other coaches cut certain children for their lack of ability, the kids were always welcome on Brian's team. Brian would then enlist the help of many dedicated parents, who worked with the children individually. In fifteen years of coaching, Brian's teams never finished worse than third place in their leagues.

During the 1981 Little League season Brian met a special woman named Kathy, whose son was on his team. They shared their struggles and hopes and came to depend on each other. A year later they were married. Now, in addition to his three children, Brian had two stepchildren. Finally Brian began looking forward once again to coming home.

Five years later his hard work with the police department paid off, and when the detectives were rotated he was assigned to the robbery-homicide division. This was the big time, the cases that involved attempted murder, bodily assault, robbery, and kidnapping. In this new position Brian hustled as he never had before, cracking one tough case after another.

There was the Barcena family of Burbank. For years police in the neighboring city of Glendale had known that the Barcenas were furnishing local gangs with PCP and other illegal drugs. But they had been unable to form a case against them.

One afternoon in 1987 some of the Barcenas kidnapped a girl who knew too much, forced a funnel down her throat, and tried to poison her with a drug overdose. Then they pushed her from a moving car and forgot about her until—after much prodding by Detective Arnspiger—she turned up in the witness protection program and brought the family to its knees with her testimony. Two adults and three juveniles were ordered to serve time and Brian was applauded by both Burbank and Glendale for a job well done.

After that there were more well-known cases until finally, by January 16, 1989, Brian Arnspiger had a reputation that few detectives ever come by.

On that day, Sergeant Bob Kight examined the file on Carol Montecalvo's murder. Detective Lynch had done a good job establishing circumstances and motive, but they needed someone obsessed with detail, someone who would leave nothing in Burbank unturned in the quest for evidence.

Finally Kight realized he had just two choices: shelve the case or give it to Arnspiger.

Quietly Kight discussed the matter with the division captain, who then walked down the hallway and stuck his head into Brian's office.

"Arnie, I need to see you for a minute," he said, motioning for Brian to follow him.

Returning to his office, the captain shut the door and sat down at his desk.

"This might not be fair, but you're my only hope." He sighed, staring down at the file on his desk and absently thumbing through the papers inside. "I'm giving you a case with no real evidence, no witnesses, and nothing more than suspicions to go on."

"What's the case, Captain?" Brian felt a rush of adrenaline shoot through his veins. A chase was about to begin.

"The Montecalvo murder." The captain paused for a moment. "What do you think?"

Brian knew the case well. The captain had been correct in what he'd said. The department had nothing to work with and the case was nearly a year old.

He pictured for a moment the helplessness of the Montecalvo woman, the horrifying betrayal she must have felt if, indeed, her husband had killed her. The thought sickened Brian, bringing out every feeling he'd ever had about maintaining the sanctity and safety of life. Brian thought the matter over for only a few seconds, imagining the sound of another jail door slamming shut, another thug taken off the streets. Slowly he reached across the captain's desk and picked up the file.

"Let's put someone in jail." And with that, the investigation into the murder of Carol Montecalvo continued in full force.

14

In the spring of 1989, with Brian Arnspiger working on Carol's murder investigation and Suzan Brown deeply in need of psychiatric help, Dan Montecalvo befriended a petite, intelligent redhead from Texas named Annette Wilder.

Back in 1982 Annette and Carol had managed different directory sales divisions for the same telephone company. They became friends when Carol was given a transfer from Wisconsin to Los Angeles. At first Annette had been impressed with Carol's appearance, her neatly tailored navy blue business suit and the confident way in which she entered a room. Carol was easy to get close to. She had a warm laugh, lively brown eyes, and a way of making Annette feel like she'd known her for years. They were both married to men they adored and they shared an interest in old-fashioned family values, Elvis Presley, and black-and-white movies. Before long they began going to matinees and exercising together.

By the time Dan was able to join Carol in California, the two couples began double-dating on the weekends. Even after Carol and Dan became involved with new friends at Overcomers' Faith Center Church, Annette and Carol remained close. Through the mid-1980s, while Annette's marriage ended in divorce, she found herself envying Carol for finding the kind of love that really did last a lifetime. When she joined the couple for lunch occasionally, she would watch wistfully as Dan held Carol's hand and pulled her chair out as they were being seated. Throughout the meal Annette would notice Dan gazing at Carol like a lovesick schoolboy while Carol basked in his attention. In 1988 Annette decided the Montecalvos were one of the few truly happy couples she knew.

So when Dan called Annette from his hospital bed at St. Joseph's late on the night of April 2, Annette was completely shocked to learn that Carol had been murdered. After hanging up the telephone, she drove furiously to the hospital to comfort Dan. But it was after visiting hours, and the nurses refused to allow her in to see him. Shocked and confused, she climbed back into her car, pounding her steering wheel in frustration. Dan needed her and there wasn't a thing she could do. With tears streaming down her cheeks, Annette began driving.

At first she drove aimlessly, but eventually she wound up in front of the Montecalvo home. A police car was still parked outside and ominous black-and-yellow police tape circled the perimeter of the front yard, making it the center ring of some macabre freak show. Annette stared at the front door, as if at any moment Carol might open it and wave to her.

Annette closed her eyes, shutting out the image before her, so she didn't see the police officer walking toward her car. He tapped on her window, startling her. Embarrassed, she wiped the back of her hand across her wet cheeks.

"Can I help you, ma'am?" he said softly.

"I'm sorry." Annette's voice was shaky and the officer knew immediately that she presented no threat. "My friend lived here." A sob escaped from somewhere deep inside her. "She was killed."

The officer nodded solemnly. "I'm sorry. Really sorry."

An hour later when Annette had finally gone home that night, she had reached one conclusion. She would help Dan. She would do all she could to see that Carol's widower did not want for company or food or a place to stay. She visited Dan at the hospital the next morning and the morning after that. Annette held Dan's hand and allowed him to talk about what had happened the night of March 31.

"Carol was all I had, she was everything to me," Dan had told her several times during their visits. "How will I ever live without her?" Annette was moved by the man's agony, his soft-spoken grief and sorrowful eyes. During those visits she found herself understanding why Carol had loved him. Dan seemed like a helpless boy, haunted by trouble and desperately in need of a woman's rescue. By the time Dan left the hospital one week later to finish recuperating with a family from church, he and Annette were fast friends.

Annette had told herself she had never met a more sincere and honest man than Dan Montecalvo. Over the next few weeks, he treated her with the charm of a southern gentleman and never crossed the line of friendship. When they were together, Annette found herself remembering Carol's stories of how Dan had been drowning in a sea of self-destruction until she came along. After that, he had clung to her like a life preserver. Now, with Carol gone, Annette thought he seemed to cling to her in the same way.

She had no reason to question Carol's description of Dan's past. Never had she heard Carol complain about the way Dan treated her. If his drinking and gambling represented a troublesome challenge, his love and devotion during sober moments more than made up for it. At least that was what Carol had always said.

Now Annette felt complete pity for the man. If sometimes his behavior, his concern about the police investigation, didn't seem appropriate for a man whose wife had just been killed, Annette decided it was because he was still in shock. She allowed him to confide in her, to share his paranoid fears.

"Those police are downright preposterous," she would say. "Please tell me if there's anything I can do to help."

"That means a lot to me." Dan hitched up his pants and humbly looked downward, moving his toe in tight circles on the ground. "I don't know what I'd do without friends like you. You're a blessing, Annette."

By the end of April, one month after Carol's murder, it became apparent to those who knew him that Dan Montecalvo was not holding up well under the pressure of being the primary suspect in the murder of his wife. He was becoming increasingly paranoid about the Burbank police, complaining to Annette that they were following him, framing him, and perhaps even trying to kill him. Concerned about his ability to handle these feelings and convinced by Annette and others that he needed help, Dan began seeing a psychiatrist in late April.

The professional counselor prescribed Valium for Dan's anxiety but the medication apparently did little to ease his fears. Less than a month later Annette was having lunch with him at the Hamburger Hamlet in Burbank when she caught a glimpse of what appeared to be a revolver tucked in his waistband.

Annette tilted her pretty red head as she set her hamburger back down on her plate. "Dan? Is that a gun?" she asked with concern.

A momentary flicker of surprise crossed Dan's face and then disappeared. "What?" He cleared his throat.

"Right there," she said, pointing to Dan's waist and sounding more than slightly concerned. "It looked like a gun."

Dan moved aside his jacket, exposing the black handle of what appeared to be a revolver.

"This?" Dan lowered his voice and leaned across the table so Annette could hear him. "I need it." He reached down and lifted his pants leg to show a small white-handled automatic pistol tucked inside his sock. "This one, too. I need 'em both."

Annette laughed nervously. "Whatever for, Dan?"

"The police hate me, Annette. They're after me. I need to be ready, need to protect myself. You never know what'll happen."

Annette nodded and shrugged her shoulders, appearing to dismiss the subject. Many people kept guns for protection, but she had never been one of them. Too often guns killed the wrong people. After all, Carol had died from gunshot wounds. As Dan changed the topic of conversation, Annette was troubled by his reasons for carrying the weapons. One did not need to carry guns for protection against the very people who were paid to keep one safe. Dan was a victim, not a wanted criminal. Yet, here he was, in broad daylight, eating in a family hamburger joint, carrying not one, but two guns for protection against the *police*.

Perhaps not ready to draw any conclusions, Annette decided to believe Dan and tried to dismiss the incident. He must be in shock, she reasoned. But as the minutes passed by, she felt her stomach tightening. When they stood to leave, Annette realized she had left most of her lunch untouched.

When Dan got home that night, back to the house where his wife had been shot and killed, he carefully placed the guns in his bedroom dresser drawer.

They're coming at me from everywhere, he thought.

He glanced around his house. "I gotta get outta here," he mumbled.

For the next ninety minutes he began performing a task that had by then become routine. He moved meticulously from room to room, carefully checking every inch of the house for taping devices or signs that police had been in his home. When he got to the spot in the hallway where Carol had bled to death, Dan stepped gingerly around it. He had taken scissors and removed the spot the day he moved back into the home. But even with the carpet gone, he never stepped directly on the spot.

Finally, in the bedroom, he found proof of police activity. A piece of paper that had been next to his telephone now sat across the room on a dresser. Dan took out a notebook and jotted down his observation.

They're closing in, he thought.

Several weeks later Dan's friend, Jack McKenzie, had an experience similar to Annette's. Jack and his wife had known Carol from church and after her death they had invited Dan to live with them while he recuperated. Before becoming a Christian in the late 1970s, Jack had been addicted to drugs. Now that he was completely clean, he empathized with people who were unhappy and did what he could to help them. During his three-week stay, Dan and Jack became friends and for months afterward the two men continued to get together.

Since Jack collected guns and frequently participated in shooting contests, police first suspected him of assisting Dan in the murder of his wife. Eventually they dropped this idea because their evidence suggested no one had left the house after the shootings. For that reason early on in the investigation police were convinced Dan worked alone.

As for Jack, he believed Dan was innocent for one reason alone—the location of his gunshot wound. Dan knew as much about guns as Jack did, only Dan had gained his knowledge in prison. No one with any understanding of guns would shoot himself in the waist. There were a hundred different ways a bullet could exit the body from that point, including several paths that might send the bullet straight out the top of the head. After listening to Dan talk about his background, Jack had decided he was a sleazy, self-destructive gambler-alcoholic. But he was convinced he didn't kill Carol.

One afternoon after Jack and Dan had gone to a movie matinee, Jack noticed Dan was carrying a gun.

"What in God's name are you doing with that?" Jack was not one to mince words.

Tiny beads of sweat broke out on Dan's forehead as he ran his fingers through his short, slicked-back hair. "I carry two. I need 'em, Jack. The cops are after me. You know that."

Jack couldn't believe his ears. "What do you think? They're going to shoot you? Like some cheap gangster movie?" He leaned closer to Dan. "Dan, if they want you, they'll arrest you."

Dan shook his head nervously. "No, no. They're

gonna kill me. They don't want me around messing up their investigation."

"Listen, Dan, if it would make you feel better I can get you some protection. Bulletproof vest, something like that." Jack would not have had trouble obtaining such protective clothing because of his connection with various gun clubs.

Dan wiped his forehead. "No, no way, Jack. Can't do it. I need these guns. For all we know, they've searched your car while we were in the movies. They're after me, Jack. I'm telling you, they're after me."

As Jack listened he remembered that Dan had told him he'd been involved in organized crime in his younger days. Connections to big-time crime families. Jack had never believed the stories before and he didn't believe them now. Dan seemed to be acting out some kind of fantasy in which he was an important crime figure and the police were corrupt villains. He seemed to have convinced himself that he would not be safe without carrying guns.

Jack shook his head sadly. "Dan, do you know what they're going to do if they arrest you and you're carrying two guns?" Jack didn't wait for Dan's response. "They'll thank you for cutting off your own head and handing it to them on a shiny silver platter, and then they'll send you to prison and throw away the key. Get rid of the guns!"

Dan shook his head. "I can't, Jack."

After that discouraging talk Jack tried again several times to convince Dan to stop carrying guns. When Dan insisted on keeping them, Jack decided the man was truly the most self-destructive person he had ever known.

* * *

In June, Dan's psychiatrist made essentially the same observation, noting these signs that Dan was in need of psychological help: depression, paranoia, and self-destructive tendencies.

Later that summer Annette had to leave town for a six-month business trip to Texas. She asked Dan—who had recently sold his house on South Myers Street—to move into her apartment and take care of the place in exchange for free rent. She hoped the move would help Dan get back on his feet financially.

The setup did wonders for Dan, who suddenly found himself in a financial situation that was much less stressful than at any other time in his life. He had $150,000 in proceeds from the sale of his home, and at about the same time he collected $220,000 from the largest of Carol's life insurance policies. Now that his budget wasn't quite so tight, Dan paid off his gambling debts and, feeling less tense, stopped seeing his psychiatrist.

Late that fall, showing a propensity for making bad decisions and exemplifying the very self-destructive behaviors his friends and doctor had observed, Dan took his newly acquired funds and on October 28, 1988, made a gambling trip to the Golden Nugget Casino in Nevada. By New Year's Day 1989 Dan was visiting Las Vegas several times a month playing blackjack with an average bet of $347 per hand.

Annette returned to Burbank in late January and was immediately notified by her homeowners' association, of which she was a member of the board of directors, that some problems had arisen while she was gone. They said her condominium had been the site of numerous loud parties in the past six months. In addition, a number of prostitutes had been seen going to and from her home. Other homeowners had complained and the association wanted Annette's word that these unacceptable occurrences would not be repeated.

"Dan?" Annette asked as he let her into the condominium later that day. She sounded hurt and betrayed. "What happened while I was gone?"

"Okay." Dan drew in a deep breath. "Now, you might have heard some stories about things that went on here. I can explain the whole thing." Annette walked slowly around her home. Smoke stains marked the walls and her once-crisp white curtains were now yellow. Cigarette burns dotted her marble kitchen countertop. The place seemed dank and dingy and was almost unrecognizable compared to the cheerful home it had been. Annette stopped just short of Dan and looked him straight in the eyes.

"I already heard the stories, Dan," she said quietly. "You know I'm on the board of directors for the homeowners' association."

She waited for his explanation.

Dan looked indignant. "Well, that's all they are, Annette. Stories. Yeah, sure a prostitute came up here once in a while. You know why?" Dan raised his voice. "To bring up a payment from one of the guys I gamble for." Dan lowered his voice again and narrowed his eyes. "Don't worry. Nothing happened. I just took the money and sent them on their way." He paused. "You believe me, don't you?"

Annette took a moment to digest Dan's version of the story. How could she doubt him? Here was the man her closest friend had loved for eight years, the man Carol had rescued and who owed her his very heart and soul. The man standing before her had gone through the sort of ordeal no one should ever have to go through. How could she even consider doubting him?

Slowly, she released a pent-up sigh and leaned over to hug Dan.

"Of course I believe you, Dan. You've never lied to me." Annette was disgusted with herself for doubting Carol's husband, even for a few moments. She looked about the condominium again. Later she would insist that Dan help her clean the place up. But she had expected it to look messy. After all, Dan was a man harassed by police and still paralyzed by grief. He also no longer had a loving wife to help him keep the place clean. Annette certainly did not expect him to handle that task all by himself with everything else he had to think about.

In the following months the friendship between Dan and Annette—while purely platonic—grew stronger. Dan had moved out of her apartment and now rented one of his own. He and Annette lunched together on a weekly basis and spent hours talking on the telephone. Annette knew Dan needed her because all he ever talked about was why the police were wrong to suspect him in Carol's murder. Sometimes Annette and Dan would play a little game in which she would be the devil's advocate and Dan would provide reasons why he was innocent.

"The police believe you did it, Dan," Annette would say uncomfortably. She did not like to doubt Dan, even in jest.

"Impossible," Dan would answer, shaking his head angrily. "I couldn't have done it, because how could I have shot myself in the back?"

"Well," Annette would say, her Texas accent thick as

she played up her role. "You might well have had a partner."

"How could I have had a partner?"

"Very easily."

"How would he have gotten in?"

"Same way you say the burglars got in."

"How could he have gotten away?"

"Very easily. He drove."

"What about his car?" Dan fired back, taking a deep breath as the questions grew more intense. "People would have seen it."

"Well, now," Annette retorted, tilting her head and raising an eyebrow. "I don't believe he would have parked it out front. He parked it several streets away, of course, and scurried out the back door over fences and through people's yards."

And so it went, this game they often played over lunch. Annette knew Dan was obsessed with proving himself innocent. And if his desire to play such a game ever bothered her or led her to doubt him, she never said so. Back then, showing even a hint of doubt made her feel as if she were betraying everything she and Carol had shared as friends.

By the spring of 1989, days before the first anniversary of Carol's murder, Dan had lost a staggering $53,200 in Las Vegas casinos, something he never mentioned to Annette. In fact, there were many things about Dan's background that Annette knew nothing about. In late July, Detective Brian Arnspiger and Sergeant Bob Kight, guessing at her ignorance, decided she should know more about her new friend. When security guards from Annette's condominium complex informed her that police had been asking questions about her involvement with Dan Montecalvo, she immediately dialed his telephone number.

"Dan, police are comin' round here asking questions." Annette's voice was urgent. For the first time since befriending Dan she wondered if she might have allowed herself to become too involved in his life. Suddenly, a seed of doubt began to grow in her mind.

"Damn cops," Dan muttered angrily. "What did they say?"

Annette paused a moment before answering him, taken aback by Dan's response. "They want to speak to me. Dan, I'm going to call them."

"What?" It was an angry, violent response and at the other end Annette involuntarily shrank back into her sofa. "Don't do it," he ordered loudly. "You can't talk to them."

Annette steadied herself. "Dan, I'm going to call them. I don't want them back around here asking questions and making a scene. The neighbors will talk."

"You don't trust me or you wouldn't do this," Dan shouted, his voice loud and defensive.

"This has nothing to do with trust. Of course I trust you, Dan. Don't be crazy. Now, I'm calling them as soon as I hang up."

Dan forced an angry sigh. "Okay. Call me right back. Soon as you get done with them."

"Fine."

Annette was angry with Dan as she dialed the Burbank Police Department. What right did he have to tell her not to call the police. What was he afraid of? Annette pushed the answers from her mind.

In the first minute of her conversation with Sergeant Kight, Dan called her back, breaking through on Annette's second line to ask what was being said.

"I'll call you when I'm done," she said impatiently. "I'm still on the phone with them."

Kight had introduced himself and told her that he and his men were investigating Dan for the murder of his wife.

"Now, what if we could tell you something you don't already know about Dan?" Kight asked pleasantly.

"You can't tell me something I don't know. I'm his closest friend. I know everything about what's going on."

"Well, I'm not so sure you know everything."

Then Kight proceeded to explain some of the things Annette did not know about Dan. Sometime toward the end of the conversation, after Annette had heard enough to question Dan's integrity and her own intelligence in befriending him, she agreed to visit the police station. While they were working out details of the visit, Dan called again to question Annette.

"I said I'd call you," Annette said calmly. Dan listened closely to her voice and thought it sounded different than before. More distant.

Annette would have agreed with his assessment. For the first time since she'd learned about Carol's death she was afraid of her dead friend's husband.

15

Brian Arnspiger investigated the Montecalvo murder as he had never investigated any case before in his life. He found it a tremendous challenge that no one else had been able to crack it. He wasted no time getting started.

The first thing Brian did the same day he was assigned the case was to lock himself in one of the station's empty interview rooms with boxes of evidence and every report written on the case. He remembered his sergeant's words: "No real evidence, no witnesses, and nothing more than suspicions to go on." Brian put them out of his mind and carefully spread the evidence along the rectangular table. For the next five hours he went over each item with the precision of a surgeon.

At 4 P.M. he struck gold. A pair of men's pants lay at the bottom of one of the boxes. Brian carefully pulled them out and stared at the numerous blood spots on the lower pant legs, including the knees. Gingerly he maneuvered the evidence tag so he could read the description. *Men's pants worn by Dan Montecalvo, 3-31-88.* Quickly, his eyes darted back to the middle portion of the pant legs, both of which were freckled with blood spots.

Brian felt a surge of excitement race through his body. Someone else might have thought nothing of the blood spots, completely missing their significance. But

Brian had just returned from San Bernardino where he had taken an extensive course on blood spatter taught by Detective Craig Ogino. If anyone knew the subject it was Craig Ogino. His reputation for unraveling murders by examining the angle and diameter of blood spots preceded him in crime-solving circles throughout the country.

Brian had been fascinated by the course. Simply put, when a bullet enters the body, a certain amount of blood sprays backward toward the origin of the bullet. The objective, as Ogino pointed out early in the course, was to learn as much as possible about that bloody back spatter. In doing so, they had fired bullets into porous sponges soaked in a red bloodlike liquid. For hours they had examined the resulting red back splash, determining how the spots varied depending upon how far away the gun was fired and the size and speed of the bullet.

When Brian returned to Burbank after three days with Craig Ogino, he had gained more knowledge about bloodstains, blood spots, and back spatter than he thought he'd ever be able to use. But that was before he discovered Dan's bloodstained pants.

According to Dan he had been outside the house that cool March evening when Carol was shot. Minutes later, after he had run into the house and himself been shot by the burglars, Dan knelt at Carol's side to take her pulse and whisper words of encouragement. In doing so, he knelt in the blood near her head, picking up splotches of blood on his knees and the lower portion of his pants. For nearly a year now Dan's explanation had gone unchallenged.

As Brian scrutinized the pants, he didn't need Craig Ogino in the room to tell him that Dan's account didn't add up. There must have been nearly fifty blood spots on the pant legs. Tiny, circular spots. Brian believed those spots told a truer version of the story.

Firearms specialists and field evidence technicians had already determined that Carol had been shot from a range of no more than four feet. One of the bullets had pierced the major artery that ran along her spine. Brian's newly acquired knowledge told him that when that happened, her blood would have splashed backward, spraying whoever held the gun.

He stared at the pants for a moment longer and then snapped into action. He walked to the other end of the table and picked up a pile of photographs taken at the scene. Quickly, he thumbed through them until he found what he was looking for. Pictures of Carol's body. Even though the pictures had been taken in a poorly lit room, they clearly showed that Carol's blood had saturated the plush carpet in the hallway of the Montecalvo home. Her blood had been so deep that closeup pictures showed a crusty ring of dried blood around the perimeter of her face. The blood had been deep enough for her face to be submerged in it. If Dan had knelt anywhere near Carol's head, as he claimed, the knees and portions of the lower pant legs would have been saturated with bloodstains. Brian put the photos down, walked briskly back to where the pants lay, and looked at them again.

If Dan had been outside when Carol was shot, how did he wind up with what certainly appeared to be back spatter on his pant legs? Brian believed the answer was obvious. That afternoon Brian made a phone call to San Bernardino and the next day he was back in Craig Ogino's office.

"Craig," Brian said. "What do the bloodstains on these pants tell you?" Brian carefully lifted the pants from a brown bag he was carrying and spread them out on Ogino's desk.

Ogino did not hesitate. "Looks like a clear-cut case of back spatter to me. Whoever wore these pants either fired the gun or stood alongside the gunman when the shooting took place. Want me to take a closer look?"

Brian nodded. "I want you to be sure. The most accurate opinion you can give me."

Ogino did not need to be asked twice. After all, he was an expert in the subject. He had even set up a miniature laboratory in a room adjacent to his office, complete with microscopes and stations for experimentation. Ogino carried the pants to the nearest microscope and began analyzing the spots.

"What's the story behind the pants?" asked Ogino, as he carefully took some measurements.

"Worn by a man I think killed his wife," Brian answered. "He says he was outside when she was shot, came in to help her and knelt in blood beside her head. Presto: Blood spots."

Ogino looked closely at the pants. "I don't think he was outside when she was shot. Unless the lady's blood sprayed twenty feet straight through a stucco wall."

Thirty minutes passed in silence as Ogino performed painstaking tests on each blood spot. When he was finished, he set the pants down and released a deep sigh.

"She was shot from a range of two to four feet," he said. Brian recognized that the man was not asking a question.

"Did I tell you that?" Brian asked, somewhat confused as to how this genius detective knew that detail about Carol Montecalvo's murder.

"You didn't have to," he said, removing his glasses and rubbing his eyes. "The spots tell it all."

"What else do they say, Craig?" Brian leaned forward. This was the moment he had been waiting for.

"If I hear them right, they say, 'Well done, Brian. You've got your man.'"

By 10 o'clock the next morning Brian was sitting in Sergeant Kight's office explaining the battery of tests Ogino had performed before he concluded that the pants were worn by a man who had indeed pulled the trigger. The excitement in the room was palpable.

"Of course," Kight said, frustrated that they had missed the detail for so long. "Those pants have been here all the time. It's obvious now. Here we've been running around trying to find some evidence to hang this guy and the best piece of all has been right under our noses."

A satisfied smile came across Brian's face. Dan Montecalvo would be locked away for a long, long time. "Now, how 'bout getting this thing to trial," he said, getting up from his chair and moving toward the door.

Kight paused for a moment. "Well, that's the thing. Because the Montecalvo case resembled the Anderson murder, sheriff's department is still checking evidence for us. They've asked us to let them look at all the evidence. Let's get the pants over to them, make sure they arrive at the same results."

Brian grimaced. "How long will that take?"

"Not long."

One morning a week later Kight stuck his head through Brian's open office door.

"Got a minute?"

Brian stood up and followed the sergeant into the hallway. "What's up?"

"Evidence technicians from the sheriff's department just sent over a report. Seems they finished running tests on Dan's pants."

The excitement was beginning to swell again. If the results were in, that meant the police were only hours away from making an arrest. Every instinct told Brian that this could be a tremendously satisfying day. In his mind Brian began making plans to celebrate Dan's arrest later that night with Kathy. Not until he saw the frustration in Kight's eyes did he snap back to reality. Kight's eyes told him that incredibly they had hit another brick wall, that somehow a blood expert at the sheriff's department had disagreed with Ogino's findings.

Brian knew that if the experts disagreed over what caused the blood spots on Dan's pants, the conflicting testimony would be useless in court. The prosecution would bring Ogino in to testify that the spots were back spatter, proof that Dan had shot his wife. Then the defense would bring in the sheriff's expert to say the spots had resulted from kneeling in blood. The autopsy had determined that Carol had been shot at close range. Without back spatter on his clothing, the defense could prove Dan had been nowhere near Carol when she was shot. This kind of conflict would likely be more damaging to the prosecution because at least one explanation for the spots would prove Dan's innocence.

Ultimately, if the experts disagreed, Brian knew he would be put back to square one. He waited a full fifteen seconds before speaking. His voice was little more than a whisper. "What'd they say?"

Kight shrugged his shoulders. "I don't know how to tell you this, Brian." The sergeant lowered his eyes to the floor. "He disagreed with Ogino. Said it wasn't back spatter." Kight picked up a report on his desk. "The report says back spatter would have covered the length of the pant legs. In his opinion, since the spots are concentrated around the knee area, they were most likely caused by Dan kneeling in blood."

16

The utter quiet of the place was driving Suzan Brown crazy. There were no appliances, no records or tapes, nothing in the tiny rented apartment that made the slightest bit of noise.

That spring 1989, she had become more dependent on drugs than at any time in her past. Since moving out of her house on South Myers Street, Suzan had not seen or heard from Ron Hardy. Occasionally, some part of her psyche continued to believe that she and Ron had somehow been involved in Carol's murder. She could picture herself rummaging through the Montecalvos' cash box just as Carol walked into the house. Carol had seen them, asked them what they were doing, and then they had fired two shots at her. Next, Dan had come running into the house and they had fired one bullet at him. Then they had left out the back door, jumping their neighbor's fence and scurrying into their own backyard.

Other times, she was equally convinced that she had not been involved, that she had been home when the shots were fired and had then heard someone running through her backyard knocking over her woodpile.

The resulting confusion had sent her into a deep, dark depression in the midst of which she had moved three times. She had also made several plans to commit suicide, but had been unable to carry them through. Drugs seemed to be her only means of escape, even if they had left her nearly penniless. By then, she was spending nearly all her money on speed and junk food. Lately, she had been writing bad checks to pay for the drugs when her pension money ran out.

On that April afternoon, more than a year after Carol's murder, two days had passed since she had been able to get her hands on any speed. Suzan glanced down at her hands and held her fingers straight out. They shook violently until she could no longer stand it, and she drew her fingers into tightly clenched fists.

At moments like this Suzan wondered if she hadn't perhaps already died and gone to hell. If she had, she knew it was because she deserved it. As far as she was concerned, hell certainly couldn't be any lonelier, any more frightening, than the horrifying quiet of her apartment.

Suzan rolled her wheelchair into the kitchen for the sixth time that hour. Frantically she pulled out drawers and emptied containers. There had to be some speed somewhere. When her search proved fruitless Suzan heard someone release a shaky deep breath and then realized the sound had come from her own mouth.

For a moment her eyes glazed over and she leaned back in her chair, almost willing herself to disappear, to no longer exist. She knew when this problem had started—or at least when it had gotten worse. March 31, 1988. The night Carol was murdered. The night she had witnessed Carol being murdered.

Maybe the authorities would arrest her for writing bad checks. At least then, in the secure confines of a jail cell, she would have someone else to talk to, and someone to take care of her meals and remind her that she was, indeed, still alive.

She wondered now, as she had hundreds of times each day since Carol's death, what Carol would say if she knew that her husband was being unfairly treated like a suspect in her murder. Dan didn't kill Carol. Suzan Brown shuddered, temporarily emerging from the trance she'd fallen into and glancing furtively about the kitchen counter for the drugs she so desperately craved. There were none.

Her eyes grew foggy again, her mind slipping back in time. Her real problems had started years ago, even she knew that much. Back in Vietnam. Back when she still had a future in the medical profession.

In the late 1960s, Suzan had just become a registered nurse. Excited, she suddenly felt bold enough to tell her parents the truth about her personal life. She proudly laid out the facts. She was a lesbian, she told them, had been for years, and thought it was time her parents knew. There had been an agonizing moment of silence.

"Is this some kind of a joke, Suzan?" her father had asked.

Suzan had shifted uncomfortably from one foot to another. "No. It's the truth. I thought you'd want to know."

More silence followed as Suzan's mother moved to stand beside her father. When he finally spoke, Suzan knew he was speaking for both of them. "Get out! No daughter of ours would ever be so sick and twisted. We won't have someone like you living under our roof."

Suzan knew then that she no longer had a family to whom she could turn. Later her friends would say that the confrontation with her parents had scarred her for life. She buried any pain she'd felt from the incident and quickly grew unfeeling toward the world. If her own parents didn't want her, no one would. After that Suzan lived life with reckless abandon, as if she no longer cared who suffered as a result of her actions.

With nowhere to live and no one to whom she could turn, Suzan enlisted in the United States Army and was promptly sent to Vietnam. She arrived in Saigon in 1968 to work at an army hospital where casualties from the Tet Offensive were being treated. Overnight Suzan found she no longer had time to think about her parents or her sexual preference, not amid life and death, blood and bandages, missing limbs and missing men. Her existence centered around the challenge of pushing herself to the limit to save one more boy from becoming another statistic in a war that made less and less sense.

By the end of each day Suzan would take off her blood-spattered coat, scrub the smell of antiseptic from her hands, and barely make it home before dropping into bed exhausted. At first this endless routine made her feel better about herself. No matter what her parents thought of her, she had her life, her ability to make a difference. Those early days of treating patients brought Suzan as close to caring about others as she would ever come again in her lifetime.

Eventually, though, she began to dread her patients, many of whom were heavily dependent on drugs. There were soldiers who used heavy amounts of marijuana to help ease their pain and others who were hooked on speed to take the edge off the depression that had settled over so many of them. There were patients who avoided drugs, too. Good boys from good homes, sent to Vietnam to stop communism from taking over the world.

It began to seem to Suzan—even if it wasn't the truth —that when she did treat such a patient, he rarely survived. Good always died, and in her life, evil always seemed to prevail. When a good soldier survived, too often both legs would be amputated, or else he would be paralyzed. Gradually, a bitter hopelessness began to make its way through Suzan's psyche. A year later, when one of her patients gave her a tablet of speed, she no longer considered the ramifications of using the drug. She slipped into the hospital bathroom, took the tablet, and waited. For the next several hours she felt as exhilarated as she had when she first arrived in Vietnam.

There was no turning back. In the hospital, certain patients made speed readily available. Before Suzan knew what had happened, the drug had not only become part of her daily routine, it had also become a part of her. Of course, after the first time she never again felt that same energetic feeling. In fact she seemed always to require more of the drug. But Suzan knew that without it her life would be unbearable.

That had been nearly twenty years ago. Now, as Suzan blinked back the memory, it seemed like a vague piece of somebody else's past. Could that really have been her life? A nurse in Vietnam? Saving lives? Suzan wondered sometimes if she hadn't perhaps imagined the whole scenario.

But then she sometimes felt that way about Carol's murder, too.

Suzan glanced at the clock on the kitchen wall. It, too, was silent, the second hand making its incessant rounds without a sound. Two o'clock. She still had time.

As if propelled into action by some unseen force, Suzan suddenly stood up, grabbed her purse, and walked out of the apartment. It was 3 P.M. when she returned. The plan had worked. Another bad check passed off at another two-bit check-cashing joint. With cash in hand it hadn't been that difficult to get hold of some speed, which she had popped immediately. Her twitching, cramping body had desperately needed its fix.

Suzan walked to her wheelchair and sat down. The silence was even louder than before and now evening was falling. Somehow Suzan knew she could not tolerate one more night alone in that apartment. She wheeled her chair into the bathroom and reached into the medicine cabinet beneath the sink. Sleeping pills. Every speed freak needed them. She remembered the first time she had used them, after three sleepless days and nights of binging on speed. Speed had given her a paranoid feeling that sleep would never come again, but even that feeling hadn't been this bad.

She picked up a dirty glass near the sink and filled it with water. Quickly, she fumbled with the bottle of sleeping pills, recoiling as the sound of rattling pills broke the silence in the room. Nervously, she sifted nearly twenty pills onto the fleshy palm of her hand and stuffed them into her mouth.

At that instant she remembered something one of the soldiers had said to her. Both his legs had been amputated and tears rolled down his face as he took Suzan's hand in his.

"You saved my life, Suzan. If you never do anything else again you can die knowing you saved my life."

But then his words became those of her father's instead. "No daughter of ours would ever be so sick and twisted. . . . No daughter of ours would ever be so sick and twisted."

The words ricocheted off the bathroom walls. Suzan reached for the glass of water and in one swift motion put it to her lips, gulping enough water to wash the pills down. There. It was over. This time she had done it.

Suzan wheeled herself into her living room and slumped forward, falling from the chair onto the floor. The silence no longer mattered.

17

On the surface Annette Wilder's relationship with Dan changed very little after her meeting with the Burbank Police Department. Throughout the summer of 1989 she and Dan continued speaking and seeing each other regularly for lunch at Hamburger Hamlet. If Dan had any concerns about Annette's July 22 visit with the police, they dissipated quickly when he saw that her opinion of him was unchanged.

But had Dan known the truth—that Annette had been terrified of him ever since meeting with the police —he would have felt angry and betrayed. The police had needed relatively little time to convince Annette that Dan was indeed guilty of killing his wife. Several officers had gathered in an interview room at the station that afternoon armed with information that Annette had never known about Dan. They had told her about Dan's excessive gambling debts and Carol's numerous life insurance policies. And they told her about Dan's past, the time he had spent in a high security prison for robbing banks. Annette knew that Dan had been in prison, but she had never known the extent of his past crimes.

To anchor their statements, the police had pulled out diagrams and flow charts and photographs of guns that Dan had been seen carrying prior to Carol's murder.

Annette was left speechless. She was also frightened. Even Carol couldn't have changed a man with Dan's background. If she herself had been fooled about him, wasn't it possible he had been able to do the same to Carol? Annette was still absorbing the shock when Sergeant Kight put away his charts and diagrams.

"Annette, you're in the position to make a big difference in this case," he said.

Annette looked startled. She had come to hear bad news about her friend, Dan, but she had never imagined that the police might be interested in her help. "What do you mean? I don't know anything."

"No, but you could if you wanted to," Kight said softly. "Remember, right now you're the best friend he has."

"That's right, but how could I help the investigation?"

Kight spent the next thirty minutes telling her.

In the days after that meeting, whenever the conversation between Dan and Annette turned to Carol's murder, Annette asked a number of questions she had never asked before.

"How long have you owned your guns, Dan?" she asked one afternoon over lunch. The clamor inside the restaurant seemed to fade noticeably as she watched him, waiting for his answer.

Dan's face took on a puzzled look and a light film of perspiration broke out on his forehead. "Not long. Picked 'em up a few months after she died. For protection."

Annette nodded, then laughed nervously. "I know that, silly. What about before? Ever have any guns before Carol was killed?"

"What's the difference?" Dan sounded abrupt and

annoyed. All traces of his gentlemanly behavior were suddenly gone. The man before her was now angry, irritable, and defensive. "Sure," he snapped. "I had guns. But there were no guns in the house that night. Believe me, if I'd had any guns in the house those cops woulda found 'em."

"But, Dan," she asked softly. "Isn't it against the law to carry hidden guns?"

Dan brushed away a bead of sweat rolling down his forehead. "Of course it is." He was getting angrier. "But the law is after me and I need to protect myself. Don't you see, Annette? They're trying to frame me!"

Similar conversations continued over many a lunch during the next few weeks. After each one, Annette would telephone the police with a report. She did not enjoy the task, but she felt it was the least she could do for Carol. It occurred to Annette that her own life might be in jeopardy now that she was acting as a police informant.

One afternoon late that summer Dan was driving Annette home from lunch when he stopped, illegally parking his car in front of a gun shop. Lately he had been acting more and more like a paranoid gangster. Annette almost never saw the gentleman Dan had first shown himself to be.

"Wait here," he said curtly, opening his car door and getting out. "I'll be right back."

Annette waited nervously in the car, her mind imagining an assortment of deadly reasons why Dan would need to visit a gun shop while she was in the car. The minutes slipped by; Annette too fearful to leave the car. *He's buying another gun. He'll take me to some remote place and kill me because I finked on him,* she thought.

By the time Dan came out of the store Annette was

convinced her life was in danger. But Dan only smiled at her and tossed her a paper bag.

"Hold this, will you?" Inside were more than a dozen boxes of ammunition.

That night after she had reported the incident to Burbank police, Annette called Shirley Brannon, one of Carol's longtime church friends. Although Annette did not attend Overcomers' Faith Center Church, Carol had introduced her to Shirley years earlier and they had become friends.

"Shirley, you're not going to believe this," she said, desperate to confide in someone.

"What is it, what happened?" Shirley was a middle-aged woman who led a quiet, conservative life in which, prior to Carol's murder, the only bad things that happened did so to people whose stories appeared in her daily newspaper.

"Well, I've been seeing a lot of Dan lately," she said, forcing herself to sound calm. "Today I was with him and he stopped and bought bullets."

Like others at church, Shirley knew Dan was being fingered as Carol's killer and she could not for the life of her understand why. Dan had been a wonderful husband to Carol. Whenever he hadn't been working, he had accompanied Carol to church. Shirley had seen for herself how the man doted on his wife, held her hand, and treated her like a queen. He was a soft-spoken gentleman who had been rescued from a wayward life by the love of a sweet, compassionate woman. It seemed clear to Shirley that Dan could never do enough to repay Carol for believing in him. He cherished his wife in a way few men ever do.

After Carol's murder, Shirley had kept in touch with Dan and he had confided in her that he had begun carrying guns to protect himself from the police. She didn't like the idea because she worried that he might accidentally shoot himself while he was cleaning or reloading the guns. But she wasn't surprised that he felt he needed protection; indeed, the police did seem to be harassing him. One officer had even tried to convince her that Dan was guilty.

"Listen, mister," Shirley had told him in her no-nonsense fashion. "I watched Dan and Carol together with my own eyes. That man loved his wife. Now, I don't want to hear another word about this, 'Dan's guilty' and 'Dan's a bad guy' and 'Dan has a bad past.' Doesn't matter. Dan loved Carol."

If Carol had been unhappy with Dan, or feared him in any way, Shirley thought that certainly she would have confided in her church friends. But Carol had never said a bad word about him. Now Annette was worried about Dan buying bullets. Shirley released a deep sigh. When would this finger-pointing end?

"He has guns, Annette," Shirley said calmly. "Guns need bullets."

Annette paused impatiently. Shirley didn't understand because she had not seen the police charts and diagrams.

"Don't you see, Shirley?" Annette's voice took on a hushed tone of conspiracy. "There's something odd about him having guns and all."

"Nothing odd about it," Shirley said. "The man fears for his life. You'd carry a gun, too, if burglars had killed your spouse and they were still roaming the streets."

"Dan's not afraid of them, he's afraid of police," Annette said firmly.

"Either way. He's afraid and he's protecting himself. So?"

"So? So, maybe he's had guns all along, maybe he had guns when Carol was killed."

Shirley could feel a wave of anger rising in her. "Annette, don't go turning against the poor man now."

"You'd turn against him, too, if you knew the truth." The words were out before Annette could stop herself. There was a moment of awkward silence before Shirley spoke again.

"What truth?"

Annette sighed, sorry she had broken the vow of secrecy she'd promised the police. "I met with the police, Shirley. They showed me charts and diagrams and pictures and told me things about Dan I never knew before."

"It's a bunch of lies," Shirley said, quick to come to Dan's rescue. "They have no leads so they're blaming Dan."

"That's not true. Dan used to be a bank robber; he has gambling debts. He had lots of life insurance on her—"

"Stop!" Shirley shouted. "If you feel this way about Dan, then why were you still with him this afternoon?"

"For Carol," she said softly. "I'm working with the police, Shirley. When Dan tells me something, I tell them."

"That's terrible!" Annette had completely betrayed Dan. "He trusts you! Do you know what this'll do to him?"

"Look, he killed Carol. So don't go telling me about betrayal," Annette said. "Anyway, he won't find out until after they arrest him and by then it won't matter."

"He's going to find out before that." Shirley spat out the words. "Because I'm going to tell him."

There was a click and the line went dead.

It was a muggy night and Annette could hear the crickets chirping loudly outside her window. Suddenly she darted across her living room and bolted the window shut. Dan was about to find out that she'd been informing for the police. *I'm a dead woman,* Annette thought to herself.

Later that night, Shirley Brannon called Dan and told him about Annette and her arrangement with the Burbank police.

"She isn't your friend, Dan," Shirley said gently. "I wanted you to know."

Dan sounded emotional. "Why, Shirley?" He pounded his fist on his bedside table. They were trying to turn his friends into enemies. "Why would she do that to me?"

Shirley had no answers.

In the following days, Annette lived in terror that Dan would retaliate. She constantly looked over her shoulder and except for work she rarely left her condominium. Dan, meanwhile, did not contact Annette. He never threatened her, visited her, or spoke to her.

Instead, he slid into what Shirley Brannon decided was a deep and sad depression. Whereas he had been distressed and grief stricken after Carol's murder, now he was despondent. Finally, Dan contacted Pastor Wil Strong.

"What do I do now?" he asked.

"You need to turn to God, Dan." The pastor was calm and quietly assuring. "The Bible tells us to expect persecution. God knows the truth. That's what matters."

From inside the kitchen of his apartment, Dan nodded silently. "You're right. Thanks, Pastor."

"You aren't alone in this thing, Dan," Strong said.

For the next three months—when he wasn't dumping money in Las Vegas—Dan spent much of his time with his church friends. By mid-November, he had befriended a woman named Maree Flores, a plump but pretty Hispanic woman with chestnut hair, bubbly brown eyes, and a contagious smile. Originally Maree had met Carol at the Women's Aglow meetings and for years had heard her speak lovingly about Dan.

The resemblance between Carol and Maree was uncanny. The two women shared the same hair and eye color, and they dressed and spoke alike. But most of all people noticed a similarity in their personalities. Maree's life had never been easy and, like Carol, she felt challenged at the prospect of helping people caught up in trouble—people like Dan.

Maree was born on August 13, 1948, in Bakersfield, California, a farming town located on Interstate-5 between Los Angeles and San Francisco. Although Bakersfield is still considered a small town, it is a metropolis compared to the way it was in the late 1940s. Maree grew up the second oldest of five daughters in a Hispanic Catholic family where—as far back as she can remember—she was something of a surrogate mother for her younger siblings. This was especially true when Maree became a teenager and her parents suffered a hostile, heartbreaking divorce. Not long afterward Maree's older sister, Mona, was diagnosed with bone cancer. After three months of suffering, Mona had one final request—to visit Disneyland. With money from his own savings account, a local Catholic priest took Mona, Maree, and their sisters to Disneyland. Mona died weeks later, her dream fulfilled.

Overwhelmed with sorrow over the loss of her husband and oldest daughter, Maree's mother began drinking and was often incapable of running the house and raising her daughters. So Maree took charge. She handled their father's alimony money, making sure her sisters were properly fed and clothed and that the cleaning got done. The experience ignited Maree's desire to help those in need—a trait that Maree knew could sometimes become compulsive.

The day after she graduated from high school in 1966, Maree signed up with the United Farm Workers of America and began volunteering fifteen hours a day for Cesar Chavez's radical organization. Maree would commute from Bakersfield to Chavez's headquarters in nearby Delano. Like Chavez, Maree firmly believed the field workers of the San Joaquin Valley deserved more than forty cents an hour for their backbreaking labor. Most of the workers were Hispanic, and Maree felt an especially strong desire to help the cause. Chavez provided his volunteers with five dollars a week, community meals, and, in some cases, shared housing. But with Maree living at home unable to provide for her mother and sisters, Chavez would quietly slip her an additional ninety dollars each month. Maree remembers it as the most exciting time of her life. She could think of nothing better than devoting herself to fighting the causes of downtrodden people.

During her five-year stint with the association, she met and married a boy who was so committed to the movement that he became Chavez's favorite volunteer. His name was Juan Flores. They shared a happy, busy life and on Valentine's Day in 1970 she gave birth to their first son, Juan Marcos. They continued their volunteer work for two years, but when Maree became pregnant again her husband decided they needed to get paying jobs. By January 1972 Juan was doing community service work for a Los Angeles County organization and Maree had begun working as a receptionist. The organizational and business skills they had attained working for Cesar Chavez paid off in the private sector and that year they bought a car and rented a large apartment in a nice section of East Los Angeles.

But their blissful lives were marred with marital trouble soon after the birth of their second son, Lino Rene. Juan began experiencing trouble and soon afterward the marriage followed suit. In 1979 the couple divorced.

By then Maree had a job as a bilingual patient advocate with Kaiser Permanente Medical Facility in Los Angeles. In many ways she was doing the same work she had done for Cesar Chavez and the farm workers. Only now she was fighting on behalf of frustrated, sick patients who were in danger of being lost in the medical system.

For years Maree remained a single mother, working at Kaiser and raising her boys alone. Then in November 1987 at a ceremony attended by Dan and Carol Montecalvo and other friends, she married Jim, her longtime friend and coworker at Kaiser. By then, Maree had been a Bible-believing nondenominational Christian for seven years. Only by following Jesus Christ did she feel she found the inner strength to continue fighting for the people who needed her.

As a child Jim had suffered from polio and the illness left him without the use of his legs. However, he used crutches and was completely self-supporting. Maree found him both intelligent and attractive. What she didn't know when she married him was that Jim was a closet drinker. Early in their marriage he would disappear for one or two days and come back with soiled clothing and alcohol on his breath. In a relatively short time Jim began to berate her sons. Maree knew that if she ever had to choose between fighting on behalf of a man she loved and fighting on behalf of her sons, her sons would win every time. She was all they had and she loved them dearly. Months after their first anniversary, the couple broke up.

After the divorce Maree welcomed her ailing mother and youngest sister to share the duplex she now owned in Los Angeles just outside Burbank's city limits. Maree's mother paid rent and Maree devoted herself to caring for the woman.

But in March 1989 her mother died, and soon afterward her sister moved out. For the first time ever, the tables were turned and Maree was in need of help. She had a $970 monthly mortgage payment and no one to share it with.

On August 24, 1989, Maree received a call from Dan Montecalvo. Dan had heard through mutual friends that Maree and her husband had split up, and during his conversation with her, he spoke exclusively about Maree and her recent trials. From the beginning, Maree trusted Dan unquestioningly. She knew from Carol that Dan had been a devoted husband, and she believed Carol was telling the truth. After all, Maree knew what it was to be in an unhappy marriage, and Carol, with her outgoing, confident manner, did not seem to be a woman suffering from an unhappy marriage.

While rumors had been taking root about Dan's involvement in Carol's murder, Maree, who attended a different church, had been too caught up in her own troubled life to hear any of them. For that reason, she had none of the doubts that Annette was by then harboring.

She and Dan agreed to meet for lunch and, in the same way he had charmed Carol and Annette and other women before them, Dan spoke in a soft, unassuming manner that quickly endeared him to her. When Maree learned that police were pursuing him as their lead suspect, she was shocked. She could not for a moment even consider that their accusations might be true. By November Maree and Dan had worked out an arrangement whereby Dan would rent the upstairs of her duplex for six hundred dollars a month. He also volunteered to make repairs on the house that Maree had been unable to afford.

In Maree, Dan found a friend who filled the void left by Annette Wilder. But there was a difference. From the beginning she could not bring herself to question him—even for the sake of discussion—as Annette had done.

"I'm praying for you every day, Dan," Maree told him one evening as they ate dinner in her dining room. "Please let me know if I can help in any way."

Dan nodded somberly. "In fact, there is something, Maree," he said. "I've been working on a manuscript, the story of my life and what's happened since Carol died. But it's hand-written. I wonder, could you type it for me?"

"Sure, Dan. Whatever you need." Maree smiled and reached for Dan's hand. "What's it called?"

Dan looked deep into Maree's trusting brown eyes and hoped with all his heart that he could trust this woman. "It's called *Grief Denied*."

18

In the course of his investigation, Brian Arnspiger began to develop a very clear picture of Dan's childhood and background. The information he found did not prove that Dan had killed his wife, but after several months of working on the case, Brian finally thought he was beginning to understand the man he so desperately wanted to put behind bars.

Daniel John Montecalvo became wise to the ways of a crime-stained lifestyle at a tender young age when most of his peers were busy joining Scout troops and building tree houses. Decades later, prosecutors would compare his later childhood to a fork that pointed in two directions, toward vastly different ways of life. Unfortunately, as those versed in the legal profession would note well after the fact, Danny chose the wrong road.

He was born May 14, 1941, in Chelsea, Massachusetts, a small suburb of Boston where his father, Nunzio Montecalvo, for reasons Danny was never proud of, was one of the most well known men in town. Other than a brief bout with diphtheria as an infant, Dan Montecalvo's troubled past didn't become noteworthy until 1950, just after his ninth birthday.

By then, he and his four-year-old brother, George, only saw their father during occasional prison visits or on rare Sunday afternoons when Nunzio Montecalvo found himself somewhere between a joyous release from the hole and the inevitable return. Up until that point, Danny, which was what people called him before he grew up, never understood that his father was a crook, a man whose idea of working for a living involved breaking into local shops after hours and taking everything of value.

Despite his father's obvious shortcomings, Danny loved the man very much. Like most small boys, he looked up to his father and tried to believe that he had never done the terrible things he was accused of.

Because his father was not home much, Danny's mother, Mary, was left to her own methods of raising her young sons. These methods involved keeping the refrigerator full of nothing but beer and inviting rowdy party friends to spend the evening with her and her sons. Several years would pass before Danny would understand why two or sometimes three men would share his mother's bed each night. At age nine, her crowded bedroom seemed simply a way of conserving space, what with the other numerous adults crashed in various parts of the two-room house.

On one such bitterly cold night in 1950, with two men asleep on his mother's bed, Danny lay wide awake in the tiny cot he shared with his sleeping brother. The younger child always fell asleep first, innocently unaware of his parents' behavior and the degree of discomfort it was beginning to cause Danny. That night as Danny worried about his mother and listened to the sounds of three distinctly different snoring patterns coming from the room next to his, he suddenly heard several loud raps on the kitchen door. Danny quickly surmised that everyone else in the house was incapable of hearing the sounds, let alone responding to them.

Moving as fast as he could, Danny threw the covers off his thin, childish body, crawled over his sleeping brother, and darted into the kitchen, his young brown eyes wide with concern. For a split second, he froze, taking in the stacks of dirty dishes, rotting leftover food, uncovered trash, empty beer cans, and clothing strewn about. This was how their kitchen had always looked, but that night the place seemed to smell even more rancid; the mixture of spilled beer and stale tobacco smoke even more pungent. Danny made a conscious effort to breathe through his mouth as he pulled his pajama bottoms up a little higher.

The knocking grew louder and the boy was brought back to the task at hand. Feeling more than slightly embarrassed by his surroundings and knowing how angry his mother would be if he woke her, Danny put his face against the door and whispered, "Who is it?"

A loud, impatient voice answered him. "Police. Open up."

The two uniformed officers standing outside the Montecalvo house that night had not been thrilled with the assignment of notifying Nunzio's family. Police knew the family well because both parents were—in their opinion—unfit. Neighbors had complained about Mary Montecalvo's wild parties and poor treatment of her two little boys. Still, no one wanted to be the bearer of bad news, even if they thought Nunzio had deserved it.

But that night, as Danny stood in his dirty kitchen, his bare feet cold on the hard, wooden floor, he knew nothing of what had happened. Police did not frighten Danny anymore. There was nothing new or surprising about the police paying a visit to his home late at night. The neighbors had complained about noise and wild partying often enough that the boy knew some of the officers by name because of their frequent visits to his home. Obediently, he opened the door and was met with a blinding spotlight.

"Your mother home, son?" one of the dark-clothed officers asked.

"She's sleeping." The little boy began to shake from the combination of cold and a sudden, inexplicable feeling of fear.

"Well, go wake her up. We need to talk to her."

As Danny turned away he heard one of the policemen mutter something about the smell. The boy dropped his head shamefully, thankful only that the officers couldn't hear the sound of mice scurrying out of sight as he made his way along the dark hallway to his mother's bedroom. Opening the door, he saw her sound asleep next to a man he knew only as Henry. Another man was asleep at the foot of the bed, despite the fact that only a few days earlier he had been in the "boyfriend" spot next to his mother, and Henry had been at the bottom of the bed. The covers had slipped off his mother, leaving her naked body exposed and causing her young son further embarrassment. Danny lifted the covers over her as he began shaking her.

"Mom, wake up," he whispered.

The woman began mumbling a series of profanities. Danny never understood how his mother could be such a gentle woman when she was sober. She never swore or lost her temper until the evening parties began in earnest.

Danny tried again to get his mother out of bed. "Mom, police are here. They want to talk to you," he whispered urgently.

As soon as Danny mentioned police, the entire room

seemed to come to life. Two other men who had apparently passed out on the floor sprang up and both men in his mother's bed jumped to their feet and began pulling on articles of clothing. His mother slowly pulled on a torn bathrobe, her eyes barely open and the effects of alcohol still evident in the way she used both hands to steady herself. While the men in her room scampered out the back door, Danny's mother led the way to the kitchen. Holding the robe tightly around her body, she came into the bright room, squinting as her eyes adjusted to the light.

"I'm afraid we have some bad news for you, ma'am. It's about your husband." The officer was doing his best to sound respectfully sorry.

Mary had long anticipated this late-night call. She knew Nunzio was a no-good two-bit thief and that many of the town's merchants had taken to arming themselves to protect against him. For years now she'd believed that one day he might rob the wrong one and wind up dead as a result. Not that there was ever any love lost between the two of them. They had split up long ago but had never divorced because neither of them had been interested in remarrying. The woman turned to Danny, standing next to her. "Son, go wake up your brother. I want both of you to get dressed and wait in your room until I come get you."

The officers watched the scene uncomfortably and then, with the child out of earshot, they told her what had happened. Hours earlier Nunzio had performed one too many break-ins, this time at an older establishment in the center of town. Police had been cruising by the building, seen the robbery in progress, and drawn their guns. What happened next was a matter of debate.

According to the local newspaper, police reports said that upon being confronted, Nunzio turned toward the officers and drew a weapon. Acting in defense, one of the officers then fired a single shot, sending a speeding bullet dead center between the crook's eyes, killing him instantly.

However, rumors around town the next day offered a slightly different version of the story, one that involved an agreement by local police to eliminate their most notorious nuisance at the next available opportunity. The townspeople were split over whether this version held any truth at all. But no one was willing to express anger at the police over the incident because even if the rumor had been true, in a town as small as Chelsea, most people would have thought it just as well. Someone like Nunzio Montecalvo was a black spot in their midst. In fact the only person who ever came to doubt publicly the role of local police in Chelsea, Massachusetts, as a result of the murder of Mr. Montecalvo was his oldest son, Danny. After his father's murder Danny's classmates began calling him Al Capone's son, and making mock gestures of putting their hands up whenever Danny walked by. Already smaller than other boys his age, Danny believed he had just one option— learn to fight.

Perhaps at this time, with his young friends' taunts and his life resembling a mobster movie, Danny began to lose his innocence. He viewed himself as something of a troublemaker. Maybe, as with many small boys, this happened because he missed his daddy and, whatever the truth about the man, still looked up to him.

Overnight he seemed to become quite good at fighting and despite his size soon had no trouble getting the best of the boys who teased him. But nearly every time he was involved in a fight, even if more than one boy was swinging back, he was forced to take the punishment for it. School officials said this was because the fights were Danny's fault. Danny said his punishments were unfairly administered with no evidence of his guilt. He was convinced his poor treatment was the direct result of his father's criminal record.

A bitter resentment began to build deep inside the little boy's heart, and finally, months after his father's death, he tired of trying to clear his reputation and began earning it. By then, he no longer cared if someone called him Al Capone's son. He quite possibly even bragged about the label.

One day, when Danny should have been in school, he and a friend discovered a department store in downtown Chelsea which had what appeared to the nine-year-old boys to be hundreds, maybe millions, of one-dollar bills pasted on a window display. It was more than enough, Danny figured, to finance his scheme of running away from home. That night he and a friend went back to the store, smashed a hole in the window, and plucked off every dollar bill in the display. The boys were giggling over their success and splitting up the money when they were arrested.

Years later Dan would dictate his life story to Maree Flores as part of a manuscript that essentially declared his grief over Carol's death. In that document, he described what happened after being arrested for the first time, several months shy of his tenth birthday:

I remember how foreboding the courtroom looked when I was ushered into it. . . . The juvenile judge cleared his throat and in a voice that I'm sure he used to sentence murderers announced he was going to straighten me out before I ended up bleeding in a gutter like my father . . .

Danny spent the next nine years—until his eighteenth birthday—in juvenile detention facilities. Each time he was released to his mother's care, he would wind up back in trouble and be ordered back to detention camp. To this day he maintains that during his nine years in the Massachusetts Youth Detention system he was beaten, the victim of perversions and cruelties at the hands of the system authorities. In telling his life story, he claims there were times when he was forced to eat soap for using profanity. He says he was wrapped in cold urine-drenched sheets for wetting the bed and forced to kneel for hours holding his penis after being caught masturbating. Using a hard, wooden stick, the wardens would administer spankings to the buttocks, feet, hands, elbows, and sometimes the head whenever Danny wouldn't stay still.

One particular warden Danny nicknamed "the Beak," because of his vulturelike tendency of springing out of dark places in the middle of the night in search of movement going on underneath the sheets. He would yank the covers off Danny and other boys, some of whom might only be scratching an itch near the genital area, and expose them to public ridicule. The next day each boy caught in the act of what appeared to be masturbation would be forced to line up, hold his penis, and remain in plain sight while the other forty or fifty boys snickered and stared at the offender. The warden's wife, whom the boys aptly named Mrs. Beak, would sit in the room and watch until the punishment was complete.

In Danny's opinion Mrs. Beak enjoyed these sessions. If any of the boys showed signs of arousal, Mrs. Beak would lash out. She would talk about burning in hell or some other fearful place and how those nasty thoughts could lead to state prison.

Even at that tender age Danny realized that a discrepancy was growing between his opinion of himself and the opinion that others held. In his eyes he was a victim of circumstances, of a crime-riddled family background, someone who had done little or nothing to deserve the punishments he'd received. Others, though, saw Danny as a bad little boy with all the tendencies of becoming a career criminal.

By then the list of crimes he had committed during various releases was long and distinguished. In fact, when he left the Massachusetts juvenile detention system, he was no longer Danny Montecalvo, Nunzio's little boy. He was Dan, with enough time served and enough trouble in his past that people no longer blamed his father for his place in life; they blamed him.

19

In addition to gathering information about Dan's background through mid-1989, Brian Arnspiger spent as much time as possible searching for evidence against him. He was still frustrated that the experts had disagreed about the bloody spots on Dan's pants. But he was determined to find another avenue—something concrete that would convince a jury of his guilt.

He went through each report again, reinterviewing neighbors along South Myers Street and talking again to every officer who had worked the scene the night of Carol's murder. When he wasn't making phone calls or visiting those people in person, he was thinking about the crime, envisioning the clues that so far no one had been able to find. At night he sometimes woke from a deep sleep with an avenue that had not yet been checked. He began to keep index cards and a pencil next to his bed for those occasions.

Gradually Brian began to gather threads of information. There was nothing terribly significant about each individual thread. But Brian wasn't just collecting them, he was weaving them together. Already Brian could see a quilt taking shape. It was one the district attorney would marvel at when it was completed.

In early November one of the officers working the case knocked on Brian's office door.

"Got the report for you," Officer Mike Gough said, tossing a bundle of stapled pages onto Brian's desk. "Dan Montecalvo's gambling habits through October '89."

"Anything interesting?" Brian leaned back in his chair and picked up the report.

"Depends on what you find interesting." Gough smiled wryly.

"Try me."

Gough took a deep breath. "Well, it seems Danny Boy has rediscovered blackjack."

"Now, there's a surprise. The slimeball."

"Yes." Gough raised his eyebrows in mock amazement. "Las Vegas pit bosses say he's one of their best customers."

"I'll bet." Brian looked disgusted. "How good?"

"Good enough to average three hundred twenty-seven dollars a hand."

"Per hand?" Brian sounded incredulous.

"He's a regular high-stakes gambler these days," Gough said.

"Winning?"

"Not exactly. He lost fifty-three thousand two hundred dollars in March and another fifty thousand dollars last month."

"Just the kind of thing I'd do if my wife was murdered." Brian was disgusted.

"What I want to know is where'd poor, old, broken-hearted Dan get that kind of play money?" Gough asked.

"Compliments of Carol."

This time Gough's look of surprise was sincere. "He's already got her insurance money?"

"Some four hundred thousand dollars of it. The rest is being contested by the insurance companies who for some strange reason suspect Dan might have had something to do with Carol's accidental death." Brian was disgusted. "Of course, just like any grieving husband, he's drowning his sorrows at the rate of three hundred twenty-seven dollars a hand."

"That stinks."

"Tell me about it."

With the knowledge that Dan was spending his time gambling away Carol's insurance money, Brian worked even harder on the case. As in all investigations one of his responsibilities was to close up any loopholes the defense might use when the case went to trial. From the beginning it was obvious to Brian that if Dan was responsible for killing his wife the prosecution faced one gaping loophole in particular. After hearing about Dan's gambling Brian's anger spurred him on so that he spent much of November finding threads strong enough to sew that hole shut for good.

The problem was this: Fingerprints lifted from a cologne box on Dan and Carol's bed had been matched by the California identification computer as belonging to a man named Kevin Bennington. A person was only listed on the computer if they had been arrested and convicted for a past crime.

Unless the prosecution could explain why an ex-convict's fingerprints were found in the Montecalvo bedroom the night of the murder, no jury would ever believe Dan was guilty. It would be too easy to prove his innocence based on the presence of a stranger in the house.

There was another problem. Other than matching his

fingerprints with his prior record and a signature card, the computer offered no assistance in locating the man. Brian checked with the Department of Motor Vehicles and used other similar means to locate him, but each attempt proved fruitless.

Brian was not discouraged. A gut feeling told him that there was a reasonable explanation why Bennington's fingerprints were in Dan and Carol's house.

The answer came the last week of November when Brian was Christmas shopping for his wife's favorite perfume. He pointed to the box and watched as a sales clerk took it from the case and began turning it in her hands to find the price. Suddenly he thought of something he hadn't before.

"I'll be back," he said to the clerk as he turned and ran from the store.

Back in the office he dug through the box of evidence until he found Carol's May Company credit card. Dan had said they'd been shopping at the store the night of the murder. One telephone call later he knew he was on the right trail. Store records showed that Dan and Carol did purchase a bottle of men's cologne the evening of March 31, 1988. Brian picked up the phone again and called the store's personnel department.

"This is Detective Brian Arnspiger from the Burbank Police Department," he said. "I need to know if a Kevin Bennington worked at your store on March 31, 1988."

"March 31, 1988?" the woman asked.

"Yes," Brian answered, trying to be patient.

"That was more than a year ago, sir." The woman at the other end sounded bothered by the request. "I'll have to put you on hold."

Brian watched two minutes tick slowly by on his office

clock before the woman finally returned. If Brian was right and Bennington worked at May Company that night, it would be perfectly understandable that his fingerprints would be on a cologne box in the Montecalvo home. The woman returned to the phone.

"Yes, he was employed with us at that time."

Brian was lacing the hole together. "What department did he work in?"

"Cologne and cosmetics."

The loophole was sewn shut.

With the New Year Brian had mixed feelings about the Montecalvo case. He was making progress, gathering pages of evidence. But everything he'd found so far was purely circumstantial. Brian began looking for a break in the case, something that would push it over the edge and give the police enough evidence to arrest Dan.

The break came January 13 just after 11 P.M. At that time, two Glendale police officers witnessed a brown sedan weaving precariously down a busy San Fernando Valley street. Switching on his car's lights and sirens, Officer John McKillop tried to stop the swerving car. Instead the driver began leading them on a chase that did not end until the driver crashed his car into a utility pole at the corner of Fletcher Avenue and San Fernando Road and tried to flee on foot.

Both officers got out of their car, drew their guns, and chased the man, ordering him to stop running or they would shoot. The man stumbled to a stop and turned around, his hands struggling to stay over his head.

"Keep your hands where we can see them," McKillop barked, noticing that the man appeared to be drunk but not seriously injured from the crash. "Stay where you are."

Carefully, their guns pointed at the man, the officers approached him.

"Let's see some identification."

The man groped about his jacket for a wallet and, after several unsuccessful attempts, finally found it and handed it to the officer.

"Take this," McKillop said, passing the wallet off to his partner. "Find his license, check it out." Then he pulled the man's hands behind his back and walked him back to his car. McKillop looked past him into the car and saw a handgun on the floor of the vehicle's passenger side. In one smooth motion he reached into the car and pulled it out. The gun was loaded.

McKillop snapped a pair of handcuffs on the man's wrists and propped him up against the car. Moving quickly and expertly, McKillop leaned back into the car and checked the glove compartment. "What have we here?" the officer mumbled as he retrieved a large wad of cash and a pager. McKillop sorted through the stack of small bills and discovered that it totaled nearly five hundred dollars. Loaded gun, excess cash. The man must have been involved in a robbery.

McKillop stood again and faced the man. "You're under arrest," he stated without emotion. "You have the right to remain silent . . ."

Back in the police car, McKillop's partner had found the man's driver's license. He was nearly fifty years old, slight build with dark hair. The officer was satisfied that the man they had pulled over was the same man pictured on the license.

"What do you have on a Dan Montecalvo of Burbank?" the officer asked. A minute later when the dispatcher had answered him, the officer felt a rush of adrenaline.

The man was the primary suspect in the murder of his wife.

Brian Arnspiger was in his office the next morning when Sergeant Kight walked in and told him the news.

"Where's his car?" Brian was already up, slipping a jacket over his shoulders.

"Over at the Glendale police yard in the East Valley. Why don't you and I go take a look."

"I'm with you." In a matter of minutes, the two men were headed toward the East Valley.

McKillop had already booked Dan's gun into evidence, but because he was suspected of a murder in neighboring Burbank he stopped short of searching the entire car. That was a job for the Burbank Police Department.

The morning was still young, chilly and overcast, when Brian and Kight arrived at the police impound lot. The first place Brian looked was inside the car's trunk.

"What's all this stuff?" Brian stepped back, taking in the scene. The trunk appeared to be strewn with garbage.

"Looks like a bunch of junk," Kight said, moving aside numerous papers as he searched for evidence.

Brian picked up one of the sheets of paper and then another. "Wait a minute," he said, reading bits and pieces of the typewritten, double-spaced document. "Look at this. It's some kind of story or something."

Brian quickly found what he was looking for. It appeared to be the front page of the document. Brian held the piece of paper where he and Kight could both read the first paragraph:

The following is a true story. It is a story of a man salvaged by the incredible love of an exceptional lady. A lady who met a violent death and how that death and the ensuing police investigation nearly destroyed his faith in God, people, and in life itself. And how he drifted back into the world of hate blinded by a rage that threatened to consume his very existence.

Beneath that paragraph was the title, *Grief Denied,* by Daniel Montecalvo.

Brian and Kight exchanged a glance and then continued reading the first page.

The hate flowed like an acid through my veins. . . . Nightmares turning into daymares, drifting in and out of insanity, trying to hold on, my grasp growing weaker. . . . Engulfed by physical pain, a constant reminder of the emotional void left by the death of my wife, Carol. . . .

It wasn't always like this . . .

The second page was somewhere in the jumble of papers and miscellaneous items strewn throughout the trunk of Dan's car. The two men stared at each other for a moment, trying to fathom the information this manuscript might contain.

"Incredible," Brian said, still gazing at the page in his hand.

"Should be a real page-turner," Kight muttered as he began sifting through the trunk, retrieving any piece of paper with *Grief Denied* typed at the top.

Brian began working beside him. "Something tells me we'll be needing the pages in order."

An hour later the ninety-one-page manuscript had

been pieced together and confiscated as evidence. When Brian had finished reading it twice through he was confident it would provide the break he'd been looking for. The manuscript was a first-person account of Dan's life and the events that led up to Carol's murder. Brian had hoped Dan might have used the manuscript to confess his part in Carol's murder. Instead, Dan had used it to tell his version of the story.

But some of what Dan wrote would obviously hurt his case. On page thirteen, he had written this: "Another escape was lying, and I became a chronic liar. Again this was to escape reality. Reality was ugly and I preferred not to see it."

Those three sentences gave Brian enough evidence to obtain a search warrant on Dan's house. The judge who granted the warrant agreed with Brian. If Dan had been a self-proclaimed chronic liar in the past, there was a reasonable chance he hadn't changed. The circumstantial evidence—Carol's life insurance policies, Dan's gambling debts and prior record—combined to make him a suspect, but it was his own words that ultimately convinced the judge a search was necessary.

The search warrant was approved just before noon on January 14 and Brian intended to spend the rest of the day combing every inch of Dan's apartment. He was on his way out the door when the phone in his office rang.

"Arnspiger." Brian sounded curt, anxious to start the search.

"Hey, Arnie, this is McKillop over at Glendale. My partner and I made the arrest on Montecalvo yesterday."

"Yeah, great break for us," Brian said.

"Something you might want to know," McKillop said.

"I'm listening."

"After the arrest we took him to the hospital section at County," McKillop said, referring to Los Angeles County Jail's thirteenth floor medical ward. "I was filling out some paperwork on him when he called me over. The guy's not too smart."

"So I'm learning," Brian said. "What'd he want?"

"I walk over and he says, 'You don't know who you're fucking with.' "

"Sounds like the Dan I know," Brian cut in.

"Wait. There's more." McKillop's voice took on a more serious note. "Then he says, 'I'm going to get you and I'm going to get your family.' "

Brian let out a deep breath and shook his head. Although the charges would be dropped and Dan would later deny making the statement, the detective knew the information would be important when they had enough evidence to take the case to trial.

"Remember that, will you?" Brian said. "Someday you're going to need to tell a courtroom full of people that same story."

"You bet." McKillop paused at the other end. "Hey, Arnie, do me a favor. Get that guy behind bars."

"I'm trying," Brian said softly, understanding McKillop's concern. "I'm trying."

20

The information in Dan's *Grief Denied* manuscript told Brian more than he'd hoped about Dan's background, including details about his early criminal days and the reasons he robbed banks.

According to Dan's story he walked away from the confinement of the Massachusetts Youth Detention system in 1958 at age seventeen, under the assumption that he would live with relatives in nearby Boston who had agreed to take him in. Dan hoped that finally his troubled past was behind him.

Instead he found himself in a prison of another kind. As quickly as he'd been set free from the juvenile center, Dan was suddenly trapped by the confines of a society that did not look kindly on those with little education and a criminal background. Rather than work to fight the odds that had quickly piled up against him, Dan continued to blame others for his place in life. When he was turned down for a job, Dan blamed the manager for not giving him a chance. When each branch of the United States Armed Services turned him away because of his criminal record, Dan blamed the system.

Finally the list of rejections became too long for him to bear. Instead of working at finding an honest way around them, Dan drew from the repertoire of skills he had acquired in detention camp. He lied. He did this by concealing his criminal record on an application for the U.S. Army's National Guard. He was accepted, but his falsified record was discovered less than six months later and, although he had caused no trouble during that period, Dan was discharged for fraudulent enlistment.

Brian found one aspect of this story interesting. After six months with the National Guard, Dan would have been trained in first aid. Yet when Carol was shot, Dan made no attempt to give her artificial respiration. Brian made a note of his observation.

Dan's walking papers in hand, he left the National Guard office that afternoon and headed for the nearest bar. During the next few weeks, he drank so much that each morning he had no memory of anything that had happened the previous day. He told himself that alcohol was an escape. In reality, the walls of his personal prison were growing thicker with each sip.

Drinking was not the only way Dan found a false sense of freedom. He also began lying.

The reality of Dan's life grew even less attractive in 1960, two years after his release from the juvenile detention system. Perhaps in an inevitable move of following in his father's footsteps, Dan began robbing banks. Until then, Dan's legal run-ins had been dealt with by the youth detention system because he was a minor. Dan's spate of bank robberies was a rite of passage, elevating him from the role of juvenile offender to that of criminal.

Dan seemed to like his newfound career. After hitting a bank in Boston he realized he'd found a job that not only paid well but also required very little effort. He began to slick his hair back and think of himself as a gangster, fantasizing, convincing himself that he had Mafia connections and an involvement in organized crime. Even though this fantasy was not true, he began to see himself as invincible, able to rob any bank he chose. He was a hero of the criminal underground world. There was one problem. He was the kind of bank robber producers make comedies about.

When he robbed his first bank, in Boston, he wrote a note demanding that the teller give him all the money in the drawer. This is a typical approach for a bank robber. However, Dan's note was written on the back of a deposit slip from his personal checking account. The slip contained not only his name, but his address and telephone number as well. When Dan realized what he had done, he had just one choice—pull up stakes.

His next bank robbery was in Cleveland, Ohio, and was relatively successful compared with his previous effort because this time he did not leave identification behind. But by then he had decided it was probably a good idea to leave town after robbing a bank, anyway. His next stop was Baltimore, Maryland.

Feeling quite confident, Dan checked into a hotel at the same busy city intersection as two of the area's largest banks. On a bright, sunny Tuesday morning he walked across the street and robbed the nearest one. Dan knew as he walked back to his hotel room with several thousand dollars that this had been his most lucrative hit of all. What he didn't realize was that he'd written the hold-up note on hotel stationery, which in addition to being free and fancy, also contained the establishment's name and address.

What with a full supply of hotel stationery and another bank right next door, Dan decided against leaving town that afternoon. Instead he waited one week—

while the police in that town were undoubtedly on vacation—and wrote another hold-up note on yet another sheet of hotel stationery. Then he walked to the other bank at that intersection and robbed it. The hit made Dan even richer, and he savored his success by staying at the fine hotel another two weeks, still oblivious of the information the stationery held. At the end of the second week, one of the Baltimore bank robbery detectives probably stopped staring at the two hold-up notes and came up with an idea: Their suspect just might be living at that hotel. The police then paid Dan the kind of visit he never expected to get. It was one that brought with it the possibility of eighty years in the state penitentiary.

With his bumbling spree of bank robberies behind him, Dan was taken to county jail, where he plunged into a deep canyon of depression. During those days, he figured that his sloppy style of leaving a paper trail behind at each bank robbery was less oversight and more the result of a secret self-destructive desire to get caught.

Perhaps for that reason, Dan waived his right to a trial and pleaded guilty to four counts of bank robbery. The judge took pity on him because of his willingness to admit to the crimes and sentenced him on April 23, 1970, to just twenty-five years instead of the maximum eighty.

Dan was immediately transferred to Kansas to serve his sentence at the U.S. Penitentiary in Leavenworth. In an effort to survive in a system controlled by powerful gangs and homosexual rapists, Dan continued to boast of his imaginary mob connections. He certainly looked the part, with his weasellike brown eyes and dark hair slicked back from his face. And his thick Boston accent completed the image. By then Dan had perfected the art of lying and his stories about his Mafia involvement became legend throughout the prison. Soon other inmates began to fear and respect Dan as a mobster. He no longer needed to worry about his safety. If his fellow inmates had known the truth, that Dan had no connections whatsoever with organized crime, they would have been shocked.

According to Dan he kept himself busy during that time by "shining lights on the system's failures." He would complain to the warden about corrupt guards and illegal activity among inmates. Though there are no records of Dan's efforts to improve prison life, Dan says his activities resulted in his being shackled in the middle of the night and transferred to another penitentiary in Springfield, Missouri.

The authorities at Leavenworth gave a different reason for moving him. Dan's prison records show he was transferred to Springfield for his own safety after having gotten in debt with several of the tougher inmates during cell-room card games. Dan's gangster reputation no longer mattered when he was unable to pay up on his debts.

Either way, Dan wound up at Springfield, where he became the target of a National Prison Project sponsored by the American Civil Liberties Union in conjunction with Amnesty International. Its mission was to set free all persons its organization deemed wrongly incarcerated by the judicial system. The ACLU believed Dan was such a person because of his troubled background. A liberal judge bought the argument and Dan was released on parole just four years after being sentenced.

Back on the streets again, Dan moved to Tacoma, Washington, and ended up celebrating his first night in town at a local bar. He returned the next day and the next, each time drinking himself into a stupor. Then, on August 6, 1974, not quite a month after his release, he was arrested for impersonating a police officer and for aggravated assault with a gun on an officer. Again, Dan's version of the incident differed from the police report. Although he was too drunk to remember the incident, Dan insisted he was minding his own business and carrying only a toy pistol. Police records said nothing about the gun's being a toy, but the judge showed pity by dropping the charges and placing Dan in an intensive alcoholism treatment program.

Two months later, on October 24 of that year, Dan broke out of the treatment center and for lack of better ideas robbed another bank. This time he was caught only a few blocks away and sentenced to serve thirty-five years at the state penitentiary in Marion, Illinois. If Dan had been uncomfortable at Leavenworth, he was miserable at Marion. He would later say this about the experience:

> With ten guys to a cell, if you ever spent the month of August in Kansas, let me tell you something. On the fifth floor of Leavenworth in a steel cage, it's agony . . . Prison is a devil's playground where nothing means anything to anybody, except survival. In prison, if you walk down a tier and you look at a guy's cell, you got a problem, alright? And the problem is . . . the paranoia is so intense in those places that the least little thing that can be thought of as disrespect is a life-threatening situation. In Leavenworth there were guys who'd (get up in the middle of the night) and use a belt to tie the door closed so the officer couldn't (burn him by) . . . opening the door, throwing gasoline on the guy behind bars and then

throw a match. Yeah, Leavenworth was a bad place.
But Marion was worse.

Marion was built to house inmates that once had been
kept at Alcatraz. It was a facility for high flight-risks and
custody problems where a thirty-five-year term made
Dan something of a goodie-goodie. Most of the men at
Marion were serving one or more life terms for crimes
like murder, murder for financial gain, or mass murder. In the world of convicted criminals, having Marion, Illinois, as an address meant there was a strong
chance of never seeing the streets again.

At Marion, Dan again convinced inmates that he was
involved in organized crime. He crossed paths with one
of the nation's most notorious criminals, Garrett
Trapnell, who was serving time at Marion for multiple
crimes including hijacking a passenger airliner.

The two men shared a cell block and, according to
Trapnell, spent many hours fantasizing about how
they'd get rich when they were released. Of course
many of the prisoners, even those serving double and
triple life sentences, enjoyed dreaming about life on the
outside. But Dan's fantasies were particularly significant
in light of Carol Montecalvo's murder when Burbank
police were still trying to decide how to prove Dan's
guilt.

The way Trapnell tells it, Dan's dream was to marry a
wallflower, insure her for a large amount of money, and
then kill her.

21

The fact that Dan had threatened Officer McKillop only convinced Brian further that the man belonged behind bars. Now as he and his fellow detectives made their way to the nearby duplex Dan shared with Maree Flores, Brian hoped they would finally find the evidence they needed. Normally it took no more than two detectives to search a suspect's residence. But for the search Brian planned to conduct, he brought five men, one holding a camera.

Brian knocked on the first-floor front door and Maree Flores answered, looking both frightened and confused as she pushed her thick black hair away from her face. Brian silently wondered at Dan's ability to gain the friendship of soft-spoken, kindhearted women like Carol and this woman before him.

"Dan's not here," she said, anticipating the reason for their visit.

"We have a search warrant," Brian said flatly, holding up the document. "We'd appreciate it if you'd open his apartment for us."

Maree nodded, retrieved a key from a jar in her kitchen, and led the way. *Dan was right,* she thought. *They're trying to frame him.* She opened the door for the officers and then hurried back down the stairs.

Once inside, Brian motioned the field evidence technician to the front of the group.

"Okay, start snapping," he said.

Brian did not want to make any mistakes in this step of his investigation. If Dan was claiming that officers destroyed his home in the days after Carol's murder, then he was likely to say the same thing about this search. Brian intended to be one step ahead of him and so had brought Field Evidence Technician Dennis Bradford along to take pictures before and after the search.

Bradford took pictures for seven minutes in each room of the apartment before Brian gave them permission to start. Brian searched Dan's bedroom, meticulously sorting through paperback books, linen closets, and dresser drawers. In less than an hour he made his first find. Underneath the right side of Dan's bed, Brian found a spiral loose-leaf notebook which Dan had apparently used as a journal. As Brian flipped through the pages he felt the blood drain from his face. It was a record of every move Brian had made on the Montecalvo case since he was assigned to it a year earlier. Each entry was specifically detailed with a date, the name of the person interviewed, and the general content of the interview. Early in his investigation Brian had often suspected that Dan was following him. The notebook confirmed his suspicions. Brian carefully placed it inside an evidence bag.

Early in the afternoon Brian made his second find. It was a receipt for a storage unit in Irwindale, nearly fifty miles south of Burbank. As Brian held the wrinkled piece of paper, he wondered if he had just struck gold.

The police returned Dan's belongings and dresser

drawers to their original places, and Bradford spent another ten minutes taking photographs.

"Let's get over to Irwindale," Brian said as they made their way down the stairs. By then bullets collected from the murder scene had proven that Carol was killed with a .357 or a .38, and Dan was injured with a .25 caliber handgun. Brian dared hope the guns would be among Dan's belongings at the storage unit.

"Now, why would poor, mistreated Dan keep his things in storage so far from Burbank?" one of the detectives muttered quietly. None of them wanted the Flores woman to know they were aware of the storage unit.

"I think I know why," Brian mused mockingly, as they reached their police cars. "Danny boy probably has a few items he wouldn't want anywhere near Burbank."

"Now what on earth could those items be?"

"Just the usual. Two guns—a thirty-eight and a twenty-five."

It took four days before the second search warrant was approved. Brian was frustrated about the delay, aware that Dan would now know police had searched his apartment. Even though Dan had no idea that they were about to search his storage unit, he might still get there before they did and dispose of any evidence.

Finally, on the crisp, sunny morning of January 18, Brian and the same four police officers who had accompanied him on the previous search drove along Interstate 5 to the Orth Van and Storage in Irwindale. Dan's unit was not very large, but it contained dozens of boxes, each of which had to be searched.

Less than an hour later Brian opened a cardboard shoe box and found loose bullets scattered among various pieces of paper, matchbooks, and other odds and ends. Carefully Brian began picking the lead slugs from the container and placing them in envelopes marked "Evidence."

"Arnie," one of the detectives said sarcastically. "Seems to me Dan said he didn't have any guns before Carol died."

"Oh, no. Not Danny boy. No guns," Brian replied. "Just bullets. Part of a personal collection, I'm sure."

The police had collected dozens of bullets, although none of them were the size used in a .38 or a .25, when they found a slip of paper that listed the telephone numbers of the Burbank Police Department and St. Joseph's hospital. It was tucked into a box of belongings that appeared to have come from the top of Dan's bedroom dresser.

Under different circumstances those numbers might have seemed insignificant. But considering the fact that Dan might have needed both numbers in the frantic seconds after he and Carol had been shot, the list took on a degree of importance. If, as Brian suspected, Dan had planned Carol's murder in an attempt to collect her insurance money, he might have thought far enough ahead to leave a list of emergency numbers near his telephone. Brian picked up the piece of paper and placed it in another evidence envelope.

By mid-afternoon, one of the detectives found a program from the Full Gospel Businessmen's Fellowship dated November 1, 1983. It listed Dan Montecalvo as the keynote speaker and said this about his background: "Out of the first 39 years of his life, Dan Montecalvo spent 24 in various correctional institutions. Convicted five times for bank robbery, addicted to alcohol, drugs and hate, Dan met the Lord at a Colson Prison Fellowship seminar and his life turned around."

Brian read the description over the detective's shoulder. "Take it," he said. "They tape those speakers, don't they?"

The detective shrugged.

"Well, if they do, I'd say that's one speech I'd like to hear." Brian made a mental note to contact the group when he got back to the office.

Next, Brian opened a box and stood up smiling.

"Well, what do you know!" The others joined Brian around the box. On top were several unopened pairs of surgical gloves.

"Dan spend any time as a surgeon?" Detective Ron Cervenka asked, his voice dry.

"Gee." Brian shook his head as Bradford stepped closer to the box and snapped pictures of the gloves. "Not that I can remember."

"If he wore gloves, that explains why there was no lead on his hands."

"Now, now. Let's not jump to conclusions," Brian said, grinning. "He probably wore them in Las Vegas. All that casino money gets so dirty, you know."

They had searched nearly every package in the shed when they came upon a box several feet high that had been buried under the rest of Dan's belongings. One of the detectives opened it.

"Full of books," he said.

Brian walked over and peered into the container. "Take 'em out. Check 'em all."

The other detectives began taking out books one at a time, fanning through pages and shaking them for hidden documents. Brian didn't know if anyone had checked the books the night of the murder, but he

Carol's 1963 high school graduation photo.

Carol and her first husband, Raj, with the children of Carol's sister in 1969. She was happy at a slim 110 pounds.

Dan and Carol in 1981 on their first trip to Hawaii immediately after Dan's prison release. They considered it their honeymoon.

Dan in front of the couple's newly purchased home at Christmas, 1985.

Dan and Carol months before she was shot to death. Carol had gained seventy pounds since marrying Dan.

BURBANK POLICE DEPARTMENT

Top, The morning after the shooting in front of Dan and Carol's Burbank home.

Bottom, The scene from Dan and Carol's bedroom: They had been packing for Hawaii and Carol's body is lying in the hallway outside, where she was found by police.

Brian Arnspiger, *right*, and partner Ron Cervenka, go through Dan's belongings in the storage shed. This was where they found the hollowed-out book.

Ben Bernard, *right*, and Brian Arnspiger chat at the D.A.'s office.

The safe and cash box as discovered by police the night of Carol's murder.

The hollowed-out book that would be used against Dan.

Above, Gene Brisco stands with Suzan Brown in front of Suzan's Ontario, California, home.

Right, Chuck Lefler in his office.

Suzan Brown at home.

didn't intend to miss anything. After the first few books had been checked, Brian reached into the box and pulled out two miniature statues. He recognized them instantly from pictures he'd studied of the crime scene. They had been in the bookcase in the Montecalvo study —the room where eight hundred dollars had been stolen from the cash box.

Brian reached into the box again and pulled out a large burgundy hardcover book titled *Howard Hughes: The Man, the Myth, the Madness.* As soon as he lifted it up, Brian knew something was wrong. The book was lighter than a paperback. He opened it slowly. The other detectives stopped what they were doing and stared at the book in Brian's hands.

It was hollow. Someone had cut a rectangular hole into the book's pages and lined the space with red felt.

For several seconds no one said a word. Then Brian snapped into motion, drawing his .38 from his waistband and placing it in the hollow space. If the other detectives had been unsure of Brian's speculations, when they saw how perfectly the .38 fit in the empty book they understood completely. A .357 would not have fit in the space, but evidence experts had determined that Carol was killed with either a .357 or a .38.

Brian lifted his right hand, holding his thumb and first finger straight out the way a child would if he was pretending to point a gun. The others realized immediately the similarity between the size of Brian's large fingers and a .25 caliber revolver. Carefully, Brian turned his hand so that his thumb and first finger fit perfectly in the empty space surrounding the .38.

"Well, boys," he said knowingly. "I believe we've just hit the jackpot."

For the next few seconds Brian dared hope the guns

might have fallen out of the hollow book and still be at the bottom of the box. They were not. But Brian felt their absence wasn't an insurmountable problem. After all, the detectives had found bullets after Dan had said he'd had no guns. They had found surgical gloves, and they had found a hollowed-out book with a secret compartment large enough to hide a .38 and a .25—the weapons very likely used in the crime. Combined, these findings were more important than any others so far in the investigation.

Brian could picture the scenario. Dan takes the money from the cash box earlier in the day and that night Carol discovers the money missing. Before she can accuse him, Dan surprises her in the hallway of their home and points a gun at her. She turns to run as Dan shoots her twice in the back of the neck, splattering blood backward onto his pant legs. He then picks up a second, less deadly gun with his right hand, points it at his back in the fleshy area just over his right hip and shoots. Next Dan pulls the hollow book from the bookcase, opens it, and places the weapons inside. A perfect fit. He slides the book back into place and rushes to the telephone to call 911 and report the emergency.

The scenario had a distinctive ring of truth.

Only two details bothered Brian as he gently placed the hollow book in an evidence bag. Why hadn't anyone discovered it in the initial search immediately after Carol's death? In crime scene investigation, a basic procedure involved a thorough search of all bookcases and books. And if Dan had disposed of the guns, why hadn't he gotten rid of the hollowed-out book as well? For an instant, an uncomfortable thought occurred to Brian. Perhaps officers had found the hollow book that March night, discovered it was empty, and returned it to the bookcase.

Impossible, Brian thought to himself, motioning for Bradford to photograph the book. *Must have been overlooked*.

The evidence of Dan's owning a hollow book with a compartment large enough to hide the exact caliber guns most likely used in the crime was just too damning to be coincidental.

Later, Brian obtained a transcript of the speech Dan had given to the Full Gospel Businessmen's Fellowship in 1983. Brian was both horrified and fascinated as several of Dan's statements caught his attention.

The first referred to his time immediately after being dismissed from the National Guard. Dan said, "I got my first taste of freedom then but I was arrested by a policeman, and in those days, if you showed me a badge, venom started to drip from my lips. I hated them, you know."

Referring to his bank-robbing period, Dan said, "I got myself two pistols, not one pistol, but two pistols. One for each hand. And I went to town. I mean, there wasn't nothin' I wouldn't do."

Another statement apparently referred to his alleged involvement with organized crime. Brian's face grew white and his hands shook as he read Dan's statement.

In my Italian neighborhood, there's three things you want to be: The pope, Frank Sinatra, or the Godfather. The first two jobs were taken so I got myself a black shirt, white tie, pointed shoes, hat and sun glasses. . . . If you kill 'em it's going to be painless. Not going to be no agony, no hurt or nothing. So you just do it, you know. . . . When they'd find the body, (he'd have) two in the head.

22

Now that he understood Dan's bank-robbing background and his pretend involvement with organized crime, Brian felt compelled to learn more about Dan's relationship with Carol. By late January 1990 Brian felt he had enough information to understand how a loving, compassionate woman like Carol Tronconi could have become involved with someone like Dan Montecalvo.

On January 18, 1978, Dan Montecalvo was taken away from Garrett Trapnell and his other cellmates at Marion, and transferred to the Federal Correctional Institution at Oxford, Wisconsin. Prison records show that Dan had again become deeply and dangerously involved in prison gambling. At Marion prisoners sometimes made fellow inmates pay for unsettled gambling debts with their lives. When officials at Marion caught wind of the increasing death threats aimed at Dan, they took the initiative and moved him to Oxford.

Dan saw the move as a fresh start—finally a chance to compile an impressive prison resume. His first move in that direction was to join Oxford's specialized communication program, designed to equip inmates to better deal with life outside prison. Dan adapted to the program so well that he was selected to teach the concepts to other inmates.

Dan then found another way to impress the parole board by joining the prison's Alcoholics Anonymous group. Wanting to seem rehabilitated, Dan eventually became chairman of the group.

In this role Dan had weekly contact with a man named John who worked with a prison ministries program. John was a Bible-believing Christian who spent fruitless hours trying to convert Dan. As desperate as Dan was to make an impression with the prison officials, he could not bring himself to submit to a God he could not see or understand.

Dan later said, "My view of religion at that particular time was . . . (you) trudge through this life . . . but you'll get your reward in Heaven. Who needed that? I liked the banks better, to tell you the truth."

Sometimes Dan would fire questions about Christianity at John that he was unable to answer. Finally John felt compelled to try another approach. He referred Dan to someone who had once worked for him during his days as an insurance broker. She was a sweet Christian woman who believed in helping others learn about God and who had enough compassion to care about a man like Dan Montecalvo.

Her name was Carol Tronconi.

Carol agreed to write to John's inmate friend, but long before her first letter, she and her friends began praying for him. They prayed that Dan would have an open heart, an open mind, and an open attitude toward the changing power of Christ's love. During that time Carol thought a great deal about Dan. She knew about his troubled childhood and figured that was the reason why he resorted to robbing banks as a young man.

"He never did anything to harm people physically," John explained to Carol in the weeks before she began writing to Dan. "He's mixed up and self-destructive. But he's crying out for help. He just needs a little push."

Sometimes Carol would wonder about Dan's troubled heart and soul and remember examples in her psychology books. She began to think about ways she might break through to the healthy person trapped inside. Carol had an abundance of love to give, no one to share it with, and the same naivete she had developed as a young girl.

On October 3 Dan received his first letter from Carol. In contrast to the time and energy she had already put into rescuing Dan, he gave Carol's first letter very little thought. He believed she was merely a good Samaritan out to save the world. By the time he went to sleep that night, Carol was long since forgotten.

But the next day there was another letter; the day after that, still another. In the wake of her divorce, with plenty of time on her hands, Carol would come home from her teaching job each evening, sit down at her kitchen table, and pour out her feelings to Dan. Persistence, she told herself, was the only way a convicted felon would believe that someone on the outside really cared about him. What she wasn't quite ready to admit was how much she was enjoying the correspondence.

She continued writing every day for the next two months. She told Dan about her strained relationship with her father and her drawn-out breakup with Raj. If not for the love of Christ, Carol wrote, she would have long ago succumbed to self-pity and depression. She urged Dan to give Christianity a try.

Receiving mail was a new experience for Dan and after a week of daily letters from Carol he found himself liking the attention. During the second week Dan began writing back. Then, after two months, Carol and Dan agreed to meet face-to-face. There was one problem. A prisoner was permitted to have only visitors he had known prior to incarceration. But Dan had not spent the past year impressing the prison board for nothing. His case worker appealed the rule to the board and days before Christmas, the visit took place.

After her murder Dan wrote about his first impression of the slim, bright-eyed woman who had so faithfully written to him for eight weeks:

One is immediately struck by beauty, and Carol certainly had that. It wasn't just surface beauty. . . . There was an inner radiance that glowed from a spring that welled deep within her. . . . Right away you knew that she was special.

For her part Carol, too, was struck by their first meeting. In those days Dan still had the dapper appearance of a small-town banker and Carol found him very handsome. He was several inches taller than she with dark hair and a neatly trimmed mustache. His soft, brown eyes seemed to be crying out for help and Carol decided he looked more harmless than the officer who had escorted her into the visiting room. He spoke with a soft voice and had a self-deprecating way of staring at his hands when he carried on a conversation. Carol was troubled to see that Dan seemed to have less self-esteem than anyone she had ever met. She had the immediate urge to take him in her arms and let him know that everything was going to be all right.

Over the next few months Carol visited as often as prison rules permitted. She told herself she hoped to accomplish just one thing with her persistence—Dan's conversion to Christianity. But there was no hiding from her feelings. She was beginning to fall in love with Dan, beginning to dream about how different their relationship might have been had they met in other circumstances.

Dan's thoughts were perhaps more self-centered. In Carol, Dan finally had someone outside the prison system who believed in him and wanted to help him. He had begun to look forward to her daily letters and frequent visits and had long since begun enjoying her attention. Later Garrett Trapnell—his former cellmate at Marion—would offer a more sinister motive for Dan's friendly involvement with Carol.

Either way, the friendship flourished and a few months later, in 1979, Dan answered an altar call during a prison presentation by members of the Chuck Colson Ministries. When he later told Carol about the spiritual experience he'd had that night, she was convinced that her prayers about Dan's converting to Christianity were being answered. Later, when he was baptized during a church service, Carol believed that finally Dan had become a Christian.

Dan's conversion started another phase in his relationship with Carol. They began spending their visits reading and discussing Scripture. If Carol had wondered about her feelings for Dan, now she was certain. She had been laid off from her teaching job and had taken a sales job at the local telephone company. Although she thrived in the competitive environment, her coworkers thought her something of a loner. Now, as her relationship with Dan grew, her coworkers began to notice that Carol seemed completely happy for the first time.

With Carol's help Dan set up a prison workshop that

offered Christianity as an alternative for kids who had been in trouble with the law. Dan would later write, "Carol and I were falling in love. She was the first thing I thought about in the morning and the last at night."

Eighteen months after Carol's first letter, the couple decided to get married. But Dan still had eight years before he would be eligible for parole, and so prison officials denied his request for a wedding ceremony. Still, the couple continued their contact as they had before, both praying that God would work a miracle and Dan would be released from prison.

In what seemed to be a miraculous answer to his prayers, Dan was allowed to speak before the parole board. As he had hoped, the board was impressed by his involvement with the prison communications program, by his conversion to Christianity, his membership in Alcoholics Anonymous, and even his relationship with Carol. Dan was granted a transfer to the federal prison camp in Terre Haute, Indiana. In contrast to the high security institutions at Leavenworth, Marion, and Oxford, the minimum security facility at Terre Haute seemed like summer camp. Here, Dan again requested to marry Carol. This time permission was granted.

On July 14, 1980, while prison guards looked on, Dan and Carol were married in the camp's courtyard. Dan would later say he was, "the happiest man alive." He would write:

> God had gifted me with the sweetest lady He could find. . . . [W]ho by her unconditional love brought me out of darkness—a place of no love. She was able to strip away the hate and bitterness that was so long a part of me.

Dan's marriage to Carol further impressed the parole board. By then Dan no longer spent much time talking about his involvement in organized crime. In fact he seemed as mild mannered as a Sunday School teacher. The communications program had taught him how to write and speak like an educated man, the Alcoholics Anonymous program had taught him how to stay sober, and Carol had taught him how to love.

Most likely the parole board was also under pressure to reduce the camp's overcrowded population. Taking everything into consideration the Terre Haute parole board released Dan just three weeks after his marriage. That day Dan promised Carol and himself that he would remain clean and begin a meaningful ministry of his own.

"One would think that with all I had going, transition (back into society) would be easy," Dan wrote later. "But it wasn't."

Before long Dan found himself longing for a drink and wondering about the nightlife in nearby bars. No matter how hard Carol prayed for him, he seemed to be drawn away from their happy home. In fact before their first anniversary Dan began dealing with his frustration by drinking and spending his evenings out on the town.

"Carol never once came down on me, although she was disappointed," Dan wrote. "She was never angry. She remained a patient and loving wife who got me over that hurdle."

In light of her painful divorce from Raj, Carol was committed to making her second marriage work. Whenever Dan disappointed her, she needed only to look into his beseeching eyes as he begged for forgiveness to know without a doubt that she could never leave this man. He just needed time to grow into the person

Carol knew he really was inside. Following Christ's example her forgiveness for her husband was always unconditional. Even after the humiliation Dan caused her in August 1981, when he was arrested while she sat home alone.

The charge against him: Soliciting a prostitute.

23

The early years of Dan and Carol's marriage were not what their friends and few family members would term happy times. The undercover police officer in Madison, Wisconsin, who arrested Dan for soliciting a prostitute wrote this in her report: "(During the solicitation) I told him I wanted to know what kind of person he was and he told me he wasn't kinky, but just wanted someone to make love to. He also asked me to give him head and he would (do the same) for me."

If Carol had read that report, it would have confirmed her fears that Dan was unhappy in their year-old marriage. But she accepted his apology and prayed for him to be stronger in the future. She probably never told anyone how Dan's close bout with infidelity had hurt her. But she clung to her belief that she had the ability to change him.

After his arrest Dan was placed on probation. His resulting depression sent him spiraling back into alcoholism. On October 7, 1981, less than two months after his prostitution charge, Dan was arrested for drunk driving and violating probation and ordered to serve thirty days in county jail. Even in these dark times when Carol must have doubted the wisdom of marrying a convicted felon, she never allowed her parents to share her pain. She had chosen to devote her life to loving Dan; like any good Christian wife she would see the marriage through.

In optimistic moments, although she hated the thought of her husband sitting in jail, Carol was thankful that Dan hadn't hurt himself or anyone else with his drunken driving. She tried to see Dan's latest arrest as God's way of forcing him to stop drinking. When thirty days were up and Dan returned home, he promised to change his ways. Just as before, Carol believed him.

Throughout 1982, Dan had no run-ins with the police. He attended weekly group therapy sessions with other former criminals and, according to Dan, he developed such a "unique insight into the difficulty that a convict faces in the transition to the streets" that the counseling center hired him on staff.

But the good life began to dissolve once again in 1983 when Dan again began drinking. Later, Dan would write, "Somehow I didn't think that I deserved the life that was being offered to me and I turned back to the bottle." Police caught up with him on January 22 and again on May 14 that year and he wound up with two more drunk driving arrests and a suspended license.

Carol began to pray for a way out, a chance to give Dan a new lease on life. She had been selling directory sales ads for General Telephone in Madison and after a successful interview quickly accepted a promotion and transfer to the company's office in Southern California.

When Dan joined Carol in Los Angeles a few weeks later, having packed up their household, Carol prayed with all her heart that California would offer a new beginning, an opportunity for Dan to blossom into the man she believed him to be. They rented a small apartment in Eagle Rock, a small community in the hills just north of Los Angeles. The weather was bright and sunny and each day as Carol drove to work she grew more convinced that Dan's alcoholism was finally behind them.

Within a month after arriving in California the Montecalvos discovered Overcomers' Faith Center Church, which seemed an appropriate enough name for the kind of shepherding Carol thought they needed. They spent several evenings meeting with Pastor Wil Strong before going in front of the congregation one Sunday and pledging their membership.

With their marital and spiritual lives seemingly in order, Carol joined a Christian group called Women's Aglow, which met once a month in Burbank and did weekly service projects. Dan, too, kept busy and managed to stay sober while working various part-time jobs and volunteering at a chemical dependency program for teenagers. He also became involved with the Full Gospel Businessmen's Fellowship group. That fall Dan's newly strengthened relationship with God had become so apparently exemplary that the group's leaders asked Dan to speak at their November meeting.

A year later, on December 20, 1984, two of Dan's church friends purchased a run-down hotel in downtown Los Angeles and hired Dan to manage it for them. Carol was thrilled to learn that Dan would receive a decent salary and 10 percent of the hotel's net profits. Finally, she thought, her prayers were being answered. Dan seemed to be a changed man who no longer desired the nightlife and drinking that had plagued his past.

During the next year, Dan worked ten-hour days to clean up the hotel. The structure had been the site of drug and prostitution rings and was on the verge of being closed down by police because it was a nuisance to the public. Its tenants were notorious for failing to pay their rent.

Dan grew to know the tenants personally. He told them about the love of Jesus and begged them to avoid alcohol and drugs. He also stressed the importance of abiding by the law and paying rent on time. Gradually the hotel began to make a profit. Still there were times when the only way a tenant could avoid eviction was by coming up with the rent immediately. On several such occasions Dan gave trusted tenants enough money to keep them off the streets. He told himself that Jesus would have done the same thing in his place.

Dan was not as lenient with the lawbreakers. If a tenant chose to continue with drugs or prostitution—even after Dan told them of his experience and God's plan for forgiveness—he would pray for the person and then turn the matter over to the police. He aided the officers in undercover operations to rid the building of its remaining narcotics and crime problems.

By the fall of 1985, the hotel had increased its profits from $27,000 a month to an all-time high of $69,000 monthly. Once the hotel was running well, Dan helped develop two Bible studies that operated out of the building's main office. He also voluntarily took on the responsibility of developing job-search and hot-meal programs for the tenants. Later, he started an Alcoholics Anonymous chapter at the hotel.

On the one-year anniversary of his employment at the Strand Hotel, the owners gave Dan his 10 percent share of the profits and Dan and Carol picked out their best Christmas present of all—a new home. They had researched the area and decided they wanted to live in Burbank. With its low crime rate, Burbank was just the place for a changed man and his devoted wife to put down roots. They decided on a 1,300-square-foot three-bedroom yellow house at 315 South Myers Street. A bushy palm tree grew in the front yard and the house was only a stone's throw from Walt Disney Studio's back lot. On the day they purchased the home, Carol took a picture of Dan standing alongside the real-estate sign, a broad smile on his face. For the first time in his life he no longer craved the things that had always worked to destroy him. The days of robbing banks, emulating gangsters, and serving time seemed forever behind him.

Carol, too, seemed in good spirits. Later she would write to her sister Roseanna telling her that she had never been happier. Dan was doing better than she had hoped and now they had saved up enough money to buy their own home.

Actually, Carol was worried sick about her own job. While Dan had been working so successfully at the Strand Hotel, the phone company had hired a bossy, short-tempered woman to manage Carol's department. For what seemed to Carol insignificant reasons, the new boss disliked Carol and began berating her in front of her colleagues. Whereas Carol's sales for the company's yellow pages had always been high, they began to slip in the atmosphere of strain and tension.

Then, weeks after moving into their new home, Dan came home from the hotel to find Carol curled up on the sofa, crying.

"Honey, what's wrong, what happened?" Dan immediately moved to Carol's side.

"I'm sorry," Carol muttered, trying to wipe away her tears. She had not told Dan of the problems brewing at the telephone company. After all, she was the rescuer in their relationship, the one who was supposed to have her life together. "It's nothing, really."

Dan was not convinced. "Sweetheart, tell me what happened."

Carol reached down and picked up a paper toilet seat cover off the floor. "I got this at work today. It's no big deal, really."

Confused, Dan wrinkled his brow and leaned closer to his wife, examining the item she held in her hand. "Why would someone give you a toilet seat cover?"

Carol tried to stop the tears that ran down her cheeks. "It's a joke. Sort of. We had a sales contest and everyone got an award." She held the seat cover a little higher. "This is mine."

Rage began building inside Dan's heart. "Honey, I'm still a little confused, you know? What's it for?"

"Don't you see, Dan? My sales were in the toilet. That's why I got the seat cover."

His face grew red as he leaned over and took Carol into his arms. Years had gone by since he'd felt the intense anger and hatred he felt at that moment. "You don't need to be treated like that, Carol. No one's going to make my wife feel bad."

Carol swallowed hard, trying not to give in to the sobs that choked her. "I don't want to go back," she said softly. "I hate it there."

"Then don't. It's that simple." Dan was suddenly calm and confident. "Tomorrow you can call them and tell them you won't be back."

"I couldn't do that, Dan," Carol said, tears welling up in her eyes again. "What would I say?"

Dan moved next to Carol and stroked her hair, his eyes still betraying his anger. "Don't worry, honey. I'll call them."

As a young woman Carol never would have allowed anyone to act on her behalf. But her rebellious behavior had long since been replaced by a biblical submissiveness toward her husband. Rather than be put off by Dan's authoritative attitude, Carol took it as another sign of his continued progress. He was finally becoming the true leader in their home.

The next morning Dan telephoned Carol's manager and told her that Carol would not be returning. Ever. As Dan hung up, Carol felt a weight lifted from her shoulders and she smiled at him from across the room. For the first time in her life, Dan had taken care of her. Never, in all her life, had Carol loved a man more than she loved Dan at that moment. He walked up to her and took her into his arms.

"We'll be okay, honey," he whispered. "The Lord will take care of us."

"Oh, Dan," Carol said, allowing tears to spill from her eyes. "I love you so much."

"I love you, too, sweetheart. I really love you."

Despite the hundreds of lies Dan had told her in the past, Carol believed him with all her heart.

Later, Dan would write, "Carol never got angry. . . . Disappointed at times, but never angry. She would say, 'We must pray for these people.' . . . She was the perfect balance for me, and I could only thank God for the gift of her, a most precious and cherished gift."

24

Brian Arnspiger was still not satisfied with all he knew about the relationship between Dan and Carol. When had things turned sour? And why had Carol agreed to purchase so many life insurance policies? It was now late January 1990, and in the days after Dan was arrested in Glendale and released on bail, Brian continued to collect answers. He was determined to solve this case and he knew he would never be satisfied until he understood the desperation which in his opinion might have driven Dan Montecalvo to kill his wife.

Brian learned that although Carol had appreciated Dan's telephoning General Telephone and informing them that she would not return, this decision resulted in a financial nightmare for the Montecalvos. Before quitting, Carol had eight years of seniority and—despite her plunging sales—had earned nearly $35,000 a year not including her stock options and bonus plan. Without her job, the couple's money problems started almost immediately.

True to her nature Carol confidently attacked the challenge of job hunting. However, despite the bravado he had shown in calling Carol's employer, Dan instantly began to panic about how the couple would handle their bills.

Less than a month later, in late January 1986, Carol

accepted a job with the Donnelly Company, a much smaller competitor of General Telephone's. Unfortunately, the Donnelly Company was only able to pay Carol half of her previous salary and the couple's financial situation continued to worsen.

Carol handled their financial woes by praying, calmly taking her concerns to a God she knew was in control of their lives. But Dan let the worries—about their increasing debt and about escalating crime problems at the Strand Hotel—eat away at him. Finally, on April 10, 1986, he passed out at work. He was rushed to the hospital where doctors diagnosed him with a bleeding ulcer and high blood pressure at a near fatal level. In their opinion, Dan was the victim of mental abuse—his own.

Dan was ordered by doctors to spend a month or more resting at home to reduce his job anxiety. Instead, when Dan awoke his first morning out of the hospital with nothing to do and only a meager disability check to look forward to, his previous panic doubled.

At the same time Dan's increasingly precarious faith in God came under direct attack. A pastor friend suddenly left his ministry, his wife, and his two small children. Then, another friend, who had lost her sight to diabetes, met someone she thought was a faith healer and, believing she was healed, stopped taking her insulin. She died days later. Dan blamed both events on God.

Carol would plead with Dan to remember how God had helped him get released from prison more than a decade before he should have been. She also reminded him that God had provided him with the hotel job and with their home in Burbank.

"You need to trust in God; everything will work out

okay," Carol would tell him. But Dan would only shake his head.

"Listen, sweetheart, God hasn't been coming through lately and I'm tired of waiting. I have you; I don't need God."

Dan's attitude pushed Carol to pray more often, but his problems only seemed to worsen. Carol's faith, though, remained unshaken because she knew God could only work in Dan's life if Dan was willing to let Him. And by 1987 Dan was clearly not including God in any of his plans.

By that time Dan had long since stopped praying and instead started thinking of ways to make money. He considered his earlier days when he had robbed banks to make ends meet, but he knew he was no longer healthy enough to do that. He had no formal education, no trade experience, and a criminal record that made most jobs out of the question. There was just one other way he knew to make a living. That year Dan began gambling.

Whether he was in prison or in Las Vegas, Dan never gambled with small change. That month he was given a $4,000 line of credit at the Mint Casino, where he played blackjack at a $100-minimum-bet table. At first, Dan did so well that the pit bosses raised Dan's credit limit to $25,000. Despite his success, Carol saw Dan's gambling as a desperate problem. She prayed constantly and solicited the prayers of her church friends Cathy Hines and Pastor Strong.

"I feel like a failure, Pastor," she would say. "Dan doesn't need to gamble. We have the Lord and He will help us through this time!"

"Hard times test a person's faith, Carol," Strong would respond. "We must continue to pray for Dan. If he survives this time and returns to God he will be stronger than before."

Instead of getting stronger Dan began to frequent Burbank bars, staying out until well after midnight several nights a week. Thus began a very dark period for Carol, who finally had begun to wonder if Dan would ever permanently become the man she wanted him to be. Still she was determined not to give up. She believed a woman's job was to stand behind her man in good times and bad. If she spent her lonely nights crying and feeling frustrated, she never told anyone. She might ask Cathy and Pastor Strong to pray for Dan but she would never complain about him.

Despite her disappointment and the hours she spent encouraging Dan to quit gambling, his efforts at Las Vegas paid off. For the next year he was successful both with his money and the money he'd received from an acquaintance of his. This man was a wealthy high roller who liked to gamble, but didn't have time for trips to Vegas. Twice this man provided Dan with as much as $30,000 as part of an arrangement in which Dan would receive a hefty 50 percent of the winnings. Of course, he would also be responsible for 50 percent of the losses.

But like all good things in Dan Montecalvo's life, his hot gambling streak eventually ended by the New Year. Because he had been a high-stakes gambler, the casinos were more than willing to give Dan loan markers to gamble with when he ran out of cash. By February 1987 Dan found himself owing $25,000 to the Mint Casino. After that he borrowed and lost $12,000 from the Golden Nugget, and another $30,000 from his gambling friend. Gasping for air in a sea of debt, Dan waited until April to tell Carol of their truly dire financial situation. She was saddened by Dan's trouble, but she was not surprised. In her opinion, nothing good ever came from gambling, even when the gambler was winning.

"I finally had to share this dilemma with Carol," Dan wrote later. "Up to that point, she had never questioned me about income; I was too ashamed of what I was doing (to talk about it with her)."

Again Carol was Dan's only glimmer of hope. By then she had left the Donnelly Company for a similar job at Pacific Bell. Her new job provided an excellent salary, valuable stock options, and a retirement plan. So they were able to slowly erase their consumer debt and catch up on their mortgage payments. But even Carol had no idea how Dan was going to dig himself out of the $67,000 hole he'd gambled himself into.

Once he had come clean with Carol about the extent of his gambling debts, some interesting events unfolded. That spring, in a six-week period, the Montecalvos began setting up life insurance policies on Carol. These included a $130,000 policy intended to cover the mortgage on their home and a $50,000 policy taken on their Montgomery Ward credit card. Next they applied for and received a $220,000 policy through Pacific Bell. Then, later that summer, they took out another policy from Liberty Life Insurance Company of Boston for $150,000.

Dan and Carol never shared this information with their friends. Carol probably knew that if she died, Dan's health and prison records would leave him completely helpless. For that reason, $600,000 didn't seem like too much life insurance, especially in the wake of Dan's overwhelmingly bad run in Las Vegas. After all, Dan might outlive her for twenty years or more and if that happened, $30,000 a year would be just enough for him to live comfortably while paying back his debts.

During that same period Dan began setting up payment schedules with the various casinos to which he owed money. These arrangements included an agreement with a man named White Mitchell at the Golden Nugget Casino. On August 24, 1987, Dan wrote Mitchell a letter agreeing to pay the casino $500 on the first of every month until the debt was paid off. If it hadn't been for this arrangement with the casino, Mitchell would have been entitled to deposit the markers—or I.O.U.s—at Dan's bank, where they would be treated like checks. If then there were insufficient funds to cover the markers, Dan could be prosecuted for having written bad checks.

"Carol thought Dan was being responsible, that he was trying to take care of whatever trouble he had with Las Vegas," Cathy Hines would later say of their discussion. "She thought he was totally in love with her and that everything was going to work out."

Chances are Carol would have been shocked and completely devastated had she ever read the letter Dan sent to Mitchell:

Dear Mr. Mitchell: Regarding our conversation as to my outstanding markers totalling $11,500, I welcome the opportunity [to satisfy] this debt. Namely, a monthly payment schedule of a minimum of $500 on the first of each month, certainly more if possible—with the perceived goal of satisfaction of my debt within twelve to eighteen months.

However, to be totally frank, there are present circumstances that I really have very little control over. The greatest is my health, having recently suffered a serious heart attack which placed me in a hospital for three weeks and precluded me from many activities. There is also my situation with the IRS, which looks very bleak and I will not know the outcome for some time.

That much alone would have upset Carol. After all, she knew Dan had not suffered a heart attack—he had been in the hospital for a bleeding ulcer and high blood pressure. But if that information would have bothered her, she would have been utterly crushed by the rest of the letter. Dan wrote:

Along with the above, there are domestic problems with my wife, and a divorce is possible—but not without a serious depletion of whatever I may have left after the IRS is satisfied.

This is not a good time for me. I do hope that you can convince management to maintain my markers in-house and not submit them to my bank—which would only cause deeper embarrassment and more pressure, for I simply do not have the funds at my disposal.

In closing, let me say that I am a person who has done and will certainly do everything in my power to maintain my reputation.

After blaming his financial troubles on a nonexistent heart attack and on divorce plans he hadn't even shared with his wife, and after assuring Mitchell he would do whatever necessary to maintain his credibility and repay his loans, Dan focused again on matters closer to home. That meant, at Carol's insistence, of course, continuing to arrange for her life insurance policies.

25

The picture was becoming clearer each day. Through the end of January 1990 Brian continued to collect information about Carol's last year, and about the degree of Dan's desperation.

Brian's information told him that at first Dan made fairly steady payments to the casinos, even keeping up with his promised $500 monthly to White Mitchell at the Golden Nugget. But by the first part of 1988 Dan had apparently decided to pay off his gambling debts more quickly. He spent his money meant for the casinos betting on horses instead.

Of course, instead of improving his financial problems, the racetrack made things worse. Dan was unable to make his January payments and on January 18 he was contacted by a debt collector at the Mint. Afterward this message was written on the log detailing Dan's account with the Mint:

"Talked with Dan. Things are better. Will be able to pay in full by April, 88."

The idea that things were looking up for Dan midway through January would have come as a complete surprise to Carol, who helped balance their bank accounts and knew the gravity of their situation. Dan had lost faith in God; he had also returned to drinking, barhopping, and gambling. Things were definitely not better.

Perhaps Dan was referring to the decision he and Carol had made to take a loan out on their house. It was quite possible that by then Dan had looked into this procedure and knew he would not receive funds until several months after applying for the loan. Say around April 1988. If that was the case, then his promise to pay off his $9,900 debt to the Mint by April would have made perfect sense.

But if Dan had been considering the home loan in January, there is no record of his having acted on it either that month or the next. Records do show, however, that Mitchell made two attempts to talk with Dan about his account at the Golden Nugget during that time, including a lengthy discussion which took place on February 6.

That February afternoon Mitchell calmly informed Dan that they had waited long enough without receiving a payment. The time had come to deposit the markers. Sounding truly desperate, Dan told Mitchell that he did not yet have sufficient funds to cover the markers. He then begged Mitchell to hold off for one more month while he tried to get a home loan to pay the debt off completely. Mitchell examined Dan's past record, noting his consistent payments through the end of 1987, and agreed.

If Carol had always been the picture of inner strength and peace, by that February she was finally beginning to fall apart. There was nothing obvious about this process, nothing anyone at church could point to as a sign that things were not well. But her close friends noticed a change in Carol's personality. She became quieter, more withdrawn. Although she continued to teach Sunday School and attend church regularly, Dan was present less and less often. Finally, one Sunday a month before Carol's murder, Cathy Hines pulled her aside after the service to ask her if something was wrong.

During that conversation Carol confided in her long-time friend that things were not well with Dan. Tearfully she told Cathy that she was worried about Dan because he had begun drinking again. Almost shamefully she asked her to pray for him.

Cathy felt that Carol was more depressed than she had ever seen her. Yet even then, Cathy noted, Carol never complained about her relationship with Dan. In fact, when the subject came up, Carol was always the first to say how very happily married she and Dan were. She seemed only concerned for Dan's health and salvation. After years of making decisions against the better judgment of her father and family, Carol had learned to hide her dirty laundry well. She would handle her problems by herself.

A few weeks later Cathy and Carol again had a chance to talk and eventually the conversation turned to Dan. This time a happier Carol informed Cathy that her prayers were working. Dan seemed to be drinking less, he was happier around the home, and he had even talked about returning to church. Most of all, Carol was thrilled about the trip to Hawaii they were planning for the first part of April.

True to Carol's words, Dan's depression did lift significantly in March. Carol attributed this to many reasons, not the least of which was her constant habit of remembering Dan in her prayers. But that month Dan learned from one of the collectors that in hardship cases casinos often accepted a mere twenty-five cents on the dollar as payment in full. This information combined with the loan application they had finally filled out and turned in that month seemed to bring new life to Dan. As their trip to Hawaii drew closer, Dan and Carol agreed that they were on the verge of a great turnaround, a new beginning in their marriage. If something else was contributing to Dan's improved spirits, Carol was unaware of it.

While the Montecalvos were busy working out the last-minute details of their trip, officers at the Burbank police station were having a rather slow week. Two of the more significant crimes that week were home burglaries—the first on March 27 and the second on March 30, when a teenage gang member stole three guns from his father's Burbank home.

Certain details about those incidents seemed unimportant at the time. These included the fact that the March 27 burglary, for which no suspect was ever arrested, occurred less than a mile from the Montecalvo home, as did the second burglary. Another interesting detail was that two of the guns stolen by the teenage gang member—who had a reputation for participating in gang shootings—were a .357 caliber hand gun and a .25 revolver. After Carol's murder, investigators could not tell whether Carol had been killed with a .357 or a .38. Dan was shot with a .25.

If these incidents received local media coverage, Dan and Carol were too busy planning their vacation to notice. Dan had errands to run and Carol busied herself with packing and making lists of friends to whom she'd send postcards. It was during this time that Suzan Brown visited the Montecalvo home with Carol's Avon order.

Dan spent the last days before their trip continuing to pacify casino collectors. Particularly bothersome to Dan was the call from White Mitchell on March 28. Although the collectors at the Mint Casino had agreed to wait for a complete payment sometime in April, Mitchell at the Golden Nugget had made no such arrangement. He told Dan that since they had not received a payment since December 6, they would have to deposit the markers immediately. Somehow Dan managed to buy three days time.

On the morning of March 31, fourteen hours before Carol's murder, Dan called Mitchell and told him a $500 payment was on its way. Dan immediately drove to his local Federal Express office and wired the money along with this note:

> Dear Mr. Mitchell: Enclosed please find a money order for $500 towards payment of my account. It is my hope that a negotiation for a loan will be finalized by April 21, 1988, and at that time I shall be able to honor my outstanding balance of $9,000.
>
> Again, due to circumstances beyond my control both in health and finances, I have not been able to satisfy this debt. However, I am certain that this situation is reversing.
>
> Therefore, I request that my markers be held until at least 4/21/88—submission of them at this time could definitely impact the loan negotiations in a negative way. Again thank you for your consideration, Dan Montecalvo.

In fact by late April Dan's financial situation had vastly improved, and not long afterward he was able to pay back each of his gambling debts. The casino collectors figured Dan's home loan must have been approved.

What the collectors didn't know until later, when

homicide investigators began asking questions, was that the payoff hadn't come from Dan's home loan—which had been turned down almost immediately. The money had come from Carol's life insurance settlement.

26

By January 1990 Dan had collected $400,000 in insurance money and spent nearly that much at various blackjack tables in Las Vegas and Lake Tahoe. The remaining $200,000 in policy money was still being contested by certain insurance companies because of Dan's role as a suspect.

The idea of Dan collecting Carol's insurance money while still being considered a suspect in her murder did not sit well with Carmelo Tronconi. By then the relationship between Dan and the Tronconi family had undergone many changes. The first was triggered by Carol's murder. During Dan and Carol's eight-year marriage, the couple had very little contact with her family. Occasionally Carol would write to her sister, Roseanna, in New York, and once in a while, around the holidays, Carmelo would call his younger daughter. But for the most part, when Carol took Dan as her husband she severed her shaky ties with her family.

However, after Carol's murder, her brother, sister, and father flew to Burbank to attend her memorial service. During their brief visit, the Tronconis were cordial and sympathetic to Dan, who appeared to be grief stricken over his wife's death.

On April 28, four weeks after she died and shortly

after returning home from the memorial service, Carol's brother, Jon, wrote to Dan.

In the letter, Jon tried to explain the separation that had taken place between Carol and her family. He said Carol was a very intelligent person and that he and her other family members could not understand why she would be attracted to a criminal still serving his prison sentence.

"Time ran out on us," Jon wrote.

He then wrote that he hoped to befriend Dan as a result of Carol's death. "I cannot change the past, but only learn from [it] and realize how foolish I was to allow this estrangement to occur."

He also offered to help Dan in any way possible and asked him to visit whenever he might have time. He also wrote that Dan should speak louder during their telephone conversations. "You don't have anything to be ashamed of. I hope the message of love and concern comes through. . . ."

But Jon's decision to give Dan a chance was short-lived. Over the next few months, detectives Kight and Lynch kept in contact with the Tronconis, apparently informing them of their suspicions about Dan.

On October 14, 1988, Carmelo Tronconi wrote to the Montgomery Ward Insurance Company requesting that Carol's life insurance benefits be placed in the control of the California courts. He also told the company that Dan was now a suspect in his daughter's murder.

When Dan learned from the insurance company that his claim was being contested by Carol's father, he told Maree Flores and other friends that he felt angry and betrayed. He requested a copy of the letter. Upon receiving it he noticed the footnote on the bottom of the page, which indicated that another copy had been sent to Detective Lynch.

Dan immediately concluded that Carmelo Tronconi was in collusion with the Burbank Police Department to frame him for Carol's murder. He even went so far as to suggest that Carmelo's real motive for interfering with the insurance policies might have been financial gain rather than any real suspicions about his son-in-law's role in Carol's death. After all, he reasoned, Carol's family hadn't doted on her over the past eight years. He had. They were only coming back now for a piece of the pie she'd left behind.

While Dan remained convinced that Carol's family had now become part of a plot to frame him for her murder, it became quite clear that the Tronconis were no longer interested in a friendly reunion with their son-in-law. They believed that Dan was guilty. Simple as that. In fact, their opinion was shaped less by what the detectives told them and more by the information they received from the insurance companies. Being Carol's next-of-kin after Dan, Carmelo Tronconi was notified by the insurance companies in late April as to the status of her policies. Since Dan was an official suspect, the companies had deemed it necessary to contact Carol's father with this information.

Carmelo learned that on April 13, 1988—less than two weeks after Carol's murder and only five days after Dan's release from the hospital—he filed a claim with Liberty Life Insurance Company. Six days later he signed a claim for the life insurance policy issued by Liberty Life Insurance Company. That same day he wrote this letter to Integrity Life Insurance Company:

To whom it may concern: The following is a brief explanation regarding the events that led to the death of my wife, Carol Montecalvo. On March 31, 1988, after returning from a walk, we surprised at least two intruders in our home. As a result, both my wife and I were shot. I survived; unfortunately my wife did not. I hope this will help you in processing this claim. Sincerely, Daniel Montecalvo.

Carmelo Tronconi believed he could read a considerable amount between the lines of Dan's request. In his opinion Dan filed the claims far too quickly. At a time when Dan should have been consumed with grief, he seemed to have just one thing on his mind—the insurance money.

Insurance records showed something else that Carmelo found interesting. The policies had been purchased within a six-week period, exactly one year before her murder. Carol's father believed this proved Dan had been planning to kill Carol for more than a year. He figured Dan had hoped to avoid suspicion by allowing a year to pass between purchasing the policies and carrying out his plans.

After learning these details the Tronconi family became certain of Dan's guilt. Especially in light of a letter Carol had written to her sister, Roseanna, in May 1987. In the past, Carol's letters had always been upbeat and positive, raving about the way Dan had surprised her by sending a dozen red roses to her office on her birthday, or gushing about how he had taken her out to dinner— almost as if she were trying to convince Roseanna of Dan's value.

But there was a difference in the tone of Carol's letter

of May 15, written during that six-week period when the policies on her life were taken out:

> I hope you have a wonderful party! I'm sure just being with the family will be great. I wish I could tell you Dan and I could be there in June, but at this point it doesn't look too good. I have started a new job with Pacific Bell Yellow Pages and . . . because of that, time and money do not allow a trip to Buffalo.
> Dan is job hunting. . . . We would have loved being there to celebrate [with you] but we will be there in spirit. . . . Maybe we will win the California lottery and things will change. Take care, and love to all. Carol.

Roseanna knew as she reread the letter after Carol's death that her sister's financial situation must have been very grim, indeed. Otherwise Carol would have brushed over the issue as she had so many other times when things were not going well in her personal life.

When Roseanna showed the letter to her father and brother, they agreed that Dan and Carol must have been desperately broke that spring of 1987, and with every additional life insurance policy, Dan must have begun planning a deadly solution to the couple's financial woes.

As the family reached that conclusion the relationship between Dan Montecalvo and his in-laws made one more, final transformation. The Tronconis were no longer angry with Dan. They hated him.

27

Now that Brian Arnspiger had a complete picture of Dan and Carol's relationship and Dan's plunge into desperation, he began weaving together the threads he'd collected. Now it was merely a matter of convincing the district attorney's office that the volumes of circumstantial evidence against Dan Montecalvo were enough to take before a jury.

By the first part of February 1990 Brian's biggest find was still the hollowed-out book. That week he compiled several other tidbits of evidence against Dan. Although these details did not prove Dan's guilt by themselves, they certainly gave Brian's suspicions a clear ring of truth.

Starting with Genios—the Italian restaurant where Sergeant Goldberg had talked with Dan on several occasions—Brian uncovered a trail of bars and restaurants that Dan had frequented. Brian heard accounts of Dan's flirtatious behavior and his animosity toward other patrons.

Manager Scott Young from the Pago Pago cocktail lounge had a particularly interesting story about Dan. The Pago Pago was across the street from Disney Studios on Alameda Avenue in Burbank. Most of its customers were stagehands and set builders and other union types who worked at the studios. According to

Young, Dan became a regular customer in the fall of 1987—the same period that the couple had been in desperate financial trouble and Carol had been working late hours trying to earn the trip to Hawaii.

Young had no trouble remembering what nights of the week Dan hung out at the bar. Saturdays, Sundays, Mondays, and Tuesdays. Always at night. Always at the same time.

"You must be quite a bright man, Mr. Young," Brian stated as he leaned against the bar and watched the manager consolidate several bottles of gin. "Remembering something like that for more than two years."

"Memory has nothing to with it." The man turned from what he was doing and stared at the detective.

Brian looked concerned. "Look," he said sharply. "This is serious. We think the guy killed his wife. You tell me he used to hang out here and you know the exact days, the exact times he'd stay. Then you tell me memory has nothing to do with it."

Young shrugged. "That's right."

"How can you be so sure, then?"

"Simple. Those are the nights Janice worked the bar." He turned back to organizing the bottles. "Dan seemed to have a thing for Janice. If she was working, he was here."

Brian thought about Carol, slaving late into the night selling yellow page ads while her husband flirted with Janice, and he felt his jaw muscles tightening. "What makes you remember Janice's schedule?"

"She's still here. Schedule hasn't changed in years," he said indifferently. "Only reason Dan stopped coming round was the fight."

Brian pulled up a stool.

"Tell me about it."

The story took ten minutes and when it was finished Brian knew his case against Dan had just grown stronger. According to Young, Dan often made a nuisance of himself, talking about his involvement with organized crime and his days in the penitentiary. One night Janice had been pouring drinks for Dan when she caught a glimpse of what looked like a handgun beneath his jacket. The more Dan drank, the more nervous Janice became. Finally she pointed the gun out to Young. In Young's opinion, the gun looked like a .32 or a .38 special—the gun police officers use.

Before Young had time to analyze the situation Dan and another patron began raising their voices. The argument escalated quickly and soon both men were on their feet shouting, inches apart from each other. Suddenly Dan reached for the gun. Then, in what looked like a scene from across the street at the studios, three stunt men relaxing nearby lunged forward and separated the men.

By then Young had decided that Dan would not be welcome back at the Pago Pago. No one was going to bring a gun into his restaurant and threaten his customers. He asked both men to leave and not to return. After that Young saw Dan just once—when he came in the next day to complain about the way he was treated.

"No one pulls a gun in my bar," Young responded. "Nothing more to say."

"Your loss, buddy." Dan spat the words and turned to leave.

"Say, Dan," Young had asked just as Dan reached the door. "Why the gun?"

Dan moved his jacket aside exposing the same handgun he had nearly pulled out in anger the night before and patted it tenderly. "Protection." He smiled.

Young never knew what Dan meant by the comment, but he figured it had something to do with Dan's much-discussed Mafia ties.

As Brian listened carefully, he began to wonder if other Burbank bartenders might have similar stories to tell about Dan Montecalvo.

Later that week he found out.

He spoke with Richard Wilkinson, a clean-cut regular at the Shaker Mountain Inn. The way Wilkinson told it Dan and he had a disagreement one night over the Monroe Doctrine. No one seemed to remember how the disagreement escalated or why it had started in the first place, but eventually the men were exchanging comments about each other's parents. Finally Dan pulled a gun and threatened Wilkinson.

"Listen," other patrons remembered Dan saying, "I'm not going to fight you, I'll just shoot you."

The manager immediately grabbed Dan's wrist and broke up the argument, asking Dan to leave.

After Wilkinson, Brian found others who remembered Dan carrying one or two guns into various Burbank bars. One man even recalled thinking Dan was a policeman because of the .38 special he carried at all times.

"Everyone knew about Dan's guns," the man told Brian. "Around here we called him 'Dan, Dan, the policeman.'"

Then there were the stories Laura Foster told. She was a waitress at Genios and she told Brian how Dan would leave late at night with other women or sit in his favorite booth necking with a woman he had met only hours earlier.

She also remembered the time Dan flashed several

hundred-dollar bills at her as she waited tables. When Laura ignored him, Dan dropped the bills at her feet.

"That could be yours," he had told her, with a suggestive smile.

Before she had time to leave, Dan took a Sugar Daddy candy out of his pocket and waved it at the pretty waitress. "How 'bout taking a trip to Vegas with me, honey? I'll take care of you."

Laura rolled her eyes, shook her head in disgust, and walked away. Later that night—while Dan was still inside drinking—Laura and a few other waitresses sneaked quietly out behind the restaurant and found his car. Trying to suppress her giggles, one of the women began writing the words "Sugar Daddy" in the dust on the car's back window.

But it was Dan's reaction that fixed the memory in Laura's mind. Dan stormed into the restaurant and demanded to see the owners, Marvin Cecchini and his son, James. While Laura hid in the kitchen, Dan ranted about her rude behavior and poor work habits.

The Cecchinis took Dan's complaint in stride. Throughout 1985 and 1986, they had seen Dan flirting with strange women—buying them drinks and making out with them. They remembered that even though Dan lived less than a mile away, sometimes he drank so late and so long that he'd spend the night in his car, parked behind the restaurant.

They also told Brian how Dan had never mentioned his wife, Carol. In fact, as they recalled, whenever the subject of marriage came up, Dan was cynical about it, laughing at the idea of being bound to a woman.

Brian listened to the men's stories and instantly remembered a magazine he'd found in Dan's home. It featured an article titled "California Break-up: When

Marriage Turns Into Economic War—A High-Powered
Divorce Lawyer Takes You Into the Trenches."

The magazine was dated March 13, 1988. Eighteen
days before Carol's murder.

In the course of a week Brian had heard enough of
these stories to close several gaping holes. All along,
Dan had claimed his undying love for Carol. Proof of
that was the blissful relationship they had shared for
eight years, and the confirmation of the Montecalvos'
church friends. Of course, those church friends only
saw Dan on an occasional Sunday morning. Their opinion of him was primarily shaped by the things Carol
said, and perhaps more importantly, the things she did
not say.

Brian had already tried to take the case to the district
attorney's office. Assistant District Attorney Ben Bernard had the task of reviewing cases and deciding
whether there was enough evidence to warrant a trial in
Pasadena's Superior Court. Brian had worked with Bernard before on murder cases and knew he was demanding. If he didn't think a case was winnable, he'd turn it
down. Three times Bernard had turned down the
Montecalvo case.

"It's good stuff, Arnie," Bernard would tell the detective each time. "One problem. You need more of it."

Brian considered trying a fourth time in light of
Dan's habit of carrying guns, carousing in bars, and
picking up women. But something told him the evidence still wasn't enough.

Late one night, while Brian was lying awake in bed
analyzing the circumstantial evidence against Dan and
trying to imagine where he might find the missing
pieces, he got an idea. Pacific Bell. That was the only
place Brian hadn't rechecked since taking on the inves-

tigation. If Carol had been afraid of Dan, someone at her former employer's office must have known about it. Women didn't spend ten hours a day at a place without talking to someone about their personal lives.

The next morning Brian paid a visit to Laura Angelino, Carol's former supervisor at Pacific Bell. The supervisor welcomed Brian into her office and immediately began searching through a file cabinet next to her desk.

"I'm so sorry," she said, sifting quickly through numerous files. "Really. I completely forgot about it until I heard you were in the lobby."

Brian frowned. "Forgot about what?"

Angelino stopped her searching and stood up to face the detective. "You don't know about Mark Paulson?"

Brian shook his head. For a moment he wondered if the woman had him confused with someone else. "Who's Mark Paulson?"

The woman drew in a deep breath and motioned for Brian to sit down. "I'd better start from the beginning."

According to Angelino, Mark Paulson was one of Carol's coworkers. On September 7, 1989, Paulson met with a man named Denis Cremins who needed help putting together an advertisement for his plumbing business. In the course of their conversation, Denis asked Mark if he knew Carol Montecalvo.

"Yeah, worked with her here at the office. Such a shame, what happened to her," Paulson had said, looking up from the ad. "You know her?"

"No, never met her," Cremins had replied. "Knew her husband, Dan. Weird guy."

"Why's that?"

"Well, one time when I was in a fight with my fiancée Dan told me how I could take care of the problem."

Mark had listened intently. "What'd he say?"

"Well, Dan told me to insure her for a bunch of money, and he'd shoot her for me. After that, we'd split the insurance money."

Long after Denis Cremins had left that afternoon, Mark Paulson pondered their conversation. He'd heard that Carol had been killed by burglars, but even so he thought the information might be important. When he had come back from lunch that day, he pulled Laura Angelino aside and explained the story to her. She made a note of their conversation, placed it in an envelope, and put it on her desk to give the authorities. She completely forgot about it until that February day nearly five months later when Brian Arnspiger showed up in her office.

Brian knew this was the piece of evidence he'd been waiting for. The next day he paid a visit to the district attorney's office and this time Bernard was impressed.

"Do we go to trial?" Brian asked when Bernard was finished looking over the new evidence.

Bernard smiled slowly and reached across his desk to shake Brian's hand.

"As soon as possible."

28

Rita Nelson had managed the Oak Tree Apartments in a run-down neighborhood near downtown Los Angeles for nearly ten years. In her younger days she had been a beautiful petite brunette with blue eyes, a soft voice, and a kind smile. But now, seven years after her husband had passed away, Rita was known for neither her kindness nor her smile. She was a white-haired wiry pencil of a woman whose soft curves had long since been replaced with sharp angles and edges. At fifty-two years old, Rita was no more than five feet tall. But something in her assertive manner and the gruff tone with which she barked commands made her tenants respond in a way that deeply pleased the apartment building owners.

In the past decade Rita had certainly seen her share of troubles at the complex. There had been drug busts, child abuse, drunken domestic fights, and occasional bursts of gunfire. Rita knew these incidents were typical of that part of town. Because of that she frequently congratulated herself on the fact that, to date, none of her tenants had died on the premises.

It was the fourth day of February 1990 and Rita was sitting in her meticulously clean office looking at a list of tenants who had yet to pay their rent. Suzan Brown's name was at the top of the list. Rita set the list back down on her desk and glanced out the office window toward a row of depressingly similar beige boxlike apartments.

Suzan Brown, Rita thought to herself. Must have been two days since she'd seen the woman. Everyone in the complex knew there was something distinctly wrong with Suzan. Almost as if she had two personalities. One that stayed in a wheelchair talking incessantly about Vietnam, and another, more conniving, personality. It was that second one—capable of drug use and passing off bad checks—that concerned Rita.

Rita glanced at her tenant records, flipping the pages to Suzan Brown's account. The records showed that for the past two months Suzan had paid her rent on time. Rita thought over the situation. Until that week, a day had not gone by when she hadn't been seen walking or wheeling herself about the property. Rita stood up and grabbed a ring of keys from inside her desk drawer. Ten minutes later she was standing outside Suzan Brown's apartment. She knocked sharply several times and waited.

"Suzan," she barked. "Open up. It's Rita."

Tenants at the Oak Tree knew that Rita sometimes paid them a personal visit if they were late with their rent. Most of them didn't bother trying to evade her. Despite her hard attitude and rigid appearance, she was usually willing to work out a deal. Rita knew the rent deals she struck were better than losing a tenant or going through the lengthy three-month eviction process.

Rita knocked again and waited. After thirty seconds, the diminutive woman let out a frustrated sigh and sorted through the keys on her ring until she found the one she was looking for. Working the key expertly into the hole, Rita opened the door.

Managing apartments in an area wrought with crime and homelessness had hardened Rita so that nothing much surprised her. So she felt neither fear nor shock as she looked at the large, bloblike woman lying face-down on the living room floor. Instead she was aggravated. Suzan Brown appeared to be dead. And that would make her the first fatality at the Oak Tree Apartments since Rita had taken over as manager.

Suddenly Rita saw the woman's hand move. As the manager stepped closer she could hear Suzan snoring. Rita performed a quick check of the apartment and verified her suspicions. An empty bottle of sleeping pills lay near the bathroom sink next to a nearly empty glass of water. Suzan had tried to kill herself.

After surviving her first suicide attempt, Suzan Brown had spent the past year making more plans to kill herself. But until that first week of February 1990 she hadn't been able to carry them out. Finally she had decided to try sleeping pills once more, but as before she hadn't taken enough to do the job. Suzan felt as if some awful force wanted to keep her alive, suffering in her constant belief that she and Ron Hardy had killed Carol.

Rita knelt beside Suzan's body and took her pulse. It was weak, but steady.

"Suzan," Rita snapped, her voice loud and bossy.

The unconscious woman writhed slowly onto her side and began moaning. Rita sighed again, realizing that she would have to call an ambulance. There was no way to tell how many pills she'd ingested. *Damn irresponsible tenants,* she thought to herself.

As Rita considered her next move, Suzan's moaning began sounding more like slurred words.

"Tell 'em wha' happened," Suzan said slowly, her

words blending into each other. "Tell 'em. Gotta tell 'em."

Rita slapped the front and back of Suzan's closest hand several times, trying to rouse her. Finally she gave up and moved toward the front door, intent on returning to the office and calling the paramedics.

"Gotta tell 'em, gotta tell 'em," Suzan repeated, her voice growing steadily louder. Rita, curious, moved back to Suzan's side.

"Tell them what?" Rita asked sternly.

"Tell 'em 'bout Carol," she said. Rita could barely understand her words. "Nobody knows about Carol."

Rita raised an eyebrow and frowned at the woman. It occurred to her that perhaps she would be better off calling a psychiatric facility. Rita had often held long discussions with Suzan Brown, simply trying to figure her out. But in all the months they'd known each other Suzan Brown had never mentioned anyone named Carol. Rita decided it was just as she had always thought. The woman was sick. She was a lesbian, a drug addict, and quite possibly a lunatic.

Suzan's body flopped back to its original position. The woman's snoring grew louder. Shaking her head in disgust, Rita returned to her office to make the telephone call. Paramedics transported Suzan Brown to Los Angeles County Hospital, where doctors took less than an hour to determine she was in the wrong facility.

The next morning Suzan Brown was checked into the psychiatric ward at the Jerry L. Pettis Memorial Veterans Administration Medical Center in San Bernardino County, southeast of Los Angeles. Upon regaining consciousness at the Los Angeles County Hospital, Suzan had told the doctors about her time in Vietnam. Although no one was able to confirm the story, Rita Nelson must have found paperwork declaring she was indeed a veteran. That would have been enough to get her admitted to the V.A. hospital.

The hospital was an old light-colored brick building set atop a rolling green knoll and fenced off from the wide residential streets that surrounded it. A visitors' parking lot was sprawled out adjacent to the main wing. Most often, the lot was empty. Broken men and women, many of them forgotten, loitered about the grounds, causing most people to look away as they drove by. There was something unbearably sad and unfair about housing America's ailing heroes in such a dreary facility.

By mid-afternoon the effects of the sleeping pills had completely worn off and Suzan Brown suddenly found herself in her element. Late into the evening she and several other patients swapped stories about Vietnam, relating death-defying incidents and numerous accounts of hand-to-hand combat and raging ground battles.

By then, whatever she had wanted to say about Carol was long since forgotten.

29

His anxiety was growing. More and more, Dan was certain the police were following him. He could swear they were listening to his telephone conversations. With each passing day, they seemed to be closing in on him, surrounding him with an invisible net. The thought scared him to death, causing his heart to beat erratically, and his hands to feel cold and clammy.

Finally, on March 13, 1990, two months after the charges were dropped, Dan Montecalvo knew that he had reached his limit. Two months of increasing tension had passed since he'd been released from jail on bail after his January arrest. Charges had subsequently been dropped, but Dan remained paranoid that police were trying to frame him. He was having difficulty breathing, difficulty concentrating. He seemed to have lost weight. No longer was he only concerned with being arrested. He told Maree he was worried the police might be trying to kill him.

"Why would they do a thing like that, Dan?"

"They're trying to frame me, Maree!" Dan said urgently. "You think they want any witnesses to something like that?"

Maree didn't understand why police would frame Dan for Carol's murder, but they did seem to be focusing their investigation on him. She didn't think they would ever find enough evidence to arrest Dan for something he hadn't done. Still, she remembered one incident in January when a telephone repair man had visited their shared duplex.

"Just here to check the wires, ma'am," he had told her with a nod and a broad smile.

After an hour he had left without saying a word. Later, Dan had been furious.

"Can't they ever leave me alone?" He shouted the words and slammed his fist on Maree's kitchen counter. "Where did they work?"

Maree showed him, and after fifteen minutes of searching the telephone wires underneath the house, Dan appeared to have found what he was looking for.

"It's a bug, a bugging device. This isn't the first time, Maree. They've been tapping my lines ever since Carol died." He paused and ran a hand through his black hair. "What are they trying to find?"

Maree had stood frozen in place, staring at the tiny device, not knowing that it would be illegal to set such a trap without approval from a judge. No such approval was ever granted in the case against Dan Montecalvo and police adamantly denied ever listening to Dan's phone conversations or planting a bug in his home. In addition, no evidence was ever introduced that came from Dan's phone conversations.

But Maree had always taken Dan at his word. Now, looking at what appeared to be a bugging device, she could finally see for herself why Dan had become so paranoid.

"Dan, we're both in this now. I'll be here for you, whatever happens," she had assured him.

Maree remembered the incident now, with Dan

glancing from the front door to the back as if at any moment he expected police to burst into the house.

"Calm down," Maree said quietly, reaching across the table. "What will be, will be. Worrying about it won't change anything."

For a moment, she thought she understood why Carol had fallen in love with Dan. He was intelligent and kind, gentle and soft-spoken. A perfect gentleman who obviously had nothing to hide or he wouldn't still be living in Burbank. Years has passed since she had thought of herself as desirable. But even in the context of their purely platonic friendship, Dan made Maree feel special. He was her constant friend and companion, he got along very well with her teenage sons and tried his best to take care of them all. He worried about them, advising them to lock their doors at night.

"If burglars could destroy my life, they could destroy yours, too, Maree," he would tell her. "Please be careful."

Many times he would surprise them all with a pizza or a rented movie on videotape. Maree knew she had begun to depend on Dan's financial contributions and his presence around her home. She wondered what would happen if police ever did arrest him.

Now, with Dan nervously drumming his fingers on her kitchen table, she closed her eyes and began to pray. Immediately, she felt a wave of peace wash over her. Everything would be all right. After all, Dan was an innocent Christian man.

"Let's get out of here." Dan's words broke the peaceful reverie of Maree's prayer. She opened her eyes and saw that Dan had begun moving toward the front door.

"Where to?" Dan's behavior was making Maree nervous.

"I don't know," Dan said over his shoulder. Maree noticed he was looking impatiently out the front window. He turned suddenly and stared at her. "I just have to get out for a few hours."

Detective Brian Arnspiger and Officer Rick Medlin were waiting on the west side of Acresite Avenue. Only a sliver of moon shone in the sky and darkness filled the parked squad car, making it difficult for the policemen inside to see the Flores home. They had been waiting there since 8:30 P.M.

Brian had decided their best plan was to wait until Dan left the house. If they could pull him over while he was driving, they would have the upper hand. If they approached the house, Dan might try to escape.

Now, as he watched for Dan to leave, Brian could hardly contain his excitement. He had obtained a warrant for Dan's arrest the day before, hours after visiting the district attorney's office. March 13, 1990, would be Dan Montecalvo's last day as a free man. Brian smiled in the dark and for the hundredth time since he'd taken on the investigation he seemed to sense Carol's presence. Almost as if she had been encouraging him to put her killer behind bars.

"You see that?" Medlin's voice was suddenly alert. Quickly, Brian focused his attention on the Flores home. Two silhouettes emerged from the pitch-black shadows. The detectives watched as the figures climbed into the car parked in the Flores driveway. The car lurched into motion just as its lights came on.

"That's our cue," Brian said.

"Here goes." Medlin started the engine and took off in the same direction. Instantly Brian flipped on the lights and siren. Medlin caught up with Maree's yellow hatchback in less than ten seconds. Maree appeared to be driving.

Another ten seconds passed and Maree still had not pulled over despite the glaring lights.

"Probably can't see us," Brian said sarcastically.

"Right." Medlin focused his attention on the car in front of him, refusing to allow a gap between them.

For nearly an entire city block the chase continued.

Inside Maree's car, Dan had been the first to see the officers behind them.

"Pull over, Maree," Dan ordered.

Until Dan had spoken up, Maree had been completely unaware of the police car behind them. Now, afraid something awful was about to happen, Maree pulled the car over and turned off the engine. Silently she reached across the space between the two front seats, taking Dan's hand in hers and squeezing it gently.

"Trust God," she whispered.

Then they waited.

Medlin's job was to take care of Maree. He placed his hand on his revolver and approached the driver's door. At the same time Brian pulled his gun and scurried around to the passenger door.

"Ma'am, you need to get out of the car." Medlin's voice was stern and Maree got out quickly. He could see the fear on her face and wondered why she had been harboring a cold-blooded killer these past months. Medlin ushered Maree to the curb and placed handcuffs on her wrists. The woman had been helping Dan for several months and the officers believed it was possible she would do something dangerous to protect him. They would take no chances.

Just then, two additional police cars arrived at the

scene. Their headlights lit up her car and Maree suddenly had a clear view of Dan's face. Something had changed. He no longer looked frightened. He looked like he had given up.

That was the instant Maree Flores's heart broke for Dan Montecalvo and she knew without a doubt that she was in love with him.

Two officers joined Brian; one pointed a rifle at Dan.

"It's all over, Danny boy," Brian said, grabbing Dan's arm and assisting him to his feet from the passenger seat. "You're under arrest."

Brian wrenched Dan's arms behind his back and clicked the handcuffs shut. It was the best sound he'd heard in a long time.

For a moment, a flicker of indignation flashed in Dan's eyes. "For what?" he snapped.

Brian shook his head in disgust. He had never worked so hard to capture one man. And now that the investigation was finally over, Dan still refused to acknowledge the truth.

"This might surprise you, Dan, so I'll say it slowly," Brian said. "You're under arrest for the murder of your wife, Carol."

Dan hung his head and released a slow, pent-up sigh. He began to nod his head in understanding. When he looked up, Brian could see that the fight had gone. What Dan said next confirmed it.

"I knew you guys would get me one day."

They were words that gave Brian a deep sense of satisfaction.

30

The article appeared in the *Los Angeles Times* on March 15 in the highly visible Metro section. The headline read, "Burbank Man Charged With Murdering Wife in 'Burglary.'"

Suzan Brown had woken up at five that morning—part of the routine she had adopted since being admitted to the psychiatric unit of the Veterans Administration hospital in San Bernardino County. Up at five. Walk the hallways. Seven times. Get the paper. Back to bed. Read the paper. Climb into the wheelchair. Watch the others rise. Wait an hour. Start the day.

Not surprisingly, doctors at the hospital believed Suzan was still in need of mental help and had therefore not permitted her release.

That morning Suzan mindlessly opened the newspaper and her eyes fell on that particular headline. It was as if someone had punched her in the stomach. In one jerky motion she closed the paper and pushed it noisily under the sheets of her hospital bed. She sat straight up, motionless except for her eyes, which began darting about at her sleeping roommates.

Had they seen her? Maybe they knew the truth and now they were only pretending to be asleep. People pretended things like that. Suzan pretended things.

Her eyes raced one way, then the other, desperately searching the room for any sign of life. There was none.

Slowly Suzan allowed her back to settle against the curved pillow behind her. Then she heard it. A loud, constant thumping. Someone was in the room, someone who knew the truth. She looked around and saw no one. The sound grew louder. Faster and louder. Thump, thump, thump, thump. Maybe someone was trying to break through the walls or the floors. Maybe they were coming through the ceiling.

At that moment Suzan recognized her own heartbeat. The sound had come from her. She relaxed a bit more and waited. Six o'clock. Seven. Eight. The minutes ticked by with no concern for the heavyset woman waiting anxiously, desperate for her two roommates to leave the room.

Finally it was 10:30 A.M. Everyone was up, dressed, and out in the yard. She waited until she was absolutely certain no one was in the hallway. Then, jerking the newspaper out from underneath the bed covers, she tucked it under her arm. Rising with quick, stilted movements, Suzan lifted herself from the bed, walked to the wheelchair, and sat down. She opened her eyes so wide that they looked perfectly round. Glancing in as many directions as she could without turning her chair, Suzan spent five minutes making certain no one was watching her.

She was alone. Trying to appear relaxed, she slowly thumbed through the pages to the article. Then, hungrily, she began reading.

A man who two years ago told Burbank police his wife was shot to death and he was wounded when they surprised a burglar in their home, has been charged with murdering his wife, authorities said Wednesday.

Police said Daniel J. Montecalvo, 48, shot himself as part of an elaborate plan to cover up his part in the March, 1988, death of his 43-year-old wife, Carol.

Suzan took a sudden deep breath and shut her eyes tightly. Something deep inside her screamed it wasn't true. They couldn't be blaming Dan for a crime he didn't commit. Impossible. She felt her wheelchair spinning in circles but when she opened her eyes everything in the room was perfectly still. Gradually Suzan's eyes made their way down to the newspaper until she found her place again.

Montecalvo, who was being held without bail in Los Angeles County Jail, was arrested Tuesday night in Burbank . . . He was scheduled to be arraigned today in Burbank Municipal Court on one count of murder.

"It's a bizarre case," Burbank Police Sergeant Don Goldberg said. "The evidence indicates he shot his wife, Carol, to death and then shot himself to make it appear they had been shot by an armed burglar."

Goldberg said the motive for Carol Montecalvo's murder was financial gain, but he would not elaborate.

It's true, Suzan thought, tilting her head back and staring at the water-stained ceiling. Carol was killed for financial gain, but not for Dan Montecalvo's financial gain. She snapped her head forward and stared at the article.

The gun used in the killing has not been found.

That was it—that moment Suzan knew everything was going to be all right. Her terror began to subside, almost as if she had finally found the perfect fix. Her heart began beating normally, and her muscles relaxed. The gun had not been found. Of course. And the gun would never be found. Everything was going to be all right.

Without a gun there was no way on earth Dan would go to prison for a murder he did not commit. Suzan drew in a deep breath and started laughing. All that worrying for nothing. She laughed and laughed until finally the sound attracted the attention of an orderly.

"Everything okay in here?" He leaned into the room and saw an obese woman with short, straight brown hair and tattoos covering her body sitting in a wheelchair laughing.

Suzan turned to stare at him, tears streaming down her cheeks.

"They can't . . . find . . . the gun!" she said, laughing too hard to catch her breath.

The orderly frowned and took another step inside the room. "What gun?"

Abruptly, Suzan stopped laughing.

"Clowns." She spoke the word flatly. All traces of laughter had completely disappeared.

"What do you mean 'clowns'?" The orderly sounded concerned. "You said, 'They can't find the gun.'"

"No." Suzan stared at him. "They can't mind the fun. Clowns."

She raised the newspaper and began shaking it in her hand. The orderly took one step back and made a note to ask his supervisor for a job transfer. He'd spent enough time in the psych ward. The woman was still staring at him and it was beginning to make him feel nervous.

"Can't a girl read an article about clowns without getting the third degree around here?" she snapped angrily.

The orderly shrugged. "Read what you want, lady. Whatever floats your boat."

"Leave." It was a command.

A chill made its way down the orderly's spine. There was something frightening in the woman's eyes. As if some part of her had died years ago and what was left was capable of unspeakable evil.

31

Dan had no trouble deciding which defense attorney to hire. Word of mouth in the Los Angeles County jail had it that a handful of attorneys took it personally when their clients were convicted. Not coincidentally, these attorneys were also the most successful. Among those Dan heard about, one name kept coming up: Lorn Aiken.

The man had an office just outside Koreatown on the poorer side of downtown Los Angeles. There in a red brick building built long before the days of earthquake safety codes, Lorn Aiken and his legal assistant rented office space. Actually the rent served two purposes because when Lorn wasn't working there, he made the place his home.

The items strewn throughout his office were normally an unrecognizable combination of personal and business belongings. Not that the status of his office bothered Lorn much. After all, most of his client meetings were held in conference rooms at the county jail, which happened to be the setting for Lorn's first meeting with Dan Montecalvo.

It was March 16, three days after Dan's arrest. Dan sat nervously in the small nondescript room where a thousand defense attorneys had met with their accused clients in the past. He gripped the arms of his chair tightly. So much hope rested on this meeting with Lorn Aiken. Dan knew that he could very possibly be convicted of murder and forced to spend the rest of his life in prison. Even with one of the most successful defense attorneys in the business. He closed his eyes and tried to shut out the frightening thought as a film of sweat began to appear on his upper lip and forehead. Dan looked at the clock on the wall. 3 P.M.

Suddenly there was a sound at the door and Dan turned to see a burly mountain of a man enter the room and then move quickly to join him at the table.

"Lorn Aiken," the man said brusquely, sitting down and stacking a pile of dockets and folders on the table beside him. "You must be Dan Montecalvo."

Dan nodded. "That's right." He had never pictured Lorn Aiken looking as he did. Lorn looked more like a renegade linebacker than a defense attorney. A generous amount of unruly dark curls covered his head and face. His beard was lightly peppered with gray and he had the most piercing blue eyes Dan had ever seen. Despite a slight limp, which he aided by using a solid walnut walking cane, Lorn Aiken was a hulking specimen of a man with a broad back and shoulders that filled out his six-foot-three-inch frame.

Lorn had finished organizing his notes and he looked across the table at Dan.

"Okay, here's my rules," Lorn stated. For a moment Dan felt like an inept athlete getting a verbal lesson on the basics from his coach. "You lie to me and it's like cheating at solitaire. It's only a win if you don't cheat."

Lorn paused until he was certain Dan was paying close attention.

"Clients don't lie to me. Ever." Dan imagined the things this man could do to him if he ever caught him lying. Lorn leaned across the table and looked directly into Dan's eyes. "You know why?"

Dan shook his head quickly. "Why?"

"Because this case is no longer about you. It's about me. If you let me walk into court and let some pencil-neck D.A. tear my case apart"—Lorn paused and his voice grew softer and more deliberate—"I'm going to rip your head off and puke down your neck."

Lorn noticed the wide eyes of the small man before him and he knew Dan believed his threat. "Understood?"

Dan nodded. "Understood."

"Good. Because I care a whole lot more about my reputation than I do about yours. My reputation depends on winning. And that depends on you telling me the truth."

"Okay." Dan swallowed hard and it sounded like a hiccup in the silent room. Lorn narrowed his eyes again.

"Ready to begin?"

Dan nodded.

"Okay, now tell me what happened. From the beginning. Don't leave anything out and don't forget the rules."

Dan nodded again and started talking.

Lorn Aiken had never planned on being a defense attorney. Growing up in northern Oregon and Washington, young Lorn was a rebel and a drifter who learned early on that he had been gifted with a lucrative talent: salesmanship. The combination of his dark looks and his quick wit gave Lorn the uncanny, natural-born ability to sell things people neither needed nor wanted.

Not long after he graduated from high school, Lorn

began making money with his talent. His first sales jobs took him door to door and he sold everything. Encyclopedias, shoes, vacuums, Fuller brushes. In the late 1960s, when Lorn was nineteen, he sold seventeen vacuums in one day, turning a profit of more than two hundred dollars. But what Lorn remembered most about the day was the occupation of four of his customers. They were vacuum salesmen.

When Lorn was twenty-two, a manager at a Portland stereo store recognized his sales ability and hired him. Lorn flourished in the job, breaking sales records and making more commission than any other two salesmen combined. But his personal life took a turn for the worse when he and an acquaintance exchanged words and the acquaintance drew a gun and began firing. Lorn took several bullets in his right leg and abdomen and was in critical condition from loss of blood when he arrived at the local hospital.

Lorn liked to say he had a little chat with Mr. Death that night and—always the salesman—sold him on the idea of returning at a later date. After several days of flirting with nurses and making a nuisance of himself, Lorn left the hospital. A month later he moved to Southern California and began working for the Federated Group selling stereos as if his life depended on it.

Later that year, Lorn befriended one of his customers, defense attorney Lawrence Davis. Whenever work permitted, Lorn began visiting the courthouse to watch Davis in action. He was fascinated. Legal defense was nothing more than a professional sales job—selling a jury on the reasons to return a not-guilty verdict. Lorn began understanding some of the more common defense tricks and before long he was giving Davis suggestions.

"Hey, Davis," Lorn would say over lunch. "Your guy's guilty, right?"

"Right. Caught him red-handed with a truckload of stolen ammunition. His partner had an alibi prepared, but the cops took care of him with a coupla quick .38s."

"It's perfect."

Davis looked up from his bowl of steaming chili and frowned. "Not from where I'm sitting. Eight cops caught him red-handed with the goods."

Lorn smiled. "Could he help it if his armed partner had forced him at gunpoint to hijack a truckload of ammunition?"

Davis raised an eyebrow and the first sign of a smile appeared on his face. Normally he would have laughed out loud at a stereo salesman offering him advice on how to defend a criminal. But something told Davis the idea just might work. A week later the two shared lunch again and Davis smiled broadly.

"Drinks are on me." He lifted his glass for a toast.

"Why?"

"Because it worked."

"What worked?"

"Your idea. The mother walked. Caught him red-handed and he walked."

Lorn slapped his leg and let out a loud whoop. "Course it worked. It's an old sales trick. Always two ways of looking at something."

Davis shook his head in awe.

"What you need is a law degree, buddy."

"Naah." Lorn took a long swig of his drink. "Too much work."

"Make you more money than selling stereos," Davis said. "Besides, you'd have a job."

Lorn looked doubtful. "Where?"

"Right here. Working for me."

Lorn pondered Davis's statement for two months before applying to the San Fernando Valley College of Law. He had never attended college, so he was required to pass a bachelor's degree proficiency test before being accepted. The test took four hours and Lorn passed it with high marks. He graduated two years later and passed the bar on the second try.

True to his word, Davis offered Lorn a partnership and the pair worked together successfully for the next eighteen months. That was exactly how long it took Lorn to realize he had absolutely no need for Davis. He set up an office in a one-room guest-house apartment in the eastern San Fernando Valley. It was impossible to see the place from the road and Lorn often said people needed more than a map to find his office. They needed a tour guide. After three years he moved into his downtown office.

By then Lorn had fully developed his legal philosophy and he liked explaining it to clients.

"I mess with cops," Lorn would say, narrowing his brilliant blue eyes and pointing his thumb proudly at his puffed-out chest. "It's my job. If I don't mess with cops, the next door they knock down will be yours. If there are no rules to follow, this will be Romania in a heartbeat."

Lorn would pause a moment and pull out a tin box of Shermans. Removing one thin brown cigarette, he would light it and take two or three deep drags before continuing.

"I'm the last line of defense between this being the good ol' U.S. of A. and this being Romania."

Lorn didn't just say these words, he believed them. And he had another rule. No rape or incest cases. Once, when Lorn was representing a man arrested on assault charges, one of his colleagues met him in the hallway.

"Changing your rules, huh?" The man gave Lorn a knowing look. At some point in their careers, most defense attorneys wind up representing criminals they never intended to work for.

"Meaning what?"

"The scumbag in there, your defendant." The attorney pointed toward the courtroom.

"In for assault, so what?"

"That's not what I heard. The D.A. worked out a deal to reduce the charges, but it wasn't assault that brought him here."

Lorn could feel his face reddening. The man had told him a story about beating up some guy who owed him money. "What else did you hear?" Lorn asked.

"Word is two witnesses saw him force some pretty little nine-year-old girl to, shall we say, perform oral copulation and a few other acts on him," the man said.

Rage began building in Lorn. He listened as his colleague continued.

"Girl wound up with gonorrhea, he winds up with an assault charge."

Lorn dropped his cigarette on the tile floor and smashed it angrily with his boot toe.

"I'll be back." He stormed into the courtroom, walked up to the defendant, and with very little effort turned the man's chair so that they faced each other.

"You lied to me." Lorn fired the words at the quivering criminal.

"Why, no, Mr. Aiken. It was just one of those—"

Lorn did not allow him to complete the sentence. He drew his hand back and released it across the man's face so hard and fast it sent him tumbling to the floor.

"Scum." Lorn seethed with rage as he stared at the frightened defendant. Then, in a suddenly controlled manner, Lorn looked up at the judge.

"Your Honor," Lorn said calmly. "I will not represent this man. He'll be needing new counsel." With that, Lorn left the courtroom in what seemed to be three giant strides.

The judge later reprimanded Lorn for his actions that day but Lorn knew he would handle it the same way again. There was nothing he hated more than a client who lied to him. He had obtained acquittals and reduced charges for seventy-one of his seventy-three defendants. Lorn believed his record was a reflection of his unquenchable thirst for truth. It was the same with any sales job. You needed to know everything about the product, good or bad. Only then could you really make a sale. The truth was so important that Lorn was always skeptical about his first meeting with any defendant, including Dan Montecalvo.

Lorn had heard about the case and had been prepared for Dan to tell him how he had been involved in his wife's murder. Lorn figured he must have shot her first and then turned the gun on himself. He had already looked at police reports. If police arrived at the scene in less than a minute and no neighbors saw anyone leaving the house, Lorn was convinced Dan didn't have a partner. Whatever the situation, Lorn was certain he could help him.

He was completely unprepared, however, for the things Dan told him during that first session at county jail. According to Dan, he'd had nothing to do with Carol's murder. He was innocent. Lorn had listened to the detailed, heart-wrenching story of a man whose circumstances made him easily the most likely suspect.

Lorn watched Dan closely as he spoke, looking for telltale signs that he was lying—twitching lips, blinking eyes, shaky voice. There was nothing. He also listened carefully to details of the story. If Dan was guilty, then how come the car's registration tag was found and photographed outside on the driveway. How did it get there if Dan was in the house shooting Carol? If Dan was guilty, then why hadn't the police found the hollowed-out book during their initial search? And how could Dan have shot himself in the waist not knowing whether he would leave a trail of blood when he hid the guns and, for that matter, not knowing whether he would survive?

There was another note of truth in Dan's story. According to Dan, Carol walked into the house and said, "What are you doing here?" Immediately after she said that, two shots were fired causing Dan to run into the house. Lorn decided that was not a statement someone would make up. When a woman surprised burglars in her house she did not typically stop to ask them the reason for their visit. Under normal circumstances she would turn and run. Unless, of course, Carol knew her killer. Lorn decided to explore the possibility that Carol was killed by someone she knew other than her husband.

After three hours of listening to Dan talk and looking over police reports, Lorn would have bet his life that Dan was telling the truth. When Dan stopped talking, Lorn paused for nearly a minute. He had represented many criminals in the past, but never had he worked for a man charged with something he had no part in.

"Far as I can tell," Lorn said slowly, leaning back in

his chair and sizing up the task before him. "You're the first innocent man I've ever represented."

Dan smiled and let out a sigh of relief. "Then you believe me?"

Lorn nodded, realizing this case would require the biggest sales job of his life. "I believe you. But getting a jury to believe you will be another thing altogether."

32

Deputy District Attorney Tricia Lynn of Pasadena's Superior Court was assigned the duty of prosecuting the case against Dan Montecalvo. Now, in the final days of March, the preliminary hearing was about to begin.

Lynn had gone over the evidence dozens of times but she was still haunted by a nagging doubt. In all her years, she had never tried a first-degree murder case solely on circumstantial evidence. Lynn ran through her notes one last time. Life insurance. Hollowed-out book. Gambling debts. Talk of divorce. Late nights on the town. Carousing. Drinking. Strange behavior since the murder. And the damaging information from Pacific Bell that Dan had previously offered to kill a woman for her life insurance money.

The circumstantial evidence was overwhelming. Lynn closed her notebook confidently. There might not be enough evidence to convince a jury of Dan's guilt, but there was enough to warrant a trial.

The morning before the preliminary hearing Brian Arnspiger was racking his brains, trying to imagine some area he might have overlooked. For all his painstaking work on the case, he was still frustrated that he had uncovered no physical evidence.

He reached into his desk and pulled out a stack of the

index cards he'd kept beside his bed during the investigation. Each card contained an idea he had already pursued. "Fingerprints on cash box?" "Blood on phones?" "Blood on hands?" "Gambling since Carol's death?"

Suddenly his eyes fell on the final card in the stack. "Second GSR test?" That was it. Gunshot residue tests always included two parts. The first part of the test—the swab test—had been negative. Brian had submitted the second test for analysis but had never received the results.

He picked up the phone. "Phil Teramoto, please."

Two minutes passed and a frustrated Brian considered hanging up and calling again. Finally someone answered.

"Teramoto here."

"Phil, its Arnspiger, Burbank P.D. I need a favor."

By that afternoon, the gunshot residue test labeled "Daniel J. Montecalvo, April 1988" was located in the Burbank Police Department evidence room. Because of an oversight, the test had never been sent in for analysis following Brian's January request. That evening Brian made sure the test was taken to the Los Angeles County Sheriff's Department crime laboratory. The preliminary hearing was minutes away from beginning and Teramoto had told Brian the test took forty-eight hours to complete. Brian knew results might come too late.

The preliminary hearing began on March 27 and took less than two days to complete. Throughout the presentation of evidence, Dan Montecalvo sat calmly in the defendant's seat dressed in an inexpensive gray suit jacket and pants. His black hair had been trimmed and was conservatively short, slicked to one side of his head.

He did not look like a man charged with murder, rather he looked like someone about to attend a Sunday church service.

If Brian Arnspiger had been there he would have noticed that the look of resignation Dan had worn during his arrest had disappeared. In its place was a confidence that his attorney, Lorn Aiken, had instilled in him. Never had anyone believed in him as completely as Aiken did. For the first time since the early days of April 1988, Dan did not seem worried about going to prison for Carol's murder.

Beside Dan sat Lorn Aiken, his walking cane leaning against the defendant's table. Aiken wore a pin-striped suit but his six-foot three-inch frame and his unruly black curly hair and matching beard made him look wild and dangerous. He looked more like a pirate than a defense attorney.

Tricia Lynn appeared cool, organized, and business-like. By that afternoon she had presented the evidence against the defendant. Finally, she called Dan to the stand and asked him to hold an unloaded .25 caliber handgun and point it at the scar on his back. The stunt was intended to prove that it was possible for Dan to have shot himself.

But during cross-examination Lorn Aiken demonstrated that there are many places on the body where someone might physically be able to shoot themselves. But some people would never be mentally capable of such a task. When Aiken was through with him, Dan appeared incapable of shooting himself in his big toe, much less an area close to several vital organs.

Lorn Aiken had been watching Tricia Lynn closely and what he saw told him his sales pitch that morning had worked. Two hours before the preliminary hearing he had met with her in her office and explained some things not mentioned in the compilation of circumstantial evidence. He had asked her of the whereabouts of the footprints collected from Dan and Carol's kitchen floor the night of the murder. They had been labeled as evidence, then sometime during the past two years they had disappeared. Why? He had told her about the footprint in Suzan Brown's backyard which was never investigated. Why?

There was a slit in the sliding screen door at the rear of the Montecalvo home, just the right size for someone to slide two fingers in and unlock the door. Yet the prosecution contended there were no signs of burglary in the house. Why? And how had the registration tag wound up on Dan's driveway if he was inside killing Carol? Lorn Aiken had questioned the evidence for more than an hour, while Lynn listened thoughtfully.

"Are you finished, Mr. Aiken?" she asked politely when he had finally stopped talking.

"Look." Lorn was going for the hard sell. "The man's innocent. He might be a lousy guy, a lousy husband, and a lousy gambler. But he's not a killer."

Long after he'd left, Tricia Lynn had sat at her desk troubled by the ring of truth in Lorn Aiken's words.

The defense was midway through its presentation when Dan Montecalvo was called to the witness stand. In tears, he recounted the last hours of Carol's life.

"I could never kill Carol," he said, tears streaming down his ruddy cheeks. "She saved my life. She was everything I had." He paused, wiping his face and trying to catch his breath. "Don't you understand? I worshipped the ground she walked on."

Lynn watched him, thinking again of the reasons

Aiken believed Dan to be innocent. She stared at the man on the witness stand and suddenly, she knew what she had to do.

At 1:30 P.M. the next day Phil Teramoto finished typing the results of the gunshot residue disc test. He wasn't sure what they would mean for the case, but he knew Arnspiger needed them immediately. He activated his fax machine.

"Arnspiger, Teramoto here," he said, holding the telephone in one hand and the results in the other. "Check your fax machine. The results are in."

"Thanks." Brian was halfway out the door of his office before he hung up the phone. He grabbed the document from the machine and searched it for the information he wanted.

Subsequent analysis of Scanning Electron Microscope—Gun Shot Residue kit No. 12760 revealed two spherical particles of lead from the right hand disc. Lead spheres are commonly found in gunshot residue.

Brian felt a surge of elation. The lead spirals were the closest thing he'd had to physical evidence so far. Even if it was only two particles. The test showed that there had indeed been lead on Dan's right hand—one indication that he had fired a gun that night. He ran back to his office and picked up the telephone. A woman answered on the second ring.

"Tricia Lynn, please."

"Speaking."

"Detective Arnspiger here. I have some evidence you need to see on the Montecalvo case."

Tricia sighed. "It's too late, Detective."

"What's too late?" Brian could feel a stirring of panic starting in the pit of his stomach.

She paused a moment before continuing. "I recommended the case be dropped for lack of evidence."

33

In the hours after Tricia Lynn's recommendation to drop the case, a frustrated Brian Arnspiger sat at his desk fuming. His office bore the proof that he did not give up easily. A bulletin board on one wall was covered with mug shots of criminals Brian had built cases against. Underneath each picture Brian had scribbled the results of his labor: "fifteen to life," "twenty to life," etc. Alongside the pictures was a photocopy of a cartoon that read, "Every day I'm forced to add another name to the list of people who can just kiss my ass."

There was also a wooden plaque given to him during his years on patrol that read, "Yea, though you walk through the valley of the shadow of death you will fear no evil, for you are the meanest bastard in the whole valley." Across from that wall was one covered with pictures of his wife and kids. Near their pictures was one of the American flag with these words, "Try Burning This One."

Brian stared at these things, thinking of everything that was important to him, and finally he came to a decision. He picked up the telephone and made a call that he knew represented his last hope. It was to Assistant Head Deputy District Attorney Ben Bernard.

For more than two years Bernard's administrative duties had kept him out of the courtroom, but he was more familiar with the case than anyone at the district attorney's office. He had reviewed the case several times. Bernard knew better than anyone the hours that Burbank police—especially Brian—had put into the case. An hour after Brian's call, Bernard was back on the phone with him.

"Relax, I talked with Meine and Foster," Bernard said, referring to his boss and his boss's superior. "We're meeting tomorrow. Ten in the morning. My office."

"What for?" Brian had been devastated by Tricia's decision and was afraid to get his hopes up again.

"To discuss Tricia's recommendation. Don't be late."

Brian was twenty minutes early for the meeting. When everyone had arrived at Bernard's office, the group moved to a conference room and began the discussion.

"I understand we have a difference in opinion about the case of *People* v. *Dan Montecalvo*," Donald S. Meine said, looking at the dockets in his hand. Meine was the senior member from the district attorney's office and he would make the final decision on whether to dismiss the charges. He looked about the small wood-paneled room at the grim faces of Bernard and Brian Arnspiger. He knew they felt strongly about taking the case to trial. On the other side sat Tricia Lynn and Bernard's boss—Joseph Foster.

"Tricia, why don't you tell us why you feel the charges should be dismissed," he said.

Tricia nodded. "Mr. Meine, I have examined the evidence and do not believe it is enough to take the case to trial." She spoke slowly and articulately, almost as if she were in court giving an opening statement. "There is no physical evidence against the man. It would be a waste of taxpayer money and court time to try him for first degree murder when there is no possible way to win a conviction."

Brian knew she was right about the physical evidence. Because there were so few lead spirals on Dan's hands, he could easily have picked them up by touching his own wound. They were helpful but they were not conclusive as physical evidence.

Her speech finished, Tricia leaned back in her chair. Beside her, Foster nodded his approval. "I have to agree," he said. "The case is completely unwinnable."

Across the room, Brian sat quietly fuming.

"I see," Meine said, gently stroking his chin. "How 'bout you, Bernard? What convinces you there's a case?"

Bernard crossed his legs casually and smiled. At fifty-one, he was a subtly handsome man of medium height and build. He was partly bald and had the kindly face of a family doctor. In fact, with the exception of his cooly intelligent brown eyes, everything about Ben Bernard suggested he was incapable of the cunning ways he had demonstrated in many courtrooms. Bernard knew how people perceived him and he had long since taken to using that perception to his advantage. It took most jurors less than five minutes to feel as if they were personal friends with the prosecutor. Often they'd nod in agreement with him, returning his warm smile. He was smiling that way now as he responded to Meine's question.

"It's an interesting thing, Mr. Meine." He chose his words carefully, responding much the same way he would have if Meine had asked him about his summer vacation. "Actually, I couldn't agree more with Ms. Lynn." Bernard smiled in her direction.

Tricia had seen that smile years before, always before Bernard won a conviction.

"In fact, I was very concerned about this case. Last thing I want is a trial that wastes time and money." He was still smiling. "Three times, maybe four, Detective Arnspiger brought this case to our office and I sent him back for more evidence. Isn't that right, Detective?"

Brian took the cue. "Right. Four times."

Meine nodded. The story was making sense to him.

"Anyway, the last time he brought the thing to me he had more than 8,600 pages of evidence against the defendant." Bernard paused and let the figure sink in. "To tell you the truth, I think I was a bit more demanding than I needed to be. We probably could have tried the case the second or third time Detective Arnspiger brought it to us. But I wanted to be absolutely sure—in my own mind—that there was enough evidence to win a conviction."

Meine made a few notes and then looked toward Bernard. "You believe there's enough for a conviction?"

"Oh, absolutely, sir. Some of the best evidence came in just a few weeks ago from the victim's employer, Pacific Bell. That evidence alone was enough to convince me."

Meine hesitated for a moment. "Mr. Foster, what do you have to say about that?"

"I'm sorry, sir, but I still have to agree with Ms. Lynn." Foster was not happy with the way the meeting was going. "There is nothing concrete to connect that man with the murder of his wife. Nothing at all."

"The reason there isn't anything concrete to connect him with the murder is that he's innocent," Tricia broke in. "I've talked with the man's defense attorney, Lorn Aiken. He is completely convinced Montecalvo is innocent. After reexamining the lack of evidence I have to agree."

Meine looked back at Bernard. "Would you like to add anything, Bernard?"

"Well, I guess I'd have to disagree. Largely because the case has already survived a nine ninety-five motion." Bernard played his trump card, watching as Meine's interest peaked. A 995 is a motion filed by the defense asking a judge to dismiss a case for lack of evidence.

"Who filed a nine ninety-five?" Meine asked.

"Defense attorney Lorn Aiken," Bernard answered. "Filed it with Judge Jack Tso, I believe. It was denied."

Meine said nothing but made several more notes.

"I guess I figure," Bernard continued, "if it's survived a nine ninety-five we might as well take it in front of a jury and let them decide if he's guilty."

Bernard had no doubt in his mind that those last words had done the trick. He watched as Meine scribbled for another few seconds.

"Well, I appreciate your different positions, but I have to say I agree with Bernard. If a judge thought there was enough evidence to go on with the thing, we need to give it our best shot. Let a jury decide."

Tricia pursed her lips in frustration. "Fine. I'll start preparing the case." She started to leave.

"Just a minute." Bernard sounded incredulous—his words stopped Tricia in the doorway. "Five minutes ago you told everyone in this room you thought Dan Montecalvo was innocent. Now you're going to prepare the case against him?" He turned toward Meine. "Mr. Meine, I believe that raises an ethical problem."

Meine nodded, looking concerned. "Good point." He

turned to Tricia. "Ms. Lynn, you're off the case. Bernard, you'll have to get someone else on it right away."

Bernard thought for a moment and then shrugged. "I'll take the case. One of the other deputies can help me out."

"I don't see any problem with that," Meine said, standing to leave. "You know it better than anyone else."

Outside in the hallway Brian could hardly contain his excitement. Bernard had done beautifully, keeping his demeanor calm and convincing throughout the meeting.

"Good job." Brian broke into a smile and reached out to shake Bernard's hand. "What now?"

"I practice up on my trial tactics," Bernard said lightly. "I'm as rusty as they come."

"Something tells me you'll do just fine."

34

Over the years Ben Bernard had earned a reputation that few deputy district attorneys ever gain. He was brilliant and thoroughly prepared for each flawlessly presented case.

In the past twenty years Ben had tried nearly one hundred felony cases and gained convictions on all but three. The way Ben saw it, trying a case was a game he practiced in the legal library and played out in the courtroom. Each time a court clerk read these words, "The jury finds the defendant guilty as charged," he wondered how he could ever have wanted to do anything but practice law.

Ben was born in northeastern Ohio in 1939. He had just turned five years old when his family moved to Southern California. He was a talkative young boy with twinkling brown eyes and an uncanny ability to debate current affairs with adults.

"You're gonna be a bright attorney one day," a teacher told him.

Ben took the comment to heart. Throughout junior high when someone asked him what he wanted to do when he grew up, he did not hesitate. He wanted to be a lawyer. But during the summer between junior high and high school, Ben began chasing girls. In the process he forgot his goal, becoming like the majority of students who had not formulated career plans.

At age seventeen, Ben focused once more on his future and decided he wanted to be a cameraman for the motion picture industry. Not long afterward he was hired as a mail boy for Warner Brothers. His manager recognized Ben's intense determination. He attacked even the smallest tasks with a fierce desire to do them better than anyone. In two years the twenty-two-year-old Ben was promoted to the television story department, coordinating between writers, directors, and producers for seventeen shows. There was even talk of his getting behind a camera one day. Then the layoffs came and Ben found himself suddenly without a job. Ben knew that if all variables had been within his control, he would have become a brilliant cameraman. Since the opportunity was simply not there, he decided to pursue something else. Ben realized that his determination was balanced by another inborn trait: realism. It no longer mattered what line of work he wound up in, so long as he did it better than anyone else.

A turning point came on Thanksgiving, just after his twenty-sixth birthday at a family gathering. After dinner, Ben found himself complaining to an older cousin about his inability to find a career niche.

"Well, my boy," the man began, stretching out in a reclining chair and adjusting his belt to a looser notch. "What was it you wanted to do before you got mixed up with that crazy show business stuff?"

Ben paused a moment thoughtfully and remembered his childhood goal. "I wanted to be an attorney," he said, sounding unsure of himself. "But that was a long time ago."

The cousin chuckled. "Nothing wrong with that, my

boy. You know I've been practicing law for many years now."

For the rest of the afternoon and well into the night, Ben did not leave his cousin's side. By the next day Ben had decided to give the legal profession a try. It might not work out, but it was worth a try.

In the 1960s, the State Bar of California offered a bachelor degree equivalency test as part of the application process—the same test Lorn Aiken would later take prior to attending law school. If prospective students passed the test, they could enter directly into law school without a college degree. When Ben passed, he decided he would not only become an attorney, he would be the best ever.

He attended night classes at the San Fernando Valley College of Law years before Aiken would wind up at the same institution. During his first year of law school, Ben was stunned by the amount of studying required. He became friends with two other first-year students, Dave and Keith. Together they held all-nighters in which they would alternately read in silence and hold raucous debate sessions in an attempt to analyze precedent cases.

Despite his heavy course load, he found some time to socialize. In 1969 he turned thirty and met and married a friend's pretty Texas niece. But the real celebration came in 1970 when he and Keith and Dave all passed the bar exam on first try. Immediately afterward, Keith and Dave went into practice for themselves. Ben wanted something different. He applied for a position with the Los Angeles District Attorney's office in January 1971 and waited for a response: The office wasn't hiring.

For the next year Ben used his law degree for odd jobs about Los Angeles but was unable to find anything satisfying. Discouraged, he and Sandy moved to Texas where his wife's father offered Ben a job in the building industry. It took Ben less than two months to realize that he could never be happy as anything but an attorney. He also realized he could never be happy in Texas. His wife, however, no longer wanted to live in Los Angeles. So Ben was alone when he returned to Los Angeles in 1971.

Ben was excited about being back in Southern California. Once more he applied to the Los Angeles District Attorney's office. This time he was hired. Overnight, Ben found himself in the center of everything he had dreamed of as a twelve year old. He drew on the verbal skills that had always come naturally to him and soon his peers began taking time from their schedules to watch him in action. What made him so good had nothing to do with legal lingo or long-winded speeches. Rather, it was the way Ben delivered a statement that struck admiration in the hearts of his colleagues. With the casual air of a trusted friend, he would deliver his lethal punch lines. Jurors did not weigh Ben's words so much as they took them to heart. His kind face and warm, trusting tone of voice told them he was merely a nice honest man, not manipulative, not overbearing.

If the truth had been known, every person in the jury box would have been surprised. Underneath his calm, casual demeanor, Ben was a ruthless fighter whose weapons were words. Trying a case was a deadly serious matter to Ben, but he had long since learned to use a casual demeanor to his advantage. It was all part of the game; one that early on Ben grew accustomed to winning.

In 1974 Ben married Laura, a beautiful, supportive woman whom he had met through a colleague at the district attorney's office. Laura was a kindergarten teacher and for the next eighteen years the couple shared their career rewards with each other. Although they had no children of their own, they enjoyed Laura's kindergartners and together their lives were rich and rewarding.

For the next decade Ben's reputation continued to grow. He sent so many felons to prison that opposing counsel used to joke that he alone was responsible for the overcrowded prisons in California. Despite his success Ben never became pompous. Other attorneys compared notes and played games of one-upmanship with each other, always ready to rattle off their win-loss records. Not Ben. For that reason, he got along with his peers as well as his superiors.

Not long after the anniversary of Ben's tenth year with the district attorney's office, the combination of his courtroom successes and his amiable attitude led to a series of promotions. He was promoted to deputy district attorney in charge of the office in Glendale and in 1988 he was promoted to assistant head deputy of the Pasadena office.

One of his duties was evaluating cases submitted by detectives. The only drawback about the managerial jobs was that they took him away from the courtroom. But by 1988 Ben had turned forty-nine, and he decided that it was time to leave the challenge of trying a case to the younger prosecutors making their way up. Sometimes a case would cross his desk that would make him hunger for his courtroom days. But none tempted him as much as the case against Dan Montecalvo.

Throughout 1989 Ben had followed the case and was aware of the hours of work Detective Arnspiger had put into it. From the beginning Ben felt fairly sure that Dan was guilty. But believing it was so and allotting taxpayer money to take it before a jury were two entirely different matters.

So each time Brian brought the case to Ben, he had no choice but to send it back for further investigation. Ben thought Brian had done a meticulous job, but there was simply not enough evidence—until the detective brought in the information from Mark Paulson at Pacific Bell. By then Ben had decided the case needed a fresh look from another district attorney and he assigned Tricia Lynn to evaluate it. After she looked at the 8,600 pages of circumstantial evidence she agreed to file it. When Ben heard the news he was satisfied that the case against Dan Montecalvo would finally have its day in court.

Later, Ben could not comprehend why Lynn wanted to drop the case for lack of evidence. Ben's feelings about the evidence against Dan Montecalvo were so strong that after his superior had agreed to allow the case before a jury he had offered to try it. The challenge of one last trial, one last chance to play the game and win, was simply irresistible.

35

Attorney Lorn Aiken had reason to believe that Dan Montecalvo did not kill his wife. In part he believed him because Dan had maintained his innocence, even after Lorn had declared his rule about clients who lie. But Lorn was not a fool. Neither was he egotistical enough to believe that the threat of his presence alone was enough to extract the truth from a person charged with murder. What convinced him were several items mentioned in the police reports.

The first dealt with the words Carol had said just before she was shot. According to Dan she said, "What are you doing here?" After years of working as a defense attorney Lorn considered himself an expert in the typical reaction of victims involved in violent crimes. In such a situation a woman might scream or run away. But Lorn had never heard of a robbery victim asking the robber, "What are you doing here?" The only reason Carol would have asked that question, Lorn reasoned, was if she knew the people burglarizing her home. Neighborhood kids, perhaps, or a business associate. Lorn was not concerned with the responsible person, as long as he could prove it wasn't Dan.

Another item that Lorn questioned was the license plate registration tag. According to Dan, he had been outside waiting for Carol to return with a wet paper towel so that he could clean off the dusty license plate and put on the sticker. He heard Carol ask, "What are you doing here?" heard two shots, and ran into the house after her.

One police photo showed a license plate tag lying on the driveway, midway between the parked cars and the front door. Dan had never mentioned the tag or what had happened to it amidst the madness that night. But there it was. Right where it would be if Dan had been telling the truth, having dropped it in his haste to get to Carol.

The longer Lorn looked at the evidence, the more certain he became that he could get Dan an acquittal. After all, if there were two likely explanations for a piece of circumstantial evidence—one demonstrating the defendant's innocence and one his guilt—the jurors were instructed to disregard it totally. In other words, if there was a reasonable explanation for a bit of circumstantial evidence, it could not be used against the defendant. Lorn could think of a reasonable explanation for everything the prosecution had against Dan—even Mark Paulson's story.

As for the Paulson story, the hearsay element would work in favor of the defense. Mark said Denis said that Dan said he would kill a woman for her insurance money. And this evidence had come forward only after the media had reported how much insurance Carol had. For all anyone knew, Denis was mad at Dan for something unrelated and had created the entire story. As far as Lorn could tell, until Ben Bernard stepped in there really was no case.

Lorn wondered why an expert prosecutor like Bernard had agreed to take on a case that technically was not winnable. If the jurors followed the rules of circumstantial evidence, Dan would walk away a free man and the resulting black mark would mar Bernard's otherwise brilliant career. After all, there was a reasonable explanation for even the most damaging pieces of circumstantial evidence against Dan.

The life insurance was easy to explain. Dan had a criminal record and health problems. That made his chances of employment virtually nonexistent. Therefore, Carol, in a manner that proved her loving feelings for Dan, had taken out a handful of inexpensive life insurance policies on herself. That way if anything ever happened to her and Dan was left to fend for himself, he would have enough money to survive two or three decades without her. Simple as that.

Dan's gambling debts were not difficult to explain, either. Yes, Dan had run into some bad luck in Las Vegas. But he was making fairly steady payments to erase his debt. Even if the collectors had deposited Dan's markers at his bank, he would only have faced the penalty one faces for writing a bad check. Since Dan was on disability and had no wages to garnish, that type of penalty was certainly not threatening enough to cause him to murder his wife for her insurance money.

In Lorn's opinion Dan's making a payment to the casino the morning of Carol's murder was of no significance whatsoever. The prosecution was pointing to the fact that the payment was accompanied by a letter in which Dan promised to pay the loan balance in three weeks. The prosecution believed this letter proved that Dan was planning to kill Carol and collect her insurance money. But Lorn thought it was logical to pay one's bills on the last day of the month before going on vacation. As for the promise to pay off the balance of the debt within three weeks, that, too, could be explained. Dan and Carol had been looking into taking a loan out on their home. Once approved, the money would have been enough to pay off the debts. Dan was not informed that the loan was denied until after Carol's murder.

Then there was the hollowed-out book, which Lorn felt only proved that the detectives were grasping at straws. Lorn was completely convinced that one of the officers must have checked the bookcase during the initial search. Since Brian Arnspiger had come on the Montecalvo case later, Lorn figured he had assumed no one had searched the bookcase. If there had been guns in that book after Carol's murder, they would have been found.

Lorn also believed that if, for some reason, the book had been overlooked, Dan would not have saved it for evidence. If he had killed Carol, shot himself, and successfully hidden guns in the book without dripping blood on the carpet or near the bookcase, he certainly would have disposed of the book when he got rid of the guns. As for Dan's character flaws—the drinking and carousing, the habit of carrying guns—they clearly were not enough to convict a man of murder.

Lorn was not concerned with whether the jury liked Dan Montecalvo. He wasn't sure if he liked Dan Montecalvo. What mattered was that Lorn produce a reasonable explanation for each piece of circumstantial evidence. If the jurors could accept his explanations, they would be obligated to return a not-guilty verdict.

But Lorn knew that to be successful in court against Ben Bernard, he would have to do more than offer explanations for the circumstantial evidence. If Dan was indeed innocent, then someone else must have killed Carol. After hearing that he was going to trial against

Bernard, he decided he would need to initiate his own investigation to produce evidence proving his theory. He picked up the telephone in his cluttered office and began dialing.

Chuck Lefler and Gene Brisco were retired sheriff's homicide detectives turned private investigators. In all of Los Angeles County there wasn't a pair of private detectives Lorn would rather have digging up information to help exonerate Dan Montecalvo. The call came in to the office just after three o'clock that April afternoon; Chuck answered the phone.

"You got some time?" Lorn sounded gruff and Chuck knew instantly who it was. Chuck and Gene had worked for Lorn several times with great success. When Lorn sent them fishing, the pond was usually stocked full of fish.

"You bet," Chuck answered, grabbing a notepad and a pencil. "What's up?"

"Remember that case I told you about? Dan Montecalvo?"

"The guy up for killing his wife?"

"Right."

"Vaguely. Refresh me on the details."

For the next twenty minutes, Lorn did just that.

"I'd bet my grandmother's false teeth that the guy's innocent," Lorn said when he finished the story.

"Where do we fit in?"

"Something Dan says he heard Carol say just before she was killed." Lorn paused. "I think Carol knew the person who shot her. That's where you come in."

"I'm listening."

"I need you guys to talk to Dan's neighbors, talk to anyone who might have seen something that night.

We're looking for hard evidence here. Anything that proves Dan didn't kill his wife."

"Who pays us?" Chuck was a bottom-line person who had no interest in working for free.

"The court. Dan is entitled to some court-funded investigation work. I'll work out the details."

"How long are we talking?"

"Three months, maybe six."

Chuck looked over his calendar. They could work it in. "Okay," he said. "You've got a deal."

Long before Gene Brisco and Chuck Lefler joined forces and began doing private investigations, they each spent nearly twenty years as homicide detectives with the Los Angeles County Sheriff's Department. As a result, they were die-hard cops who even after becoming private investigators still looked and acted like deputies.

They became friends in the late 1970s when both men were working in the City of Industry station. Each detective had his own unique and successful knack for solving murders. In 1985 Chuck retired with twenty years experience and opened his own private investigation office, south of Los Angeles in La Mirada, an industrial city near Disneyland. Two years later, Gene also retired.

Chuck suggested that Gene come to work with him, doing private investigations and adding a little money to his retirement pension. Just before Christmas 1989 Gene made up his mind and accepted Chuck's offer. The two men made an exceptional team, Gene drawing on his instincts to come up with leads; Chuck carefully fitting them into a variety of possibilities. Calm and analytical, Chuck believed in keeping an open mind. The way he saw it, every murder investigation had at least six possible solutions, and he never narrowed his search to anything less. A pleasant-looking man, he had a thinning head of dark blond hair, warm sky-blue eyes, and a kind smile. He was a neat dresser and had the gentle demeanor of a small-town traffic officer. Born and raised in Southern California, Chuck had wanted to work in law enforcement for as long as he could remember.

Gene was nothing like Chuck. His wife often said that Gene looked like the quintessential tough cop. Dark hair, dark neatly trimmed mustache, and dark eyes full of suspicion. Whereas Chuck analyzed every angle of a case before making a conclusion, Gene solved dozens of cases by instinct.

Gene had grown up in Graham, Texas, a town of three thousand people where acting on one's instincts was the proper thing to do. When he moved to Los Angeles County and began working for the sheriff's department it took him two years before those instincts clicked into action. By then Gene had fallen in love with detective work. After twenty years of investigations, there was still no place Gene would rather be than roaming the streets of Los Angeles looking for clues to solve a murder.

"If I ain't a son of a gun," Gene would remark to his coworkers, his Texas accent thick and slow. "There's more killin' in these parts than in all of Texas combined."

In 1987 Gene began having heart rhythm problems and his superiors insisted he take a desk job at the station. He then began looking into early retirement. At forty-six, he worked his last day as a sheriff's detective. Within two years, his heart trouble eased and he felt well enough to continue investigating murders. His stir-crazy days of retirement ended the moment he agreed to be Chuck's partner.

When Lorn Aiken showed the investigators the volumes of circumstantial evidence against Dan, Gene and Chuck had to refrain from laughing out loud. The man was obviously guilty. Chuck and Gene were, after all, cops at heart. Their job had always been to catch the criminal. But these days they were often paid by the defense to crack cases. This was not an easy transition, especially for Gene. They took the case on June 9, 1990, and from the beginning, Gene was convinced Dan was guilty.

"The guy's a scumbag, I don't care what you say about him," Gene would say in his slow monotone.

"We're not being paid to determine whether he's a scumbag or not," Chuck would remind him.

"I know, I know."

No matter how hard he tried, Gene could not bring himself to believe Dan was innocent. Still, he went through the motions; looking for leads, talking to neighbors, and trying to find evidence that would prove Dan innocent.

Gene and Chuck agreed there was something odd about Carol's last words, *"What are you doing here?"* Of course, it was possible Dan had made up the words. But they seemed an unlikely piece to the story. If Dan was innocent and his story true, Carol must have known her killer. In that case the killer might have known that Dan and Carol were leaving for Hawaii and mistakenly thought they were already gone. That would explain why the burglary had taken place with two cars in the driveway.

Also, if the burglars were familiar with the Montecalvo home, that explained why they would have gone straight to the cash box instead of rummaging through the house. Chuck and Gene began interviewing everyone in Carol's neighborhood.

Early in their investigation Gene and Chuck heard one neighbor's name mentioned time and again—Suzan Brown. Neighbors said she had moved away days after Carol's murder. They said she was a drug addict with severe mental problems. One neighbor said she thought Suzan might have sold Avon to Carol.

"Big deal," Gene said flatly. "So they used to have a crazy Avon lady in the neighborhood."

Chuck shrugged. "It might be nice to find her."

"And it might not make a difference. Dan's in prison because some honest detective broke his back finding evidence against him. He belongs in prison. Why are we even wasting our time on this?"

"Okay," Chuck said, turning to face his partner. "But let's say Dan's innocent—even though it isn't likely. Then this might be the hottest investigation of our lives."

This time it was Gene who shrugged. "You're the boss. Let's find her."

So while Dan remained in county jail awaiting trial, Chuck and Gene started by talking to people who knew Suzan Brown. They obtained a list of her previous addresses and began interviewing her former roommates. In August they spoke with a shabbily dressed woman who said that she and Suzan had once been lovers.

"I can tell you this much," the woman said. "Everyone in that house was doing drugs big time. When they was low on cash, they broke into houses. Happened all the time." She lowered her voice and leaned close enough that Chuck and Gene were suddenly assaulted by her putrid breath. "I think any one of those people living with Suzan coulda killed her. Hell, Suzan coulda killed her."

Outside the woman's apartment Chuck and Gene went over their notes in the front seat of Chuck's car.

"I'm not convinced," Gene said. "We have no reason whatsoever to believe Suzan's anything but a lunatic."

"I feel the same way," Chuck said. "But we can't rule her out. Let's find her."

It took the investigators several months of checking government records before they located Suzan Brown at the Jerry L. Pettis Memorial Veterans Administration Medical Center in Loma Linda, a few miles from San Bernardino. Her doctors still felt she was suicidal and they had kept her an inpatient since her last suicide attempt. By then Chuck and Gene knew Suzan had talked with police about footprints she'd found in her backyard after Carol's murder. So they asked Suzan's doctor if she would be suitable to testify as a witness.

"I can't guarantee she'll tell the truth," he said. "The only reason she's here is because she's still a threat to herself. She's also somewhat paranoid. But I would give her permission to testify."

They passed the information on to Lorn and he arranged for her to be served a subpoena to act as a defense witness.

"See," Gene said after they'd talked with her doctor. "She's nothing more than a neighborhood nut who heard strange noises when Carol was killed. So what?"

"Maybe so, maybe not," Chuck said calmly. "I want to see her in person."

"You call the shots," Gene said. "Long as we're getting paid."

"Set it up, will you?" Chuck said, mulling over the clues that could come from meeting the woman.

Gene nodded, picking up the phone in Chuck's office. He spoke to the hospital director and five minutes later had arranged a meeting with Suzan Brown for September 1. By then she would have already received the subpoena.

"All set," Gene said as he hung up the phone. "I can hardly wait."

"Listen, the day we stop checking every lead is the day we stop being investigators. Who knows, maybe we'll walk in and she'll confess on the spot."

Gene laughed. "Don't get your hopes up."

36

One of Suzan Brown's favorite times of day came when the mail arrived. This was odd because she rarely received any mail. But every day she would walk to the main desk at the Veterans Administration hospital and check, just to be sure.

"Any mail today, Ed?" she would ask the orderly who worked behind the desk.

"No, 'fraid not," he would reply.

The question was the same each day and sometimes the orderlies would hand her a coupon book or other junk mail. Suzan would scrutinize the label on the item and smile.

"Resident," she would say approvingly. "That's me. Definitely a resident, wouldn't you say, Ed?"

"Definitely a resident, Suzan."

Suzan's doctors knew that her parents had not made contact with her for nearly twenty years. Nevertheless Suzan liked to talk about how they lived in Florida and how her dad was a doctor, or sometimes a lawyer—depending on different versions of the story. In any event Suzan no longer had any family ties, and her transient friends either didn't know or didn't care that she was being treated for paranoia and suicidal tendencies in the psychiatric unit of the Veterans Administration hospital in Loma Linda. Once in a while the government would write her requesting her signature to verify she was indeed receiving government-sponsored mental health treatment. But otherwise, there was nothing.

One morning in August Ed Casaba, the orderly who most often worked the day shift, was surprised when an official-looking envelope came addressed to Suzan Brown. He looked at the return address. Pasadena Superior Court. Why would the court want anything to do with a woman like Suzan Brown? Ed shrugged and looked up just as Suzan turned the corner heading toward the front desk—this time via wheelchair. Ed noticed that she was wearing her straight brown hair cropped even shorter to her head these days. She was stocky in addition to being obese, dressed in long, baggy shorts and a tank top that clearly exposed the tattoos covering her fleshy arms. More than once it had occurred to Ed that with a little hard work and iron, Suzan would make a fine offensive tackle. She wheeled herself over to the desk.

"Any mail today, Ed?" she asked, standing up and leaning her heavy body across the counter.

Ed smiled. "Why, yes, Suzan. The mailman left this." He had seen the displays of excitement Suzan sometimes put on when she received a piece of junk mail— hooting and shouting as if she had just won a million-dollar lottery. She was the kind of patient who offered comic relief in an often dreary job. He handed her the envelope. He could hardly wait to see her reaction.

She looked puzzled as she studied the return address. Suddenly, the orderly saw her eyes fill with recognition, and then terror.

"What are you looking at?" she blurted angrily, staring at Ed and stuffing the letter into her pocket.

Ed was not sure how to respond. He had seen Suzan do some very strange things, all in keeping with her paranoid condition. But he had no idea what had brought on this surliness. "I thought you liked getting mail," he said.

Suzan stared at him as if he—and not she—belonged in a psychiatric ward. "What mail?"

Here we go, Ed thought. "The letter from the court," he offered. "You know, your mail."

"What mail? I got no mail." Suzan began raising her voice. "You understand what I'm saying, Ed? I don't got no mail. Understand?"

It was a no-win situation. He shrugged. "Okay, Suzan. Sorry 'bout that. No mail today. Maybe tomorrow, huh?"

Suzan stared at him for several seconds. "Yeah," she grunted, satisfied with his response. "Maybe."

With that, she plopped down into her wheelchair and rolled down the hallway humming some unfamiliar tune.

Back in her room Suzan broke into a cold sweat. Her heart began beating in strange, erratic patterns and she felt as if someone were trying to strangle her. She wheeled herself to her bedroom window and took a deep breath. Everything was going to be okay. There had been no mail. Ed had told her so himself. Then Suzan stood up. Her hands brushed by her shorts and she felt the envelope.

The letter was real and it was trying to kill her. Suzan reached into her pocket, grabbed the envelope, and quickly tossed it onto the floor as if it were scalding hot. She sank into her chair, turning her back to the envelope.

No one must know, she thought. Her eyes began darting about while she made absolutely certain she was alone. Suzan closed her eyes and shuddered. The court knew what had happened to Carol and now they were going to make her tell the truth. But what was the truth? Hadn't she heard people running through her yard the night Carol was killed? No, wait. She hadn't been at home—she'd been at the Montecalvo house, kneeling beside the cash box when Carol walked in and said, "What are you doing here?" Or had she only read that in the newspaper?

Suzan wheeled her chair 180 degrees so that she was facing the envelope on the floor. "Is that you, Carol?"

Suzan stood up and took two shaky steps toward the paper. With one final deep breath, she bent over and picked it up. "Is that you?" she asked again.

The room seemed to grow quieter, silence filling it like a poisonous gas. Suzan waited but when there was no answer, she carefully tore open the envelope. The word "Subpoena" appeared in large letters across the top of the page. Quickly, Suzan shut her eyes, willing the word to disappear. She opened one eye. "Subpoena." It was still there. Her eyes moved quickly down the page.

"You are ordered to appear at Pasadena Superior Court as a defense witness in the case of *People* v. *Dan Montecalvo*. . . ."

Suzan's eyes grew wide and she let the letter fall back to the floor. They didn't want her, they wanted Dan. It occurred to Suzan, even in her unstable psychological condition, that Dan's defense attorney must want her to talk about the sounds she'd heard in her backyard.

"That's not fair," Suzan heard someone say. She looked around but the sound seemed to have come from her own mouth. Suzan clenched her fists. It wasn't

fair for them to accuse Dan of ⸺
done.

"Never happen." There it was aga⸺
voice. "They can't find the gun." The voice⸺
sense of the situation. Of course. No jury woul⸺ ⸺ct
Dan of something she knew he didn't do. Not with⸺ut a
gun.

Suzan smiled, her body relaxing. How many patients
at the hospital were asked to testify in a murder trial?
Suddenly the idea sounded exciting. She wheeled herself back into the hallway. As she went by the front desk
she smiled pleasantly at Ed Casaba, the orderly.

"Thanks again for the mail, Ed."

37

Chuck Lefler and Gene Brisco arrived at the Veterans Administration hospital on September 1 at 10 A.M. Gene was not looking forward to the interview. He still believed Suzan was nothing more than a crazy Avon lady.

They were ushered down a narrow hallway toward the psychiatric unit visitor room where Suzan was waiting for them. She was slouched slightly forward in her chair, her hair combed straight back with what appeared to be a greasy gel. She wore a short-sleeved men's shirt, the tails of which covered her thick waist. There were tattoos on her bulky arms and she wore a man's watch.

"Here she is," the orderly said. "Suzan, I'd like you to meet detectives Gene Brisco and Chuck Lefler."

Suzan sized them up. "Well, come on in. Let's talk."

Gene's first thought was that Suzan could not possibly have been successful in her Avon career.

She is singularly the most unattractive woman I have ever seen, Chuck thought.

Aloud he said, "Fine, let's talk." He turned to the orderly. "We won't be needing you anymore, thank you."

The detectives worked best with Chuck asking questions and Gene taking notes, developing hunches.

"Hello, Suzan, I'm Chuck," he said amiably. "This won't take much of your time. Just a few questions."

Suzan wondered if she looked as scared as she felt: first the subpoena and now this interview. She had agreed to meet with the private detectives because they were working for the defense. They would ask her questions about the sounds she'd heard in her backyard. Not about her recurring belief that she had been in the Montecalvo home when Carol was killed. Suzan tried to look disinterested.

"Fine," she barked. "I don't need to stand or nothing, do I? Lost feeling in my legs in Vietnam. Can't stand or walk or nothing." She belched loudly, unaware that on this morning she was not sitting in her wheelchair.

Chuck caught Gene's look of surprise and knew his partner was trying not to laugh. "You're fine right where you are, Ms. Brown. Okay, how long did you know the Montecalvos?"

Suzan swallowed hard and coughed several times. *This is all Carol's fault,* she was thinking, *walking in on us like that.* Out loud she said nothing, but began humming.

Gene raised an eyebrow in Chuck's direction. Chuck gave him an imperceptible nod and cleared his throat loudly. "Excuse me, Ms. Brown. We need your complete cooperation here. Now, how long did you know the Montecalvos?"

Suddenly Suzan snapped to attention and turned to face Chuck. "What are you trying to say?" she asked angrily.

Chuck drew in a deep breath. "Okay, let's start from the beginning. Dan Montecalvo is in jail facing murder charges in the death of his wife, Carol. Did you know that?"

"No." Suzan snapped the answer. Dan wasn't in jail. She had convinced herself that he had been released long ago. Suddenly she forgot everything she had planned to say about the sounds in her backyard. "Why is Dan in jail?"

"He's being charged with murder," Chuck answered patiently.

Suzan stared straight into his light blue eyes and began to speak very deliberately. "Mister, I ain't letting Dan go to prison for something he didn't do. Dan didn't do it."

Chuck nodded matter-of-factly. "I see. Who did do it, Ms. Brown?" Chuck was fishing. "Can you tell us that?"

"I don't know," she shouted. "Why you askin' me?"

Chuck decided to play it safe. "We've read police reports that say you had a woodpile fall down the night of Carol's murder," Chuck said, taking papers from a folder. "Oh, and something about seeing footprints?"

Suzan felt her body relax into the chair.

For the next ten minutes she told the detectives an elaborate story about hearing gunfire, then the sound of someone running in her backyard a few minutes later. She told them about the fallen woodpile and the shoe print.

"I told the officers they oughta take pictures or something of that there print." Suzan shook her head regretfully. "But they never came back."

When Chuck and Gene had finished their interview they thanked Suzan and stood to leave. As they did, Suzan also stood up, her useless legs quite capably bearing her considerable weight. She shook both their hands heartily.

"Pleasure talking with you boys," she said, her voice noticeably deeper than it had been before. They nodded and made their way to the parking lot.

"Well, she's certainly in the right hospital ward," Gene said as they left. "Like I said, a waste of time."

Chuck chuckled softly. "She's definitely interesting."

"Interesting? I had the feeling we were talking to at least two different people in there. None of them Avon ladies."

"I keep thinking of the first thing she said." Chuck paused a moment. " 'Dan didn't do it. I ain't letting Dan go to prison for something he didn't do.' "

"The woman is a loony tune, whacko, off her rocker." Gene was getting excited. "You can't believe her, Chuck."

"She's strange, all right. But we don't know if she's lying."

"Oh, yeah? What about her cockeyed Vietnam story?"

"What about it?"

"Either she's lying or we just witnessed a miracle."

"You lost me."

"Don't you remember? She lost feeling in her legs back in Vietnam. Then when we leave, she stands up."

"You're right," Chuck said. "I wasn't paying attention. Watch her tomorrow and see if she does it again."

"What?" Gene looked confused. "We're going back?"

"No. You're going back."

"Why?"

"Because, she didn't open up to me. You might get her talking. See what you can find out."

"Chuck, she's a lunatic. We're wasting our time."

"Not until we hit a dead end."

Gene knew from Chuck's voice that the subject was

closed. He would be back at the hospital the following day.

The next day Gene and Suzan had been talking for twenty minutes when she began asking about the murder scene.

"Was it pretty bad in there?" she asked, her face devoid of expression. "You know, bloody and messy and everything?"

Gene felt a stirring of curiosity.

"Uh, yeah, I think it was in fact," he answered.

"Find much evidence in the hallway or the office, any clues or anything?"

Suzan had fallen for Gene's casual style of questioning. Since they'd started talking, Suzan had listened as he shared his own experiences, trying to relax her. Now that her guard was down, Suzan's curiosity was getting the better of her.

Gene cleared his throat. He had no intention of telling her anything about evidence left at the scene, especially the empty cash box, which according to Dan was missing eight hundred dollars. The media had never known about the cash box. Investigators on the case had agreed to keep quiet about it. That way, if anyone ever mentioned it the police could reasonably assume the person might be a witness or even a suspect.

"Well?" Suzan interrupted Gene's thoughts. "They find anything or not?"

Gene shook his head. "Nothing at all, no clues."

Suzan frowned. "That's not what I heard. What about the cash box? Beige cash box with a bunch of missing cash?"

Gene stared at her unable to believe what he had just heard. There was no possible way Suzan Brown had obtained a police report. Even if she had, the reports hadn't mentioned that the cash box was beige.

Suzan looked nervous, like she had said something she regretted. After several moments of silence, she stood up.

"Gotta get going, now."

Gene nodded and shook her hand, thanking her as he left. His hunch about Suzan Brown had been wrong. It occurred to Gene that the woman was not only crazy, she was quite possibly dangerous. But more importantly, he thought, Dan Montecalvo was an innocent man.

Gene burst into his office—he couldn't wait to tell Chuck what the woman had said.

"She did it, I know she did it," he said after he had finished the story. He paced the small office as he spoke.

Chuck looked at him calmly. "My, my. This is certainly a different tune from the song you were singing yesterday. What's our proof?"

"Proof?" Gene was flabbergasted. "She knows about the cash box. Knows it was beige. What more do you want?"

"The cash box was mentioned in the police reports."

"She's been in a mental hospital. How could she have seen the police reports? Anyway, the police reports don't say that the cash box was beige. How did she know that?"

"She was Carol's Avon lady. Probably saw it lots of times. Look, Gene, I'm with you on this but we need hard evidence or a confession. Otherwise we don't have a thing."

Gene shook his head angrily. "Montecalvo's in prison for something he didn't do. I'm calling Lorn Aiken."

He picked up the phone and started dialing.

"You were right, Lorn, Montecalvo didn't do it," Gene said after he'd told him about Suzan.

The news did not surprise Lorn. He released a deep sigh. "I'm sure Ron Applegate will appreciate your work."

Gene frowned in confusion. "Who's he?"

"Dan's new defense attorney."

"What? You're his attorney."

"Correction. I *was* his attorney," Lorn stated flatly. "He fired me this morning."

38

The falling out between Dan Montecalvo and Lorn Aiken came as a result of Dan's stubborn pride. Early on, Lorn had agreed to file papers granting Dan the authority of *propria persona*—making him cocounsel.

Despite the arrangement Lorn never intended for Dan to utter so much as a single word in the courtroom. Defendants who had chosen to help represent themselves were allowed to spend their days in the county jail law library while other inmates were doing work detail. For those benefits alone, in an effort to make Dan more comfortable, Lorn set up the paperwork allowing Dan to be cocounsel on the case.

The falling out came less than a month before the trial. After months of browsing about the jail's law library and talking to other defendants who were preparing to represent themselves, Dan began to like the idea.

"Lorn, there's a couple people I wanna question in court," Dan mentioned nonchalantly one afternoon.

Lorn let out a hearty laugh. "Right."

Dan frowned at his attorney's reaction. "Lorn, I'm serious. I'm *pro per* now. Legally, I can represent myself. All I'm saying is when Kight and Arnspiger are up there, I wanna ask the questions."

Lorn stared at him as if he were the dimmest man he'd ever met. "Over my dead body," he said evenly.

That was the moment Dan's pride overcame his common sense.

"What are you saying, Lorn?" he said. "Anyone can ask questions. I know what those guys did to me. They framed me. No one could ask questions like me."

Lorn shook his head, his dark curls moving with the motion, and his blue eyes blazing brightly. "Maybe you're not hearing me, Dan. I'm the attorney. I'll do the talking; I'll do the questioning; I'll do everything." Lorn's tone was condescending and Dan's anger grew with each word. "Did you forget? You're the defendant, the accused. You're not exactly a sweet-faced choirboy, either. You sound like an ex-con. You look like an ex-con. Open your mouth and you're finished. Understood?"

"No." Dan was livid. "You work for me. You will sit beside me and give me legal help when I need it. And if I want to ask some questions I'll do it."

Lorn leaned back in his chair and stretched his long legs in front of him. "Let's go back to the beginning," he said flatly. "This case is no longer about you, it's about me. I will not walk into that courtroom as cocounsel on some suicide mission. You open your mouth in there and Ben Bernard will eat you for lunch. I will not sit calmly by while you destroy yourself and take me down with you. If you want me beside you, you'll keep your mouth shut."

Dan picked up the folder full of reports in front of him and slammed it shut. "Fine. You're fired. If you won't let me ask a few questions, I'll find someone who will."

Lorn knew without a doubt that if Dan opened his mouth in court it would be a major disaster. In all his ignorance, Dan was choosing to defend his innocence and in doing so Lorn feared he might very likely lose his freedom.

Dan stood up. "You can go now, Mr. Aiken," he said curtly. "I'm not going to change my mind. You're fired."

"You're making a big mistake, Dan," Lorn said, reaching out and shaking Dan's hand regretfully. Lorn had been looking forward to winning an acquittal for a man he deemed his first innocent client. "Call if you change your mind."

Dan did not change his mind in the following days. If anything he became more anxious to take matters into his own untrained hands. One of the defendants he'd met at the jail's legal library recommended an attorney who didn't mind sharing the courtroom with his client. His name was Ron Applegate.

Applegate was a liberal-minded former social worker with tall good looks and the rumpled appearance of someone who had been up all night. Over a year had passed since he'd had a drink, but his long, elegant fingers still shook from the effects of alcoholism. Life had not been easy for Ron Applegate. He grew up in Oklahoma City, a shy kid who didn't feel like a normal teenager until he started drinking. Alcohol seemed to bring him to life and soon he needed it for every occasion. In 1979 Ron discovered that more than 90 percent of the criminals he represented were dependent on either alcohol or drugs. Disgusted, he quit cold and for eight years he avoided liquor. Not coincidentally, his law practice grew both reputable and lucrative during that time.

Then, in 1987 he represented a client during an out-of-town murder trial. One night, after a particularly grueling day in court Ron met with a few attorneys for dinner. When the time came to order drinks, Ron found himself joining in. For Ron it was like jumping into a deep, dark abyss which seemed for the next two years to have no bottom. Alcohol alienated him from his family, his law practice, and his very self. One evening in early 1989 Ron found himself standing up at an Alcoholics Anonymous meeting and saying something he had never imagined saying in all his life.

"My name is Ron," he told the others in the room. "I'm an alcoholic."

Overnight, Alcoholics Anonymous became the focal point of his life. He attended as many meetings as he could and talked about his addiction with anyone who would listen. By the end of 1989 he was happier than he had ever been in his life, but the income he had received from his law practice was less than half of what it had once been. Ron knew this had happened because his first priority was no longer making money or practicing law, but visiting jails and telling inmates about the pitfalls of alcohol. Quite often, Ron represented those inmates. Word of mouth around the jail's legal library was that Ron would let a defendant do the talking.

The day after firing Lorn Aiken, Dan got wind of Ron Applegate and decided the attorney would be perfect for his case. Three days later the two men met to discuss Dan's upcoming trial. Unlike Lorn, Ron did not care whether Dan was guilty. He was aware that Dan claimed to be innocent, and he had no reason to disbelieve him. Still, he felt the issue was irrelevant. He cared only about whether the prosecution could prove guilt. From what he'd seen of the circumstantial evidence against Dan, he doubted the prosecution could do that.

Ron was granted a brief extension allowing him just

four weeks to prepare for the case. The trial was set to start Monday, September 24. When Lorn Aiken heard this he was disgusted. Ron was completely unfamiliar with the case and Lorn was sure he would need months to prepare it.

"Dan, you guys will never be ready on time," Lorn said one morning when he stopped by the jail. He planned to follow the case and keep in touch with the investigators, Chuck Lefler and Gene Brisco. "Ask for three months. Six months. Whatever you can get."

"I don't need your opinion, Lorn." Dan's pride was still hurt by Lorn's refusal to let him work as cocounsel.

Lorn bent over and stared into Dan's eyes. "Forget my opinion. It's suicide for the two of you to go up against Bernard with only four weeks preparation time."

"We'll be ready long before then," Dan said defiantly. "Applegate knows the law. I know the rest. I'm going to do most of the work, so that's all that matters."

Lorn threw up his hands in mock surrender. "Fine. But don't say I didn't warn you. See you at the hanging."

39

On the hot, smoggy morning of September 24, 1990, testimony got under way in the case of *The People of the State of California* v. *Dan Montecalvo.* Jury selection had been relatively simple, neither side using its allotted twenty peremptory challenges. Ron Applegate seemed to have intentionally filled the jury box with women. This confused Ben Bernard, who had long since decided that women would more quickly convict Dan than men.

Women would feel the agony of Carol's loneliness. They would hate Dan for spending his evenings at bars and flirting with other women. Most of all, Bernard believed that women would not trust Dan. Men, however, would understand more quickly how flirting with other women did not make one a killer. So Bernard was surprised when the combined legal intelligence of Ron Applegate and Dan Montecalvo removed one man after another with peremptory challenges. It occurred to Bernard that Dan must truly have believed himself to be a lady's man, even though he had lost weight and was gaunt and unattractive. In the end the jury was made up of two men and ten women of all different ages.

That morning at 9:47, minutes before the trial would begin, Ben Bernard wheeled a shopping cart through the double doors of Division J, Judge Jack B. Tso's courtroom. In it were six notebooks—each several inches thick—containing 8,600 pages of circumstantial evidence against the defendant. The prosecutor wore a fashionable dark gray suit and smiled warmly at the jurors, who were already in their seats. He had the happy look of a weekend shopper who had just stumbled onto a tremendous bargain.

As they watched him move the shopping cart toward the left side of the table where the prosecution would set up camp, it was all the jurors could do to keep from waving to him. As it was, many of them smiled and nodded at him.

The picture Bernard was presenting to the jury was no accident. As far as he was concerned, one started trying a case the moment one walked into a courtroom. But for all his calm appearance, Bernard was intensely focused on the task that lay ahead of him. He had prepared for it better than for any case he had ever tried. Hours had been spent talking with Brian about the voluminous amount of evidence. They had agreed that Brian would sit at the prosecution table because he knew the information better than anyone. That way if Bernard suddenly needed to see the report from a particular bartender who had seen Dan threaten a customer with a gun, Brian would be able to locate it instantly.

Bernard knew that regardless of how well prepared they were, chances were still high that Dan would be convicted of nothing more than voluntary manslaughter. Bernard had never heard of a first-degree murder conviction based entirely on circumstantial evidence. Next to Bernard, Brian Arnspiger sat ramrod straight, his energy emanating across the courtroom. He wore a navy blue suit that looked uncomfortable on his large frame. Bernard looked at him and decided he might as well be wearing a uniform and badge. The two men shook hands and Bernard sat down, nodding politely toward the jury.

From the right side of the table, where the cocounsel for the defense were sitting, Ron Applegate and Dan Montecalvo bent their heads and shared some last-minute strategy. Dan was dressed in a black pinstripe suit which on other men might have looked sophisticated. Instead the suit made Dan, who was wearing his black hair slicked back in a 1950s style, look like a two-bit gangster. Ron Applegate looked nervous in a slightly wrinkled beige jacket and dark brown polyester pants. His hands had started shaking the moment Ben Bernard pushed the shopping cart into the courtroom. Now Applegate wondered why they hadn't insisted on taking more time to prepare. The moment he saw Bernard's shopping cart of information and the calm look in his friendly brown eyes, Ron Applegate had a feeling of impending doom. If only Gene Brisco and Chuck Lefler had been able to find something concrete in their doubts about Suzan Brown.

Ron noticed the courtroom filling up with spectators and other attorneys. He glanced toward Ben Bernard and realized that this would probably be Bernard's last time in a courtroom. He understood why the other attorneys were there. They had come to see his final performance and they expected it to be brilliant. Ron Applegate swallowed hard and tried to regain the confidence he had felt just hours earlier.

Several members of the press were arriving in the hallway. Cameramen checked the setting on their cameras and reporters looked over their notes. A few minutes before 10 A.M. they filed into the courtroom and sat down in the worn-out theater seats that made up the small spectator section. Any murder in Burbank was a story, but when Dan had been arrested for killing Carol and shooting himself to cover it up, the press had attacked the story with ravenous interest.

Lorn Aiken also sat in one of those seats. He wore lizard-skin cowboy boots and a tweed jacket with suede elbow patches. He had been unable to resist the drama of seeing Ben Bernard destroy an innocent man. Already he could sense what was about to happen—Dan was about to be railroaded and he was helpless to stop the oncoming train.

A hush fell over the courtroom as Judge Jack B. Tso walked in without ceremony and took his seat. Tso was a small man of Asian descent in his mid-fifties who stood not quite 5 feet 5 inches. Soft gray hair framed his round face. He had a dark gray mustache and round gold-rimmed glasses through which his deep black eyes peered intelligently. There was something kind about Judge Tso, something that suggested he might make a wonderful grandfather. Until he began to speak, it was not difficult to picture Judge Tso playing with small children or animals.

When he opened his mouth, however, the image disappeared. Judge Tso had little compassion or understanding for people who wound up in his courtroom. Neither Ben Bernard nor Ron Applegate had ever worked with a more no-nonsense man than Judge Tso. He was known to hand down ruthlessly tough sentences for misdemeanors, advising defendants that their punishments were for their own good and warning them not to show up in his courtroom again unless they wanted to grow old in prison. Convicts believed Judge

Tso. He did not mince words and he did not let common criminals and their attorneys make the rules in his courtroom.

Tso looked over the upper rim of his glasses and cast a disgusted look toward Dan Montecalvo. There were many things Tso did not like about criminals, but among them there was nothing he hated more than a defendant who had chosen to represent himself. *The man's a fool,* Tso thought. He sorted through several dockets on his desk and then looked up, first at the prosecution and then at the defense.

"Are all parties present for *The People* v. *Dan Montecalvo?*" Tso asked matter-of-factly. Both attorneys nodded and Dan Montecalvo stood up.

"Your Honor, we have just a few questions here before we . . ."

Judge Tso took off his glasses and leaned over the edge of his bench toward Dan Montecalvo. "Sit down. Immediately. This is my courtroom and you will ask questions at the proper time. Is that understood?"

Dan remained standing. "Your Honor, I just . . ."

"Sit down!" It was a command and Tso stared at Dan incredulously. "Sit down immediately before I charge you with contempt of court."

Ron Applegate tugged inconspicuously on Dan's suit jacket and reluctantly Dan sat down. At the other end of the table, Ben Bernard shrugged his shoulders imperceptibly and cast a confused smile toward the jury.

Judge Tso was furious. He placed his glasses back on his head and continued to stare at Dan.

"I understand, Mr. Montecalvo, that you have chosen to be *pro per,* to represent yourself in this murder trial. Well, I have said it to others like yourself and I will say it again now," Judge Tso stated. "A man who represents himself has a fool for a client." He paused. Every eye in the courtroom was on Dan Montecalvo.

"Are you absolutely certain you want to do this thing?"

Dan nodded proudly. "Yes, Your Honor."

"Very well. I will warn you ahead of time that I intend to make you follow the same rules of argumentation and cross-examination as any other attorney. I will give you no preferential treatment and I expect you to conduct yourself in a professional manner. Do I make myself clear?"

Dan nodded again.

"There will be no talking out of turn," the judge added. "This is my courtroom; you will follow my rules."

Ron Applegate watched his client receive the verbal lashing and looked across the room at the jury. They were looking disapprovingly at Dan. Ron wished he could fade into the brown paneled walls and disappear. If this had been a football game, they would be well on their way to a blowout. Ron hoped it was not an indication of things to come.

"We will hear from the prosecution now," Judge Tso said as he leaned back in his chair.

Ben Bernard stood up and smiled pleasantly toward the judge. "Thank you, Your Honor." He turned calmly toward the jury and made eye contact with each person as he began to speak. Bernard always opened with the kind of statement his opponent might give. This tactic did two things. First it made him appear humble to the jury. Second, it took the wind out of the defense's opening statement.

"Mr. Montecalvo, Mr. Applegate, Your Honor, ladies and gentlemen of the jury." Bernard nodded toward

each party. "As the *court indicated to you* during jury selection, nothing I say to you at this time or, in fact, at
any time during the trial is evidence. All the evidence
comes from the witness stand by way of testimony, by
way of exhibits. That's what we will urge you to listen to
and look at very carefully.

"What I will give you is something of a road map to
help you notice the points of interest along the way."
He looked like a tour guide about to take his passengers
on a trip through Disneyland. "It is by no means complete nor will it cover everything that we intend to
prove. But it is an overview of what I believe the people's case will show."

Ben Bernard proceeded to introduce the points of
interest. He told the jury how Dan answered the telephone with a "jaunty" hello when the 911 emergency
operator called him back the night of the murder. In
what sounded like an afterthought, Bernard added, "Of
course, Dan's first call to 911 came a full five minutes
after the neighbors heard gunfire."

Bernard cocked his head at a curious angle. "I wonder what Dan was doing during those five minutes?"
He shrugged pleasantly, then directed the jury toward
another landmark on the road map. Sounding embarrassed for the defendant, Ben told the jurors how Dan
had lied to police from the beginning of the investigation.

"We believe our evidence will show that Mr. Montecalvo tried to throw the police off from the beginning,"
Bernard said. Several of the jurors were nodding in
agreement.

He continued, telling the jurors that there was absolutely no sign of anyone else having broken into the
house. Again he drew on the very information his oppo-

nent had been planning to use by mentioning the slit in the screen door. "No one has any idea how long that slit was there," Bernard said, again shrugging his shoulders. "It certainly doesn't indicate there was a burglary." Again the jurors appeared to agree with their friend, the prosecutor.

Bernard discussed how none of the neighbors had seen anyone leave the Montecalvo home after they heard gunshots. This, of course, was not the whole story. After all, Applegate would present Suzan Brown's testimony that she had heard someone in her backyard that night. But the opposing side could not object to information in opening statements since these statements were not considered official testimony.

"Dan told the police he rushed to his wife's side, knelt down, and took her pulse." Bernard's voice grew softer. "Mrs. Montecalvo was shot twice in the back of the neck. There was a lot of blood. Especially on her face and neck. If Dan took her pulse, why didn't he have any blood on his hands? By the way, there was no blood on the telephone he used to call the nine-one-one emergency operator, either. We don't know if he wore gloves, but we did find surgical gloves in his storage items after the murder."

Ron Applegate could hardly believe how badly things were going. The jurors were practically hypnotized by Bernard's monologue. They were nodding and smiling and frowning on cue.

"Please listen carefully to the evidence. This, as you know, is a case of circumstantial evidence," Bernard said, not a bit ashamed of the fact. "Every little bit and piece of the puzzle is important to this case. Listen carefully. Use your common sense." Bernard smiled. "One more thing."

Twitching anxiously in his seat, Ron Applegate rolled his eyes. He knew that Bernard was about to deliver one of his infamous punch lines. Ron was sure it was the first of many to come during the trial.

"Two years later, when Mr. Montecalvo was arrested and taken to the Burbank Police Station, Detective Arnspiger will testify that Mr. Montecalvo lowered his head and said, 'I knew you guys would get me some day.'" Bernard shook his head sadly. "Listen to all the evidence very carefully. I think you will find it a most fascinating case. Thank you."

It was all the jurors could do to keep from applauding in anticipation of the fascinating show the prosecutor had just promised them. They were preparing to enjoy the tour.

"Mr. Montecalvo or Mr. Applegate, do you wish to address the jury?"

Ron Applegate took a deep breath and stood up. "Yes, Your Honor." Dan had agreed that Ron should make their opening statement.

"Mr. Bernard, ladies and gentlemen of the jury," Ron began without emotion. "As you already know, everything that Mr. Bernard just told you is not evidence. None of it is evidence. It is merely his opinion of what he feels the case will show in his interpretation of the evidence." From his seat, Bernard noticed that several jurors looked doubtful. "Likewise, what I am getting ready to say is my interpretation of what I feel the evidence will or will not show in this matter.

"The evidence in this case will show that Daniel Montecalvo's wife, on March 31, 1988, was killed by an intruder. That in June of 1989 Mr. Montecalvo filed a wrongful death suit against the city of Burbank naming certain police officers for negligently allowing his wife to bleed to death." Ron waited for a moment before delivering his own punch line. "Nine months later Mr. Montecalvo was charged with first degree murder."

The jurors did not appear to have understood the significance of the statement. For the next twenty minutes, Applegate bored the jury with numbers and technicalities. No longer were the jurors on a thrilling sight-seeing tour. They were back in the confines of a courtroom anxious to get on with the trial and back to their own lives.

When Applegate finished, Judge Tso ordered the prosecution to call its first witness. The jury looked relieved when Ben Bernard stood up. After all, the prosecutor had promised them that the case would be fascinating.

"The prosecution calls William Strong."

Pastor Strong walked into the courtroom and took the witness stand. He was conservatively dressed and honest looking. As Ron Applegate watched the man adjust the microphone before him he wondered what plan Ben Bernard was about to unveil.

The prosecutor asked Strong about his relationship with Dan and Carol and their relationship with each other.

"Every time I talked to them—on a friendship and a ministerial level," Strong was saying, "it was very clear to me that the most important thing in Dan's life was his wife." As the pastor spoke, Bernard maintained eye contact with him, nodding agreeably. "They had a good relationship. There were some difficulties, of course, as with any relationship. But based on my experience with both of them, they had a lot of love for each other."

Bernard looked concerned. "Did Mr. Montecalvo ever express what those difficulties were?"

"No. I would say they were my observation, not his."

Bernard nodded in understanding and smiled at the pastor. "What did you observe, if I may ask?"

"Well, Carol was very active in church and Dan did not attend as often. She was always trying to get him to follow the Lord in a closer manner; the way he had after his conversion when he was formerly incarcerated in prison."

Bedlam instantly filled the spectator section and Dan turned angrily toward Ron Applegate. Both sides had agreed early on not to disclose Dan's prior record. An article about Dan's background had appeared in that morning's newspaper, but the reporters knew the topic was considered taboo inside the courtroom. Now it was out in the open.

Judge Tso rapped his gavel on the bench. "Silence!" he said. "This courtroom will come to order."

Bernard contained his excitement. He had not planned for the minister to mention Dan's prison record. His reason for putting Strong on the stand was to prove that at least in some circles Dan expressed a fervent love for Carol. That being the case, his actions at various bars would prove those expressions of love to be inconsistent.

But since Strong had mentioned Dan's record, Bernard was not about to touch it. Everyone had clearly heard what Strong had said. Now the defense would probably use the incident to request a mistrial. Bernard quickly switched topics. When he was finished, Ron Applegate approached the bench.

"Your Honor, Mr. Bernard was told to admonish his witnesses not to reveal things regarding my client's past prison and jail history. And that either was not done or in any case the evidence came in through this witness." Applegate paused. "Therefore I request a mistrial."

Bernard broke in. "Well, as the court saw, I tried to stop him from saying it. Everyone had been told we are not getting into any prior record. Of course, I think it is rather humorous that the defense brings this up now. Because the *Los Angeles Times* this morning has splattered Mr. Montecalvo's prior record all over the front page."

"Well"—Judge Tso did not look amused—"the jury has been admonished not to hear, read, or look at anything in the press and I will assume they have complied with that. However, I am sure the revelation of the defendant's past history was not intentional on the part of the prosecution. Therefore, the motion for a mistrial will be denied. I am suggesting we leave it at that because to bring attention to his record now would only highlight it to the jury."

Ron Applegate could feel his stomach turning. There was no way he could leave the pastor's statement alone. He would have to ask Dan about his background so that the jury would not wonder whether Dan had been in prison for a previous murder. He wondered if the situation could possibly get any worse.

The answer came later that day when Judge Tso held a bail-reduction hearing to have Dan's bail reduced from one million dollars to no more than ten thousand dollars. Several witnesses testified for and against Dan out of the presence of the jury. Included among them was Officer McKillop, who told the judge how Dan had threatened him and his family after he had arrested him in January for carrying a loaded weapon. When Judge Tso had heard all the testimony he looked at Dan.

"Why should I reduce bail for you, Mr. Montecalvo?"

"Your Honor, I have been a suspect in this case for two years. I knew I was going to be arrested any day, sir. I defied the police to arrest me. I wanted them to arrest me, to give me my day in court so I could clear my name and my marriage."

Judge Tso frowned curiously. "You did what?"

"I told them, 'Arrest me!' " Dan looked ready to burst into tears. "I told them, 'let's go to court with this case.' I'm not running from anybody, sir. I am not a flight risk."

"Very well," Tso responded, and Applegate thought he looked unaffected by Dan's emotional plea. "The court has considered the seriousness of the charges against Mr. Montecalvo, and the fact that other than one or two associates and the Reverend Strong, the defendant has no roots in our state. Based on this incident of January as well as the threats attributed to the officer, I believe the defendant is a flight risk. For that reason bail will no longer be one million dollars. Instead this defendant will be denied bail at any amount. That is all. We will resume tomorrow," Tso said, rapping his gavel once and rising to leave.

Across the room, Lorn Aiken stood up in disgust and left the courtroom. He had seen enough to make him sick. Dan was going to go down in hot, searing flames, and there was nothing he could do. He had never dreamed the first day would go so badly. Especially when Dan had not yet asked a single question.

40

In the following days Ben Bernard painted a very careful picture of what had transpired at the murder scene. He called every officer and paramedic who had been there to testify. Each one had a useful observation.

There was Officer Rick Medlin, who had watched from a side yard as Dan appeared to walk without a limp down the hallway. The man had obviously been shot, but there was a question as to whether his limp was real or manufactured.

"As soon as he looked up and saw the police activity and the helicopters outside, he immediately grabbed his right side and began yelling that he had been shot and needed help," Medlin stated sincerely. The jurors were hanging on every word.

Ben Bernard nodded as if trying to make sense of this new bit of testimony. "That strike you as rather strange?"

"Yes, sir." Medlin searched for the right words. "It was almost like it was . . . show time, you know?"

Bernard nodded again, casting a sad glance toward the defendant. "Yes. I believe I do know."

Next came Officer Glen Sorkness, who had interviewed Dan that night at St. Joseph's hospital.

"Were you present when Mr. Montecalvo was told

that his wife had died?" Bernard lowered his voice respectfully.

"Yes, I was," the officer answered.

"Could you describe his demeanor at that time?"

"He immediately appeared to become very upset. He started sobbing." The officer's voice grew quieter as his mind seemed to drift backward in time, remembering the incident. "However, I looked closely at his eyes at the time."

"Did you observe anything noteworthy about his eyes?" The jurors were rapt with attention.

"Yes," the officer stated. "His eyes were dry. There were no tears."

During cross-examination Ron Applegate tried to instill doubt about the officer's testimony because he had not mentioned the lack of tears in his initial report. But the damage had already been done. The jurors—especially several of the women—were staring angrily at Dan for having shed no tears over the death of his wife.

Bernard called Patrick Lynch, who had recently been promoted from detective to sergeant, to the stand and began asking him about his initial investigation and finally about the first of several conversations he'd had with Dan in the days after Carol's murder. That discussion had taken place in the hospital and midway through it, Lynch had mentioned that police were still searching Dan's home.

"At that time he just got very irate, he blew up."

Bernard looked surprised. "What did he say?"

"He told me he wanted all the police officers off his property, he didn't trust the police. He wanted us out of his house and off his property. For a man in his condition he was very upset."

Before Lynch left the stand, Bernard asked if he or any other officer had checked the bookcase for hidden guns.

"No, sir. It was an oversight."

"Thank you. No further questions."

At first Dan allowed Ron Applegate to cross-examine Lynch. But when Dan became frustrated with watching, he intervened and on the morning of October 1, he took over. The moment he did, Applegate knew their position had just gotten worse.

Every time Dan tried to phrase a question, Ben Bernard would stand politely and object to its wording, its content, or its intention. Dan tried to give the appearance of an attorney, walking about the courtroom as he asked questions and using words that lawyers sometimes use. But as soon as he began cross-examining Lynch it became evident that he knew nothing about what was legally permissible.

Dan was asking Lynch about the entry log that kept track of the officers who came and left the Montecalvo home in the days following the murder.

"Sergeant Lynch, would it refresh your recollection to review the entry log again and tell me what time Sergeant Madrid went into the house?"

Judge Tso took a deep, exasperated breath. "Counsel, he can only testify as to personal knowledge. If you are asking him to testify as to the document itself, that is hearsay. I will sustain all objections on the basis of hearsay, which I am mandated to do." The judge threw his hands up in the air. "You are going about it all wrong and you are wasting the court's time."

"It is not my intention to waste your time, Your Honor. I thought police reports were an exception."

"Those reports are only exhibits, they are not in evidence," Tso said.

"Sergeant Lynch . . ." Dan tried to sound professional as he continued pacing in front of the jury. When he turned back toward Lynch his question sounded like an accusation. "You never wrote in your report that Sergeant Madrid pronounced my wife deceased at a certain time?"

Judge Tso shook his head in frustration and leaned toward Dan. "Is that another question? Or does that relate to time of entry, or what?"

Dan's face went blank as he continued to pace the courtroom. "Excuse me, Your Honor?"

"Listen," Tso said, and Bernard shrugged questioningly toward the jurors. "I will run this courtroom. You may go back and stand near your seat. This is not a television show. I do not permit the attorneys to wander up and down before the jury. That is not permissible by court rules."

Dan's cross-examination went on in this manner for more than an hour, frustrating everyone in the courtroom. It was like watching someone with a thimble bail water from a sinking ship. The more Dan worked at correcting his interrogative skills the deeper he sank.

Later in the afternoon Judge Tso stopped the proceedings altogether to admonish Dan after Ben Bernard had objected to another of his questions.

"Mr. Montecalvo, I think it would be wise for the court—on your behalf—to sustain Mr. Bernard's objection." The judge leaned over the bench again and removed his glasses. "Mr. Montecalvo, you are asking questions that are only harmful to you."

Thirty minutes later Dan was still questioning Sergeant Lynch when he began drawing on terms no one in the courtroom had ever heard before.

"In the course of turning over your investigation to Detective Arnspiger did you apply due diligence in contacting various agencies that assisted you that evening in crime-scene workup, if you will?"

Bernard stood up, his face twisted in confusion. "Your Honor, I'm not sure I understand what the question means."

Judge Tso rolled his eyes and released a deep sigh. "I will sustain the objection as to the phrasing 'due diligence' being vague and nonsensical. Please restate the question if you wish, Mr. Montecalvo."

And so it went. By the end of the day, Dan actually thought he had made progress in showing Lynch to be a dishonest man whose single goal in 1988 had been to frame Dan Montecalvo for the murder of his wife. Of course no one else who had been in the courtroom that day saw the proceedings that way. Ron Applegate, for instance, felt as if he'd spent the past four hours in some kind of hideous torture chamber. In his opinion Dan had come across as an angry, defensive, bitter man who wanted only to seek revenge on the men who had caught him and sent him to jail.

The next day Ben Bernard began disputing the idea that someone else had been in the Montecalvo home that night. Bernard knew the defense intended to show that Carol could have been killed by their gardener, the cologne salesman from the May Company, or the local wild teenager who had stolen guns from his father's house. Bernard started by putting the gardener on the witness stand.

"Mr. Gomez, in the late hours of March 31st, 1988, at

approximately eleven o'clock at night, do you remember where you were?"

The small Hispanic man shrugged blankly. "No."

"Did you kill anyone that night?"

The gardener thought long and hard before answering. "Yes, señor," he said. "A cockroach."

Laughter filled the courtroom and Bernard grinned knowingly toward the jurors.

"What I mean, Mr. Gomez," Bernard continued, "is did you kill a human being that night?"

The man's eyes grew wide with concern. "No. No, señor."

Bernard nodded warmly toward the man. "Thank you, Mr. Gomez. No further questions."

When Bernard had exhausted that angle, he introduced testimony proving that the guns stolen by the teenager had been recovered and the May Company salesman had merely sold the Montecalvos a bottle of cologne. Next he brought evidence technician Phil Teramoto in to testify about the lead spirals found on Dan's hands based on the second gunshot residue test. Yes, he could have gotten the lead from touching his own wound. But the evidence was also consistent with having fired a gun—especially if the shooter had worn gloves. When the gloves were removed, one or two lead spirals might have fallen onto Dan's hands. Bernard then marched in a string of witnesses to talk about Dan's habits of carrying guns, frequenting bars late into the night, and flirting with other women.

"Did you ever see Mr. Montecalvo in the Pago Pago with a gun?" Bernard was questioning one of the bar's frequent customers who had become an acquaintance of Dan's.

"Quite a few times."

A rash of whispers filled the courtroom. This was the first time anyone had heard testimony that Dan carried guns. Already several officers had testified that Dan had told them he never had guns.

"Was the first time you saw Mr. Montecalvo with a gun some time before March 31, 1988?"

"Yes."

Bernard nodded as if understanding the information for the first time. "Can you tell us under what circumstances you first saw that gun?"

"Sure. He had it out lying on the bar showing a couple of the guys the bullets in it, telling them they were special-made bullets and stuff like that."

"What kind of gun was it?"

"A .38."

Another wave of whispering rose from the spectator section as people made the connection: Earlier testimony had proven that Carol had most likely been killed with a .38 caliber handgun. Bernard continued.

"Did there come a time in the Pago Pago when the defendant threatened you?"

"Yeah, sure did. You name it."

"I would like you to name it, sir. What did Mr. Montecalvo say?"

"He was saying how he didn't like police officers and he didn't like me, either. I told him, 'I'm not scared of you and I'm not scared of guns.' "

"What did he say he was going to do with his gun?"

The witness turned and stared at Dan. "He said he was going to blow my head off."

On Monday, October 15, Bernard released his most potent testimony. Mark Paulson was on the witness stand, describing what Denis Cremins had told him about Dan Montecalvo. Bernard was refreshing Paulson's memory about Sept. 7, 1989.

"On that day at approximately noon did you have a meeting with a client, Denis Cremins?"

"Yes, we were putting together an advertisement for his plumbing business."

"And did Mr. Cremins ask you if you knew Carol Montecalvo?"

"Yes."

"Did Mr. Cremins tell you that he had met Mr. Montecalvo?"

"Yes. He said that when he lived in Burbank he used to frequent a steak-house bar, and I guess Dan Montecalvo used to go there also."

"Did Mr. Cremins ever tell you that Mr. Montecalvo made any comments about taking out insurance on anyone?"

The jury was hanging on every word. Meanwhile, Applegate did not object to Bernard's leading his witness. Although Paulson's testimony was hearsay, Judge Tso had allowed it because Cremins would later testify that he was unclear on the details of his conversation with Dan.

"Yes. As I recollect, Denis said he and his fiancée were having some problems and he had told Dan about these problems." Paulson was obviously uneasy as he took a deep breath and continued. "Denis told me Dan told him to take out an insurance policy on her and that, you know . . ."

Bernard was waiting expectantly. "I'm afraid I don't know, Mr. Paulson. Please finish your statement."

Paulson swallowed loudly. "Well, that Dan would kill her and they would split the insurance money."

The courtroom erupted into a symphony of surprised gasps and whispered discussions. Judge Tso sat up straighter in his chair and rapped his gavel on the bench. "That is enough. Come to order."

Gradually the commotion settled down and Bernard, looking astonished by the revelation, continued.

"Did you think that was a little bizarre?"

Paulson nodded quickly. "Oh, yes. I really did. I mean, the story that I had heard in the newspaper was that Carol had been killed in a burglary. The whole story Denis was telling me was really bizarre because it was possibly another explanation for Carol's murder."

Bernard paused a moment and sorted through his notes. "Let me clarify something before I go on," he said, enunciating each word. "Mr. Cremins told you that Mr. Montecalvo had offered to kill his fiancée so they could split the insurance money?"

"That's right."

A look of genuine disbelief crossed Bernard's face. "After he told you this information, did you think you'd better report it to somebody?"

"Well, I finished writing up Denis's advertisement and I thought about it for a while—about twenty minutes. Finally, you know, at about twelve-thirty I decided to see my supervisor and tell the story to her."

"What did your supervisor say about the story?"

"She said she'd pass the information along to the detectives."

"Thank you. Nothing further."

Carol's supervisor took the stand next and admitted that after promising to pass the story on to detectives, she had forgotten about it for several months. Denis Cremins was subsequently called up to tell the jurors that he had, indeed, had the conversation with Mark Paulson. The details, however, were vague. He was obviously not happy about testifying and kept glancing nervously toward Dan.

In what Ron Applegate had to admit was perfect witness placement, Bernard called Cathy Hines to the stand next. With the vivid image in their minds of Dan's suggesting he would kill Denis Cremins's fiancée so they could split her insurance money, the jurors listened to Cathy Hines tearfully recount Carol's deep love for her husband.

"Ms. Hines . . ." Bernard sounded sympathetic and understanding. "Was there ever a time when Carol and you were in church and she kind of broke down and was crying?"

"Yes, I believe it was in February of 1988."

"Approximately one month before her murder, then?" Bernard appeared distraught and it seemed he had become Cathy's friend, sharing an intimate conversation in the privacy of her living room.

"Yes." Cathy's voice cracked with emotion. "I had seen Carol in the back of the church, and I went back to see her. I asked her how Dan was doing and at that time she had tears in her eyes. She said Dan wasn't doing too good, that he was drinking heavily. She asked me to pray for him. I told her that I would and, well . . ." Cathy paused to wipe the tears off her cheeks. "She said she was really concerned for him and she started crying."

Bernard shook his head sadly. "I'm sorry, Ms. Hines," he said softly. "Nothing further."

If that evidence wasn't damaging enough, in the following days Bernard paraded a host of witnesses through the courtroom who carefully detailed Dan's gambling debts. When they were finished, the jurors heard from insurance agents who had records of policies totaling $600,000 on Carol's life. Annette Wilder was next, testifying about the two guns she had seen Dan carrying after Carol's murder.

Bernard's guided tour was almost finished but he wanted to point out one final landmark. He called Brian Arnspiger to the stand.

"Your Honor," Bernard said, lifting a bag containing a worn-out hardback book. "I have what appears to be a book called *Howard Hughes: The Man, the Myth, the Madness.* I'd ask the book to be marked as Exhibit one fifty-one."

"It will be so marked," Judge Tso stated.

"Thank you, Your Honor." The prosecutor turned toward the witness stand. "Detective Arnspiger, have you seen this book before?"

"Yes, during our search of Mr. Montecalvo's storage unit in Irwindale."

"Did you ever open that book, sir?"

"Yes. It felt very light, and when we opened it, we found that it was hollowed out."

"I see. And did you ever take two guns—the same types of guns Ms. Wilder indicated Dan was carrying after Carol's murder—and place them in this hollowed-out book?"

"Yes. If you arrange them the right way, a thirty-eight and a twenty-five will fit perfectly inside that book."

Again the courtroom burst into a chorus of exclamations. A question that had haunted the jury was that if Dan had killed Carol, why hadn't the prosecution been able to produce the guns? The answer lay between the covers of the hollowed-out book.

Dan wisely chose not to cross-examine Brian, leaving the task instead to Applegate. The defense wanted to show that if guns had indeed been hidden in the hollowed-out book, detectives certainly would have found them the night of the murder—regardless of Lynch's earlier testimony that the bookcase had been accidentally overlooked.

"Detective Arnspiger," Applegate said in a monotone voice. "You've been to the scene of a lot of homicides?"

"Yes, I have."

"You search bookcases for weapons?"

"I search everything." Brian sounded very sure of himself and Bernard knew instantly what the defense was trying to do. "In fact," Brian continued, "some detectives don't like to take me along because I spend too much time searching."

Applegate nodded. "So, if you would have been there that night, you would have searched the bookcase?"

"Yes. I would have gotten to it. If that had been my assigned room, I would have checked it."

"I guess if you would have been there, we would have known whether or not there were weapons in that book, wouldn't we?"

Brian paused, realizing the picture taking shape. "Yes. If there were weapons in that book, I would have found them."

"If the book had been empty, you would have probably found that, too, wouldn't you?"

Brian nodded. "I'm sure."

Applegate looked at Judge Tso. "Nothing further."

If Arnspiger would have checked the bookcase, it was reasonable to assume that other detectives would have checked it, too. Just because Lynch didn't check the bookcase didn't mean that no one else had. Ben Bernard was on his feet immediately, hoping to correct that impression.

His smile suggested he was willing to allow for the inexperience of his opponent. "Detective, you weren't there that night, were you?"

"No, I was not."

"So, you have no idea if anyone checked the bookcase, do you?"

"No, sir."

Bernard gave a single nod of his head as if Brian's answer had clarified the issue. "Your Honor, I have nothing further. The prosecution rests."

41

On April 28, 1980, convicted felon Garrett Trapnell—
serving time in the U.S. Penitentiary at Marion, Illinois
—made the decision to turn over a new leaf. Nearly ten
years after receiving a life sentence for hijacking a passenger airplane, Trapnell suddenly knew he could no
longer live without a moral code of conduct. For the
first time in his life he felt the need to atone for his past
wrongs.

A week later Garrett knew what he had to do. He had
heard through the prison grapevine that Vic Santinni, a
runner for the Gamboda family, had been picked up for
murder. The Gambodas were Chicago *Mafiosi*, heavily
involved in narcotics. Someone in the family had hired
Santinni to knock off a district attorney who had been
working overtime to put the family out of business. Santinni had rigged a car bomb one night and set it to go
off when the prosecutor started his car the next morning. There was one problem. The next morning the
district attorney handed the car keys to his eight-year-
old daughter, Juliana. The blond-haired, blue-eyed
child loved the occasional privilege of starting her
daddy's car.

Investigators who later searched through blown-up
bits of the prosecutor's car found very little of Juliana's
body for identification. The grief-stricken attorney had

suspected Santinni in other cases and, working with
detectives, he quickly put together a case against him.
But talk on the street and in prison had it that Santinni
had suddenly come up with an alibi for his whereabouts
that night.

Garrett Trapnell knew otherwise. One of the
Gamboda brothers was serving time at Marion. Like
other inmates Joe Gamboda found some kind of per-
verse enjoyment in sharing war stories with his fellow
convicts. A week after the prosecutor's daughter was
killed, Trapnell found himself sharing a lunch table
with Joe Gamboda.

"Darn shame," Gamboda was saying, wiping the back
of his hand across some crumbs of food on his upper
lip. Gamboda was a strict Catholic and he never used
foul language. "Stupid old fool, that Santinni. Set the
whole thing up perfect like, you know? Perfect bomb,
perfect timing. Then he puts it in the flippin' car."

He paused a moment and stuffed an enormous bite
of mashed potatoes into his mouth. "Coulda put the
darn thing in the D.A.'s briefcase or his office. Some-
thin'."

"Look, Joe, maybe he didn't do it." A man sitting
across from Gamboda broke in, waving his fork for em-
phasis. The man was also involved in organized crime.

"No way, Louie boy." A grin flickered across
Gamboda's scarred face. "I helped him design the
bomb last year."

Now, one week after his moral turnaround, Garrett
Trapnell remembered every detail of Gamboda's conversation. He knew the consequences of squealing. He
would be banished from the common criminals, set
aside like some kind of freak. He would be hated,

mocked, and quite possibly killed. Trapnell thought the possibilities over and decided they had never seemed better in his life. Juliana's death would not be in vain. The prosecution needed someone to dispute Santinni's alibi and Garrett Trapnell had the information to do it. He made up his mind. His atonement had begun.

A year later it was Trapnell's testimony that provided the prosecution with a stunning victory and put Santinni away for life. It was the first in a series of convictions that eventually brought the Gamboda family to its knees.

Ten years passed and everything Garrett had imagined about the consequences of finking on fellow inmates had taken place. With one exception. They hadn't been able to kill him yet. But he had been placed in the Federal Witness Protection Program for convicts, which had meant being moved to a special unit at the Federal penitentiary in Missouri. He had received death threats and had been made an outcast among prison inmates. For his own safety, he had to eat, sleep, and live in quarters set off from the others.

This treatment did nothing to change the way Garrett felt about finking. He had since had the opportunity to act as a Federal witness in two other cases. Each time he testified, prosecutors raised a suspicious eye his way. What did he want? An amended prison term? Special privileges? But Garrett surprised them. He wanted nothing in return—only the wonderful, peaceful feeling that came with knowing he was finally doing the right thing.

In the past decade Garrett Trapnell held no illusions about being released from prison. The life term he was serving held no clauses for parole or good behavior.

But none of that mattered. Garrett believed that a person did not need to be behind bars to be imprisoned. Likewise, a person did not need to be on the streets to be free.

At age fifty-two, Garrett enjoyed his freedom in many ways, but his favorite pastime was watching true crime shows each evening on television. These shows would detail terrible crimes and the people who solved them. Garrett could relate to those people and he knew that if his life had been different he would have been happy as a detective, or perhaps a prosecutor. On the evening of October 16, 1990, twenty-two days into the trial of *The People* v. *Dan Montecalvo,* Garrett Trapnell was watching such a true crime show.

"Next up," the announcer was saying, "the story of Dan Montecalvo, a Burbank man accused of killing his wife and shooting himself in what prosecutors say was merely an attempt to collect her insurance money."

Garrett could hardly believe his ears. He had shared a cell block with Montecalvo and spent hours playing cards with him. Garrett remembered Dan's dream of marrying a middle-aged woman, insuring her, and killing her for the payoff.

The announcer began telling the story.

"Carol Montecalvo never loved anyone like she loved her husband, Dan. . . ." Pictures of Carol and Dan flashed across the screen. Garrett studied the woman, the trusting look in her soft, brown eyes. Nausea began to build in his stomach at the injustice that had been done to her.

". . . and because evidence against Montecalvo is purely circumstantial, he is optimistic about being acquitted."

Garrett had nothing against Dan, personally. The

man had always treated him with respect, and they had been prison buddies back at Marion. But suddenly Garrett knew what he needed to do. The peaceful feeling that always accompanied his acts of atonement began washing over him. The next morning he was granted permission to contact his attorney and by October 18 he was on the telephone with Sergeant Kight at the Burbank Police Department.

Kight was expecting the call. He had been informed about Trapnell's background and his flawless record of testifying in previous cases. When he learned that Trapnell had information about Dan Montecalvo, Kight decided Christmas had definitely come early. The sergeant wanted to take no chances with the conversation. That morning he began tape-recording as soon as the call came in.

"Sergeant Kight, here."

"Yeah, this is Garrett Trapnell."

"Okay, Garrett. Give me a minute here." Kight paused, glancing at the recorder until he was certain it was working properly. "I understand you have some information on one of our boys."

"Dan Montecalvo."

"Correct."

"Yeah, well, I did time with Dan Montecalvo."

"Yeah." Kight was determined to say as little as possible, to let Garrett do the talking so that later no one could accuse him of leading the conversation.

"And, well, at the time I knew him in Marion, he uh . . ." Garrett paused and coughed into the telephone. "He had told me about his uh, his plans to get rich. Get married. And, well, he was a notorious gambler at Marion. The minute I saw him on TV I knew who he was."

"Were you cell mates with him?"

"Yeah, same row. Many times he borrowed money from me and this sort of thing. We were good friends."

"Uh-huh. How long were you guys incarcerated together?"

"More than two years."

"When was this?"

"I'd say about 1976 or '77."

"And what did he tell you about?"

"Well, first let me tell you, uh, they did a lot of cooking on the range."

"Cooking on the range?"

"They'd hide their cooking utensils in the books. The minute I saw that carved-out book on TV, I knew what the story was."

"What do you mean the carved-out book? What did that have to do with what happened in the cell?" Kight was playing it safe.

"He liked to cook. There was a bunch of Italians together. You know, we used to cook at nighttime. We'd hide our hot plates or, you know, our cooking utensils in our books. Then, uh, we'd get together for steaks late at night."

"Uh-huh. You guys ever get caught?"

"Sometimes. I talked to the lieutenant here. He worked at Marion back then and he remembers it."

"He remembers that Dan Montecalvo and some of his cronies would hide cooking utensils?"

"Right, yeah."

"In hollowed-out books?"

"Yeah."

"Uh-huh." Kight penciled the words "hollowed-out book" across a notepad on his desk.

"We used to fantasize about making money."

"Okay."

"And he told me, he says, one of the best tricks was to get married, insure your old lady, and knock her off."

"Did he say how he'd knock her off?"

"Well, you had to make it look like an accident. Make it look like, you know, like a robbery or something like that."

"Uh-huh. Did he ever talk about how he'd plan this?"

"Oh, yeah, many times."

"You heard about this case on television, is that right? It brought back old memories?"

"Right. I knew what the story was immediately. Didn't have to think twice about it. Didn't even finish watching the show."

Garrett paused and there was a sudden change in his tone as if he'd forgotten a very important detail.

"Look, first off, Mr. Kight, I'll tell you straight. I don't want anything from you. I'm not looking for anything. So this isn't one of those jail house, uh, you know, let's-trade-something-for-something deals."

"I understand. How much time do you have to do?"

"I'm doin' a life sentence, so there's no way in hell you could do anything for me."

"Okay. Because we'd want to know the motive for this."

"Well, I have no motive. It's just that I know this guy knocked her off. There is no doubt in my mind whatsoever."

"Okay."

"He talked about it so many times. He used to dream up ways, how he'd make money."

"Uh-huh."

"He told me the insurance scams are the best way.

You know, either getting a member of the family to do it, or make it look like a burglary or boat accident."

Kight suddenly thought of the trip the Montecalvos had been planning to Hawaii. They would have had plenty of opportunities to go boating.

"Uh-huh."

"He was fed up with bank robberies. The percentages were too risky. Then one day he came out and said he wanted to marry some woman, a certain kind of woman, and that was one way to make money. Marry her, insure her, knock her off and make a fortune. But it had to look like an accident."

"A certain kind of woman?"

"Yeah, you know, wallflowers. Lonely women, maybe in their early to mid-thirties. Maybe widowed, or divorced, maybe just not very sociallike."

"Did he talk about working when he got out of prison?"

"No, he had no intention of going to work. He was a flashy kind of guy, used to talk about Vegas all the time. And organized crime. But he was always broke."

"Broke?"

"Yeah, he owed everybody money."

"Okay, I understand you've testified in other cases?"

"Yeah. Testified for the government against the nation's top narcotics organization."

"Okay, you're in for aerial piracy. What else?"

Garrett thought a minute. "A couple of attempted escapes, but that was a while ago. There's been nothing in the last ten years. Absolutely nothing. Not even an incident report."

"You'd be willing to testify?"

"Yes, sir. But I couldn't stay at a county jail."

"Because of your jacket?" Prison finks were considered to have a jacket. A fink's jacket grew more colorful and more dangerous with each convict he brought down. By then, Garrett's jacket was a vivid rainbow of colors.

"That's right. I would need a special facility."

"Okay, one more thing, you're in prison because you're a notorious criminal. Why testify against a good friend?"

"All right . . ." Garrett took a deep breath. "I had a day, about ten years ago, when everything came together and I just turned my life around."

"When was that?"

"April 28, 1980. That was the day I faced up to the fact that I couldn't keep abiding by the convict code and sit on my keester while somebody killed someone else. I decided if I could prevent it I would. From that point on I alienated myself from the rest of the prison population."

"Okay." Kight could hardly believe it. The interview had gone far better than he had ever hoped. "I want to make one thing absolutely clear for the record. You're not asking for any favoritism for this, is that right?"

"Nothing at all."

"No special treatment?"

"I want nothing."

"You were never in a fight with Dan Montecalvo?"

"I have nothing against Dan. Nothing. The fact is, in my own heart of hearts, there is no doubt in my mind that he killed her. Now, if I know facts that would be helpful in solving a crime and don't come forward, that leaves me back on the side of the outlaws. Understand?"

"Certainly."

Garrett paused a moment and his voice softened.

"Sergeant, I'm not doing this because of Dan Montecalvo. I'm doing it because of his wife."

Later, Brian and Bernard weighed the options of interrupting the defense's case to bring Trapnell in as a last-minute prosecution witness—a move that would cost the court twenty thousand dollars because of the special security he would need. In the end they agreed to wait until the defense had presented its case before making a decision.

"He'll be our little secret," Bernard smiled. "Imagine Trapnell sitting up there telling the jury about Dan's get-rich-quick fantasy."

42

Suzan Brown sat nervously on the wooden bench outside Department J. For the past ten minutes she had been trying unsuccessfully to button the cuffs of her striped men's dress shirt. Her heart was beating wildly and each time the elevator door opened to the sixth floor she looked up expecting to see Carol Montecalvo.

It was just before 10 o'clock in the morning, Tuesday, October 24, 1990. Suzan Brown was about to be the first defense witness. She closed her eyes and silently rehearsed the happenings of March 31, 1988, the way she now remembered them. The gunfire, the sound of someone running through the backyard, the falling woodpile, the shoe print.

Dan would certainly not go to prison for something she knew he was innocent of—not unless the police had found the guns. She smiled complacently. There was no way they would find the guns now; she had long since sold them and by now they were most likely out of the country. Just then a bailiff opened the courtroom doors. On this occasion Suzan had decided against using her wheelchair. She took a deep breath and stood up.

Inside, Ron Applegate was hurriedly going over some last-minute notes. The strength of his case rested on the stories Suzan Brown and a handful of other neighbors would tell about someone running through their yards the night of the murder. If he could prove the house had been burglarized, the jury would have to return a not-guilty verdict. Applegate did not plan to ask Suzan how she knew the color of the cash box. She had not admitted to any kind of involvement and that line of questioning would make her look like an unreliable, crazy woman. Which was, of course, exactly what she seemed to be. But her doctors had released her from the hospital six weeks earlier and there was no reason the defense couldn't use her story about the falling woodpile to support the theory that the Montecalvo home had, indeed, been burglarized.

Dan's testimony might help, also. The jury would be more likely to believe Dan in light of evidence that someone had burglarized his home. He was also planning to call on Sergeant Lynch for verification that the police had suspected a burglary when they first responded to the call. Then he would bring up the footprints on the Montecalvo kitchen floor, which after being lifted by evidence technicians that night had somehow disappeared.

Still, Ben Bernard had done a significant amount of damage to their case. Applegate didn't need a degree in psychology to read the looks on the faces of the jurors. They thought Dan was despicable. Worse, they thought he was guilty. And apparently, so did Judge Tso. Early in the trial, the judge had called the defense attorney into his chambers.

"Listen, Applegate," the judge had told him. "I know you took on the Montecalvo case with the understanding that you would be paid by the defendant only if he won."

"That's right, Your Honor," Applegate replied, looking slightly embarrassed.

"Rest easy, Applegate. When this thing's over and Mr. Montecalvo is sentenced, I'll appoint you as counsel retroactively so you can be compensated for your effort."

Applegate hadn't been quite sure what to say. The judge was in essence telling him that he believed that the jury would find Dan guilty. But at the same time, he took comfort in knowing that his work wouldn't be for nothing—just in case they lost.

Applegate had stared at Judge Tso. "Thank you, Your Honor."

Now the attorney glanced about the courtroom at the bored faces of the jurors who had just taken their seats. He looked over the spectator section and his eyes fell on Gene Brisco, who had made a point of being in court that morning.

The more Gene and Chuck had researched Dan's version of the story, the more credible they thought it was. Especially after Suzan's statements about the cash box. Gene and Chuck thought the recent evaluation of her mental health which determined she was fit for release was a tremendous mistake. Since her release Gene had kept track of her, meeting with her at the Glendale motel where she was currently living and constantly trying to learn the truth from her. Gene kept his eyes on Suzan as Ron Applegate called her to the stand. *I'll get to the truth one day,* he promised himself as he watched her take the stand. *And someday everyone will know it.*

The testimony of Suzan Brown was mundane and anti-climactic. She slumped over in the stand, her shoulders bent forward and her eyes only half open. She seemed so bored with the questions that several times she appeared to be falling asleep.

Tediously Applegate extracted from her the story of how she had been sitting in her garage earlier that March evening and seen Dan and Carol walk by. She knew they were going to Hawaii and she testified that she had spoken to them and asked them to bring her back a souvenir. She then testified about hearing gunfire and someone running through her backyard. This was the first proof that burglars might indeed have been in the Montecalvo house and the jurors seemed interested.

When Applegate finished, Ben Bernard stood up and began asking questions that shed light on Suzan's character, if not the truth. Aware of Suzan's background of mental illness, Ben was asking about her clothing that night.

"How were you dressed when you were sitting out in your garage?"

"I had on a pair of shorts and a tank top."

Ben tilted his head and the jurors could read the confused look on his face. "Would it surprise you that the National Weather Bureau said it was fifty-one degrees that night?"

Suzan could feel her eyes beginning to widen. This man did not believe her. *Carol has gotten to him,* she thought. Aloud she said, "Yes, I'd be surprised."

"You wouldn't dress that way if it was fifty-one degrees?"

"Yes, I would," Suzan said. "I also sleep with my window open."

Ben switched topics. "You were recently in the hospital, weren't you?"

"Yes, I was. At the Veterans Administration hospital."

Fear was beginning to make it difficult for her to answer.

"For what?"

Suzan racked her brain and then came up with this answer: "I have osteosarcoma of the right femur," she said matter-of-factly.

Ben wrinkled his eyebrows. "What's that?"

"Cancer."

Gene hung his head angrily. He had heard Suzan talk about cancer before but her doctors knew nothing about it. He was convinced Suzan was lying, or allowing her imagination to overtake reality.

Ben's look of surprise was truly genuine. "That's what you were in the hospital for?"

Suzan nodded. "Yes."

Ben did not challenge her. "Why did they release you?"

"I walked away on my own."

"Why, if I may ask?"

"Well . . ." Suzan straighted herself in the witness chair. "If someone told you they were going to cut your leg off, wouldn't you be scared and walk away?"

"So you discharged yourself?"

"Right." Suzan was lying and Gene shook his head.

Ben glanced at the jury. They got the point. The woman was beginning to look like someone whose candles weren't all lit.

"Isn't it a fact, Ms. Brown, that when you heard the woodpile go down, you also heard a helicopter overhead?" Ben asked.

"I never heard the helicopter," Suzan answered firmly. "Didn't see one, didn't hear one."

"Okay," Ben said, making an effort to understand the

information. "You didn't hear a helicopter, but you did hear a woodpile fall down."

Applegate grimaced as Bernard poked yet another hole in Suzan's story. Police testimony had already established that a police helicopter was on the scene within minutes of Dan's 911 call. It seemed unlikely that Suzan had heard her woodpile fall down if she hadn't heard the helicopter.

"Ms. Brown," Ben continued, "what did you do when you went out to the garage that night?"

"I was putting my hobbies together."

"Your what?" Bernard wanted the jury's attention.

"My hobbies. I had converted my garage into a patio area where I make lampshades out of Popsicle sticks."

This time Ben did not smile. The jurors were doing that for him. "Popsicle-stick lampshades? That's your hobby?"

"Yes. I made them every night till about eleven o'clock."

"And you worked on that hobby wearing shorts and a tank top in fifty-one-degree weather?"

"Yes." Suzan did not appear to be bothered by this line of questioning. After all, there was no connection between having a hobby of making Popsicle-stick lampshades and the events of Carol Montecalvo's murder.

By the end of the morning Applegate sincerely wished the defense hadn't called Suzan Brown as its first witness. If Applegate's impression was correct, the jury had been more interested in the woman's hobby of building Popsicle-stick lampshades and her style of dress than in her testimony about the noises in her backyard.

The next neighborhood witnesses did much better,

especially the man who testified about a ladder that had been knocked off his fence that night. When they had exhausted the neighbors' testimony, the defense called Jerry Vogler to the stand. Jerry was one of the two men who had hired Dan to manage the fledgling hotel in downtown Los Angeles back in 1984.

Dan decided he should question Jerry. The process was tedious and stilted, peppered with objections both from Ben Bernard and Judge Tso. Dan was asking Jerry why he had hired him as a manager for the hotel.

"At the time you went to interview me, Mr. Vogler, what exactly were you looking for in a manager?" Dan asked, pacing in front of the defense table.

"Objection. Relevance," Bernard said. In the interest of time, he had resorted to one-word reasons for objecting to Dan's questions.

"Sustained," Judge Tso said with a sigh.

"When you said that you realized in a week or so at the hotel that dealing with the homeless was not your strong suit, could you expound on that a little, please?" Dan asked, apparently unfazed by his lack of success.

"The court will interpose an objection; sustain the objection. Irrelevant. Next question," Tso said.

Dan and his attorney shared a whispered conversation. When Dan stood up, he looked confident. "Can you tell us why you thought I would make a good manager?"

"Objection," Ben said. "Relevance."

Dan nodded. "Do you recall the purpose of a meeting at the Rampart Police Department?"

"Yes," Vogler said, finally able to answer a question.

"Purpose of that meeting to discuss the clientele of the hotel?"

Judge Tso took off his glasses again and leaned over

the bench. "Don't testify, Mr. Montecalvo; ask questions."

"Was there a concern raised by the local Rampart Police Department regarding the clientele of the hotel?"

"Objection," Ben responded. "Hearsay."

"Sustained."

"Were you informed by local police departments—"

Judge Tso interrupted Dan before he could continue. "Mr. Montecalvo, that invites hearsay. Restate the question."

"After the purchase of the hotel, Mr. Vogler, did you discover what kind of clientele was at the hotel?"

"Objection," Ben said politely. "Relevance."

"Sustained."

And so it went for more than an hour. Relief finally came when Judge Tso called for a lunch break, ordering all parties back in the courtroom in two hours. But if Dan's questioning had hurt his case, it was nothing to what happened in the afternoon. Just after 2 P.M. Judge Tso ordered the defense to return Vogler to the stand. Applegate cleared his throat nervously.

"Uh, Your Honor, may we approach for a moment?"

Judge Tso appeared to be on the verge of losing his patience. "No. You may not. Have your witness come forward, counsel. Is he outside?"

"No, sir. He's not."

Judge Tso strained forward, his eyes wide in astonishment. "What do you mean he is not?"

"Well, he had to meet with people out of town, a business meeting, I guess," Applegate said softly. "I told him that we would tell you that."

Judge Tso was clearly furious. "Our jury has returned, defendant and counsel are present. We had put the matter over until two P.M. The hour is now two-twenty-five. We will call Jerry Vogler once again."

The court clerk bent her head toward the microphone. "Jerry Vogler, please enter the courtroom."

There was no response.

"The jury may be excused," Tso said. The jurors filed out of the courtroom. When they were gone, Tso continued. "It is against the law for a witness to ignore a judge's order to return to the courtroom. Therefore, I want to issue a bench warrant for Mr. Vogler's arrest. I will set bail in the amount of fifteen thousand dollars." Tso spat out the words.

"I have never had anything like this in fifteen years on the bench," Tso continued, staring at Applegate. "I will not have it again."

"Well, Your Honor, I don't know what to say," Applegate sputtered. From the other side of the room, Ben Bernard appeared to be busily sorting through paperwork. He had never seen Judge Tso this angry and he thought it best to stay out of the conversation.

"Do you have his business address?" Tso asked.

Applegate shook his head. "I have no idea what it is."

"Then give me his phone number. Give it to the clerk immediately." He turned to the court clerk. "You give that phone number to the sheriff's department to reverse trace it to an address."

The courtroom was utterly silent while Applegate and the court clerk responded to the judge's orders. When the court clerk took the phone number and left the room, Judge Tso continued. "I want that person here. I can't believe this is happening to me." He shook his head in disgust. "We will resume with the next witness."

*　*　*

Although the jurors did not understand exactly what had transpired in their absence, they were certain of one thing. The defense had made another lethal error. Judge Tso still looked angry when the proceedings continued. They heard again from Pastor Wil Strong and then from Maree Flores, who had rented part of her home to Dan, been with him during his arrest, and was now in love with him. Applegate hoped their testimonies would rebuild what devastation the prosecution had wreaked on Dan's character.

Maree was on the witness stand, her thick black hair hanging below her shoulders and draping her face so that it was difficult to see her eyes. During her testimony she mentioned that she and Dan were in love. Neither Dan nor she had admitted their growing feelings for each other until his arrest. That weekend, Maree had visited him in prison, bereft that the man who had come to be her best friend was being treated so unfairly. Speaking over a telephone and gazing through thick glass just as he had presented the question to Carol years earlier, Dan asked Maree to marry him and she agreed. No matter that everything was working against them, no matter that police thought he'd killed Carol. Maree loved Dan and wanted to do whatever she could to help him fight the charges against him.

Now, with Ben Bernard about to begin cross-examination, Maree looked like a frightened deer on the first day of hunting season. Bernard did not waste time taking aim before firing his first question.

"Ms. Flores, you said you had fallen in love with Mr. Montecalvo," Ben said pleasantly. "When did that happen?"

"I would think over a period of time, gradually," she answered quietly.

"When did you realize you were in love?" Ben asked. He was trying to paint a sordid picture of Dan killing Carol for her insurance money only to take up a relationship with her closest friend. Maree knew this was not the truth. While Carol was alive she had never been interested in Dan.

Maree fidgeted on the witness stand. "Well, I think after the arrest," she said sweetly. "I think that's probably when I, you know, when I realized it."

"Something about an arrest that causes you to realize that you are in love?" Bernard asked plainly. He caught a few of the jurors smiling at the notion.

"Well, crisis does that. Yes, I think I fell in love because of the crisis situation."

"Dan ever express his love for you?"

"After his arrest, yes. We began to realize the depth of our feelings for each other after that."

The connection had been made. Before Ben finished he could feel the jury's contempt for Dan. By the day's end, Ben Bernard believed the defense witnesses had helped the prosecution as much as anything he had presented. At this rate they were going to save the court that twenty thousand dollars it would have cost to put Garrett Trapnell on the witness stand.

On the following day Vogler returned to court and—after a verbal reprimand from Judge Tso—continued his testimony. After that Applegate brought forth a string of witnesses who further testified to Dan's good character, and a maid who had worked at the Strand Hotel who testified to seeing stray bullets in Dan's desk drawer. This was intended to confirm Dan's story that the bullets found in his belongings in storage were from his desk at the Strand and not an indication that he had kept guns in his house.

Bernard was not concerned. After all, the prosecution had presented witnesses who had seen Dan with guns on many occasions. Finally, only Dan Montecalvo was left. It was the afternoon of October 25, and Applegate was trying to convince Judge Tso that they needed more time to prepare.

"I cannot allow him to take the stand today, Your Honor," Applegate said earnestly. "I have not had an opportunity to talk to him in more than two weeks."

"We have an hour left before we recess for the day," Judge Tso explained impatiently. "If you do not put him on the stand now, I will rest your case for you."

"Your Honor . . ." Applegate sputtered. "Your Honor, the court knows the problems I have had communicating with the defendant in the jail. I can't let this man testify without at least spending a day with him."

Judge Tso raised an eyebrow. "Remember, you are only cocounsel on the case, Mr. Applegate. This was his wish, right from the beginning. I am not going to waste another hour as I did yesterday."

With that, Judge Tso again dismissed the jurors. Ben Bernard understood why. The judge's sharp words might prejudice the jury. When the jurors had filed out of the courtroom, Judge Tso turned to Applegate.

"Your Honor," Applegate said, "I feel that it would be grossly unfair for the court to rest our case for us until we have had time for Mr. Montecalvo to prepare to testify." Applegate paused, taking Judge Tso's silence for acceptance. "If I can have a day at the jail with him. As you know, I was denied that last weekend. If we were not going to be here tomorrow, I could meet with him tomorrow."

"Fine," Tso stated, mistakenly believing that Applegate had agreed to question Dan the next day. "We will begin the defendant's testimony tomorrow at nine o'clock."

Applegate stared blankly at Judge Tso, realizing that he had been misunderstood. "Your Honor, how can I interview him tonight? He does not even get back to the county jail until nine o'clock at night. I believe you misunderstood me. I need tomorrow to interview him."

Judge Tso sighed. "Counsel, at first you said tomorrow. We are going to do it tomorrow."

Dan stood up. "Your Honor, I have been under this pressure for three years. I am trying to clear my name, here. That is why I wanted to come to this courtroom. Do you have any idea what it's like to be in this county jail on a daily basis here, sir?"

"Look, Mr. Montecalvo . . ." Judge Tso sounded tired. "I have warned you of the disadvantages you would face by acting as your own attorney. You are your own attorney, therefore you are prepared. You know what you are going to testify to. I am going to treat you as I treat any lawyer that appears in this courtroom. That means I expect you to be ready." The judge turned to the bailiff. "Bring the jury back in, will you?"

The bailiff moved toward the jury room. Dan looked on the verge of a nervous breakdown as he made one final attempt.

"Your Honor, if you could just give us tomorrow. One day to prepare so that—"

Judge Tso interrupted Dan's plea. "We will resume in the matter of *The People* v. *Dan Montecalvo*."

The argument was over. Dan would have to testify the following day. Ben Bernard was not surprised by the judge's decision to deny more time for the defense.

What did surprise him was that the defense was still not ready to produce the very testimony on which they had built their case.

In the end Judge Tso studied his calendar and agreed to put testimony off until Monday, giving the defense a three-day weekend. The extra day did little to allay Applegate's concerns about putting Dan on the witness stand.

The advantages of doing so were easy to recognize. Dan would tell the story about what had happened to him and Carol the night she was killed, offering the jury an alternative to the picture that had already been painted by the prosecution. The disadvantages were more subtle. If the jurors didn't like Dan—and Applegate had no illusions that they did—they might discount everything he said.

There was also the issue of Dan's prior record. Wil Strong had already mentioned that Dan was an ex-convict, and now it was up to Dan to explain his past in a way the jury would empathize with. That Monday morning Applegate cringed at the thought and listened as Judge Tso ordered the proceedings to begin. He called Dan to the stand and asked him to describe his duties at the Strand Hotel in 1984.

Dan wore a plain gray suit. He looked composed as he took a deep breath and began. "Well, my duties were to manage the hotel, to accommodate the clients at the hotel, to supervise the employees of the hotel, to bring a semblance of some sort of a hope into the hotel for the clients—most of which were homeless people, welfare recipients." Dan stopped to take another breath. "My job was to establish, and if possible, to fulfill ministries in the hotel, to try and serve the people in the hotel, to reduce the crime in the hotel, to reduce the violence, to eliminate the welfare fraud that was running rampant in the hotel. Eliminate those people who were not paying their rent, to get them into drug programs, alcohol rehabilitation programs, and also to direct them to employment, if they were seeking that."

From his seat Ben Bernard felt exhausted by Dan's long-winded explanation. He wondered if Dan was trying to impress the jury with his numerous abilities. If so, judging by the jurors' tired faces, he had failed miserably.

Dan's testimony wore on. After establishing how Dan's poor health had resulted in his job loss, Applegate next asked Dan about his gambling debts, trying to imply that the collectors were not pressuring him to make a payment as the prosecution had implied.

Just before lunch, Applegate asked Dan about his emotional state after Carol died. Ben sat peacefully in his chair, aware that his opponent was trying to make an emotional plea in the moments before a break.

Dan's eyes filled with tears and he appeared to be struggling to answer. "What was my mental state of mind?"

"Yes."

Dan dropped his head into his hands dramatically and a loud sob echoed into the microphone. The jurors stirred restlessly in their seats.

After several seconds, Dan lifted his head and tried to answer the question. "Well, you've got to understand the type of lady Carol was," he blurted out. "You had to know this lady. I mean, to lose something like she was, the impact she had on my life . . ." He shook his head and seemed to drift back in time; then suddenly he turned back toward Applegate. "Don't get me wrong.

I'm not trying to say I'm a saint. I truly wasn't. But she was." Dan sniffled loudly. "The impact she had during the ten years we were together . . . and to have to lose her like that and then . . ."

Ben Bernard considered objecting because Dan was not specifically answering the question, but he decided against it. Past experience told him that whenever Dan opened his mouth for any period of time the end result was worse for the defense than if he hadn't.

Dan paused again and more tears filled his eyes. "I mean, I could have dealt with it better if it was a heart attack, or an accident, or something. But to have her shot like that and to . . . to know she is not going to be here anymore and going through that every day." He wiped a tear from his cheek. "Then when you put that on top of what the police were doing as far as walking around telling my friends that I did it, telling my wife's family, telling my church friends that I executed my wife. After that, people started to stay away from me. People in my own church were afraid of me. They didn't know who to believe."

Dan's tearful emotion was gradually being replaced with a vengeful anger. Bernard smiled to himself as he glanced at the jury. They appeared to be having an easier time than Dan's friends had in knowing whom to believe.

"And then to have the threats from Sergeants Kight and Lynch, to know that the people who did this was still running loose, to be followed by the police, to have my phone monitored and tapped, to have the police show up at my neighbors' doors wherever I moved, and to have the police telling them I was a murderer." Dan's voice was rising steadily as he revealed the reasons for his anger. "Well, after a while I didn't know what to do so I went back to Vegas. It was an escape. Booze was an escape," Dan said, turning angrily toward the judge. "These people had no right to do anything to anybody . . ."

Ben Bernard still had not moved to make an objection, but Judge Tso had heard enough. He stared at Dan, amazed at the man's gall. "Wait just one moment. You were asked one question. Now, answer the question, please. I want to hear what your state of mind was."

Dan leaned back in the witness stand and visibly tried to compose himself. "Immediately afterwards, Your Honor, I had this rage in me. I wanted to get even. And I just thank God that I never met the people that did this thing," Dan said, his Boston accent thick. "But I also was enraged at the police. You can imagine being there in the house with your dying wife and asking them for help and they just stay outside for no reason. And then, knowing my wife might have lived. . . . And to come home to a house that was totally destroyed by these supposed public servants and then I . . ."

"Mr. Montecalvo"—Judge Tso interrupted him again —"please answer the question."

"I went to a psychiatrist, a therapist," Dan said. "I stayed in therapy for a while and I was very depressed. But I was also very mad."

Throughout Dan's testimony, Ben Bernard continued to sit calmly in his seat. His appraisal had been correct. In his opinion, Dan sounded like a whining, complaining liar who had chosen to blame his own mistakes on decent law-abiding police officers.

After lunch Dan tearfully told the story of what he remembered about the night Carol was murdered. Applegate was asking him about what happened after he was shot.

"I went to her," Dan said.

"What position was her body in?"

"She was lying on her back. I could see her face, her eyes." More tears trickled down Dan's cheeks. "The glasses was down by her chest because she wears a chain, one of them loops that hold glasses in place, you know?" Dan's accent grew more pronounced. "I remember looking at her—her eyes were opened—and I just remembered saying something like, 'God, please.' And I remember running to the phone."

"What phone did you go to?"

"I went to the telephone in the study at the end of the hallway. But it didn't work. Then I ran to the phone in the living room and called nine-one-one. And I told them something has happened, we need some help. Then I remember running back to my wife." Dan sobbed again, taking several seconds to compose himself. "All I know then was, she wasn't conscious. She was breathing, though. And I felt her pulse. I know she was alive. And all I remember is praying for her. I just prayed whatever I could pray, whatever." Dan gulped back another sob.

"I just asked God to please let her be okay, and I opened the door and I expected people to come in to help us. Then the phone rang again and it was the nine-one-one people. We talked and I told them again what happened and she asked me if the people that shot us were still in the house and I said no."

Dan was crying louder now. "And still nobody . . . nobody came. And then I heard a helicopter and I went to the front door and looked out. Police officers were everywhere but no one was helping us."

Dan wiped his face again as fresh tears flowed from his eyes. "I asked them for help. I said, 'My wife is bleeding and she needs help.' But the officer only told me to come out and keep my hands where they could see them. All the while I kept saying they had to send someone inside. My wife was bleeding to death."

Everyone in the courtroom was disturbed by Dan's testimony, picturing Carol bleeding to death while police officers did nothing to help. Bernard wondered whether the jurors believed Dan's story.

Dan continued, his voice strained from the force of his sobbing. "I told them my wife needed help and finally I got up and tried to run back into the house to be with her. But they knocked me down and tied me to a stretcher. I kept asking them about my wife and they wouldn't tell me nothing. Not until later. At the hospital. That's when they told me that my wife died."

Applegate thought about the direction the proceedings were taking and decided the timing would never be better. "Mr. Montecalvo, have you ever been convicted of a felony?"

Dan was busy trying to dry his wet face with his sleeve and he appeared not to have heard the question. "I'm sorry. Could I have a tissue or a towel, please?"

Applegate moved toward the witness stand with a box of tissues and repeated the question. "Mr. Montecalvo, have you ever been convicted of a felony?"

Dan was clearly upset, but he now had his tears under control. His answer was quiet and humble. "Yes, sir."

While still wiping an occasional stray tear, Dan recounted his bank robbery convictions in the 1970s. Applegate hoped the jury would see Dan as a man of sorrows who had not only had the misfortune of losing his wife but had been confused in his early years and paid for his mistakes with prison time. He looked at the jury but the expressions on their faces gave nothing away.

As the afternoon testimony continued, Ben Bernard began to see a pattern. Dan was refuting everything that suggested his guilt. If the jury was to believe Dan, they would have to believe that numerous police officers, detectives, and sergeants, as well as the patrons and employees of a handful of Burbank bars and restaurants, and some of Dan's personal friends had all conspired to frame him in the murder of his wife. Ben made a mental note to point this idea out to the jury in his closing remarks. Before the day was over, Ben was able to cross-examine Dan. He started by asking Dan about his love for Carol.

"Now, you say that you worshipped the ground that your wife, Carol, walked on?"

"That is right," Dan answered. By this time, his tears were gone.

"You thought she was a saint?"

Dan nodded emphatically. "I knew she was a saint."

Ben cocked his head to one side and wrinkled his eyebrows. "Then, Mr. Montecalvo, let me ask you this, sir: Why did you find it necessary to be out trying to hustle other women?"

"I never was out trying to hustle other women, sir." Dan's answer sounded angry and defensive. "Bring those women in here."

"Well, I believe we've done that, sir. Did we not? You've heard the testimony about you dropping hundred-dollar bills on the floor."

"Ask people who know me. That's ridiculous," Dan said.

"Did that waitress make up the part about you waving a Sugar Daddy lollipop around?"

"Yes, she certainly did," Dan answered defiantly.

"Did she make up the part that you were seen—for want of a better word—hustling other waitresses in that establishment?"

"Yes. Again, if I hustled those people, bring those people in here."

Ben ignored Dan's statement. "Did she make up the fact that you were seen necking with women in this same establishment?"

"That never occurred. Come on, please." Dan seemed disgusted by the idea. "Bring these people in here. This is all innuendo."

"In a court of law we call that testimony, Mr. Montecalvo. Not innuendo."

When the cross-examination continued the next day, Ben Bernard's questions seemed even more pointed and ruthless than usual, as if he had seen his opponent's weakness and was moving in for the kill. The prosecutor had done his homework and found a document stating that Dan had once been penalized in prison for concealing a razor blade in the heel of his shoe. He picked up the document from the table and walked closer to Dan.

"Mr. Montecalvo, did you ever conceal something in a hollowed-out place, say, in 1975?"

A fleeting look of panic seemed to cross Dan's face. "In 1975?"

"Yes."

Dan shook his head. "No, sir."

"Well, then, let me show you a document. United States Government. Has your name on it, certified by the custodian of records, Department of Justice. I will ask you to read this to yourself, sir."

Dan took the piece of paper and read it. "Yes, sir?"

"I will ask you again, sir. Did you conceal a razor blade in a hollowed-out heel of your shoe, sir, on or about the eighteenth day of January 1975?"

"No, I did not."

"Then this report is a lie?" Ben's gaze was focused directly on Dan.

"I think the report was explanatory. I mean, I explained it to a particular committee involved. I think they were satisfied that the shoes were not mine."

Ben raised one eyebrow. "You were wearing them, weren't you?"

"Yes, sir, but if you notice the reason I was wearing them. I was in transit in 1975."

"You were wearing somebody else's shoes?"

"That's right."

Ben nodded sarcastically. Now that Applegate had introduced Dan's prior record, questions about his time in prison were fair game. "So then, when they transfer a federal prisoner from one institution to another, they don't let you wear your own shoes?"

"It really depends, sir. In my particular case, my shoes were totally gone. When I got to Washington or Oregon, they gave me another pair of shoes. If that razor blade was in those shoes when I started off at the U.S. Penitentiary, it wouldn't have been discovered until we arrived in Tacoma, or whatever.'

Ben looked confused again. "Somebody else put it in the shoes?"

"Who knows who put it in there. I just know I didn't. They gave them to me to replace my old ones."

"Where did you get these shoes that somebody else put this razor blade in?"

"At one of the stops. When we were in transit."

"The federal government gave you used shoes to replace your old worn-out ones?"

Applegate watched the questioning and wished, once again, that he could disappear from the room. The jurors could make the connection. If Dan had been caught with a razor blade in the hollowed-out heel of his shoe, then he might very well have hidden guns in a hollowed-out book. By then Applegate was certain that he should have trusted his hunches and not allowed Dan to take the witness stand. His testimony had served only to damage their case.

In fact, the single redeeming bit of testimony that day did not come from Dan. It came from his psychiatrist, Dr. Desmond Fung, who testified that Dan was indeed in a depression after Carol's murder.

"Dr. Fung, what facts did you consider in coming to your conclusion that Mr. Montecalvo was suffering from depression after his wife's murder?"

"I think he had—still has—a tremendous fear that he is going to be killed."

"Anything else?"

"Well, he has tremendous difficulty because he feels he is being persecuted. Examination proved that he was very depressed. He was crying; he was tearful. He reported he was drinking a lot just to cope with this problem. He was unable to sleep. He was taking prescribed tranquilizers."

Applegate was not satisfied. "Was there anything else that caused you, in your professional opinion, to believe he was suffering from depression?"

"Well, he felt like he was being accused of murdering

his wife. And based on what he has communicated to me, he could not have done this. He feels like he is being wrongfully accused of something he hasn't done. At the same time, I also feel that the marriage between him and his wife was perhaps the best thing that ever happened to him in his life. And he had lost that. He was still mourning over the loss of his wife even after two years."

Applegate wanted to walk up and thank the man personally, but he refrained. "Thank you, sir," he said. "Nothing further."

Ben Bernard recognized that Dr. Fung's testimony had been the most damaging so far to the prosecution's case. A professional had determined that Dan had indeed loved Carol and mourned her death. Still, he was not terribly worried. The trial had been completely one sided so far. Later that afternoon, the defense rested its case. The following day both sides would give closing arguments, drawing the trial to a close. Dan's fate would then be in the hands of the ten women and two men who made up the jury.

43

On the windy morning of Halloween Day 1990—a full seven weeks after jury selection had begun—prosecuting attorney Ben Bernard gave his closing argument. If Bernard was good during the trial, he was brilliant that morning. Talking smoothly and making eye contact with the jurors, Bernard expertly recapped each bit of circumstantial evidence. He also reminded the jurors of information that was not evidence.

"If you noticed, during Mr. Montecalvo's testimony from the stand," Bernard said, raising an eyebrow, "he was sobbing and crying—emotional on direct examination. But under cross-examination, he was angry and mad. He wants to know what we're doing to him. Why is Arnspiger framing him? What am I doing here?"

Bernard paused a moment and looked like a teacher about to answer the question that had stumped the class. "This is why: The man has two personalities. And I suggest to you now, the man led two lives."

Several jurors nodded in agreement with Bernard's assessment. Bernard continued. "I agree with Mr. Montecalvo, the best thing that ever happened to him was Carol. But he didn't know how to deal with her. He lied to her. He cheated on her. He was out playing and drinking and gambling and chasing women, while she worked day and night to support him. She was insured for six hundred thousand dollars."

Bernard stared at the jurors and knew they shared his contempt for the defendant. "Mr. Montecalvo was in debt. He was in trouble with the casinos. This was his way out."

As Bernard continued, he questioned why Dan felt compelled to accuse many of the prosecution witnesses of lying. "Mr. Montecalvo characterizes himself in the manuscript he wrote as a chronic liar. . . . Yet he wants us to believe that everybody is lying about him, out to frame him, out to kill him."

The jurors sat in rapt attention while Bernard accused the defense of using court time to try their civil suit against Burbank. "He is not defending himself on a murder charge. He is picking on the Burbank Police Department. He is attacking them. That is his entire defense."

Finally, Bernard pleaded with the jurors to remember their common sense.

"You will be able to use the exhibits and the testimony. But you get to take something else back in that jury room with you." He lowered his voice as the jurors strained forward, hanging on his every word. "Your common sense and logic. Do that. Please, do that. This does not all happen in a glass bubble. Your life experiences apply."

Ben continued, full of emotion. "The evidence—I suggest to you—is overwhelming. I also suggest to you, ladies and gentlemen of the jury, that the only just verdict, the verdict that Carol Montecalvo calls out from her grave for, is a guilty verdict. Thank you."

Ron Applegate was next. For nearly an hour he droned on about the tedious details of Carol's murder.

The position of her body, the way she clutched the registration papers and the paper towel in her hand, which bullet entered her body first. Even Judge Tso appeared to be bored by the proceedings.

But after lunch Applegate underwent a transformation. For the first time in the trial, he came across as both interesting and rational. The jurors noticed the change and sat straighter in their seats, listening to his reasons for thinking the defendant innocent.

In the spectator section, Gene Brisco and Chuck Lefler sat near Lorn Aiken. Despite their hunches about Suzan Brown they had been unable to produce anything concrete during the trial. Now Gene and Chuck wondered if Applegate would be able to convince the jury of the truth. Lorn Aiken wondered the same thing. He was busy with other cases, but he couldn't put Dan Montecalvo out of his mind. *If there is justice, Dan will be acquitted,* Lorn thought to himself. He watched with interest as Applegate continued.

Applegate reminded the jury that although Suzan Brown testified that she had seen Dan and Carol walking that night, Dan had testified that he had not seen her. Police did not believe that Dan and Carol had taken a walk because Dan was too busy planning her murder. When Suzan testified that she saw them walking, Dan could have had a perfect alibi.

"He told the truth," Applegate said, his voice rising passionately. "He honestly told you that he didn't recall seeing her that night. He could have lied and said, 'Sure, I saw her.' But he told the truth. That's an example of someone who is not trying to hide something, ladies and gentlemen. Mr. Montecalvo is telling the truth."

Applegate summed up the prosecution's case in a way that made it seem ridiculously full of holes.

"If it happened the way the prosecution says it did, Dan had to plan it like this: He had to shoot his wife twice with a thirty-eight, shoot himself in the back in just the right place with a twenty-five—not knowing which way the bullet would go, not knowing whether he would even be conscious, not knowing whether the bullet would miss a vital organ, not knowing whether he would be bleeding and dripping blood everywhere while he tried to find some place to hide the weapons."

For the first time since the trial began, Ben Bernard felt slightly concerned. The jurors seemed to be making a connection with Applegate. As if they were seeing the prosecution's case in a different light for the first time.

Applegate continued. "Of course, Dan also has to know that he can hide his weapons in the bookcase because Burbank Police do not search bookcases. He has to figure they will never find the weapons in a bookcase." Applegate's voice took on a note of mock brilliance. " 'I know, I'll hide the guns in the bookcase. They'll be safe there. It will be the perfect crime.' "

Applegate rolled his eyes. "Then, in that short time after dialing nine one one, Dan has to cut the screen, jimmy the file cabinet, jimmy the cash box, hide the guns, take the paper towel and registration documents and put them in Carol's hands, run outside, drop the registration sticker on the driveway, and finally"—Applegate caught his breath—"go back inside to answer the nine-one-one call."

Strolling in front of the jury, Applegate looked angry and frustrated. "This is their theory. It is why this man is sitting here today. This is what they think happened."

Applegate then asked the jury to do something that

the other attorneys in the room would likely have agreed was a very smart move. He asked the jury to consider the testimony they'd heard and assume for a moment that there was no insurance on Carol.

"With that assumption in mind, look at the evidence as to whether or not Mr. Montecalvo killed his wife. Then I would like you to understand that adding a motive does not bring any more evidence to that crime scene."

Applegate stood still for a moment and stared at the jury. "This has been a trial on motive and character assassination. We've spent all this time with people coming in to tell you why you shouldn't like this man." Applegate pointed to Dan, who carefully kept his gaze away from the jury box.

Applegate shrugged. "He is not a likable person. He does things we don't like. We don't like his lifestyle. We don't like the people he associates with. But having a drinking problem does not make him a murderer. Being a gambler does not make him a murderer. Please, when you examine the evidence, don't confuse it with the character description and motive."

Later on Applegate dealt with the inadequacy of Dan's questioning. "He is on trial for first degree murder and he is cocounsel. He has that right. Because he is not an attorney, you may not have liked the way he handled it. However, that does not make him guilty of murder."

Applegate brought his final argument to a close. "Please do not convict Mr. Montecalvo because you don't like his lifestyle. Look at the evidence and see if you have been convinced beyond a reasonable doubt. I am certain you have not. Thank you."

As with all such trials, the burden of proof in the

Montecalvo case lay with the prosecution. For that reason, Ben Bernard was entitled to a final rebuttal argument after the defense was finished. Bernard used the time to attack everything Applegate had said. As for the sequence of events, Bernard reminded the jury that by some accounts, five full minutes passed between the time neighbors claimed to have heard gunshots and Dan's first call to 911.

"What was Dan doing during those minutes while Carol bled to death?" Bernard asked the jury. "Perhaps that's when he cleverly hid the guns and made certain the registration tag was in the driveway."

Bernard raised one eyebrow and shook his head incredulously. "As for some kind of frame because police are worried about being sued, it makes no sense at all. Police get sued all the time. That is no reason to put careers on the line by manufacturing evidence against a person."

Fifteen minutes later, Ben Bernard finished his rebuttal. "Dan Montecalvo is an admitted liar. Dan Montecalvo doesn't know the truth when it hits him in the nose. And I suggest the evidence points to the fact that Dan Montecalvo killed his wife, that woman whom he called a saint, the woman who meant everything to him. He said he worshipped the ground she walked on," Bernard said softly. "But the truth was he treated her like dirt. Thank you."

The jurors received their final instructions later that afternoon and early the next day. After that they set about the task of sorting through the overwhelming circumstantial evidence against Dan Montecalvo. The process took all day Thursday, Friday, and part of Monday.

Both Ben Bernard and Ron Applegate worried about the time it was taking the jury to reach a verdict. The jurors had been advised that if they could not agree on first degree murder, they could agree to a lesser murder charge.

Finally, just before lunch on Monday, November 5, the jury foreman presented the court clerk with a verdict. Both attorneys and various members of the press were contacted; Dan was moved up to the courtroom, and by 1:40 P.M., all necessary parties had arrived at Department J. The jurors were in their seats when Judge Tso entered the room.

He cleared his throat and sorted through the documents on his desk. Looking up, he addressed the jury. "I understand we have a verdict?"

The jury foreman stood. "Yes, Your Honor. We do."

Judge Tso nodded. "Will you hand the verdict slips to the bailiff, please?" For several seconds a tense silence filled the courtroom. "We will have the clerk read the verdict now."

Dan closed his eyes, looking small and insignificant next to Ron Applegate. Ben Bernard appeared relaxed, leaning back in his chair as if he were about to take in a good football game in the comfort of his living room.

The court clerk held the verdict slip in her hand and began reading. "We the jury in the above entitled action find the defendant Daniel J. Montecalvo guilty of murder in violation of penal code one eighty-seven A, a felony, as charged. We further find the murder to be in the first degree. . . ."

The clerk kept reading, but everyone had heard enough. Dan dropped his head dramatically into his hands. Those sitting near him heard him quietly moaning to himself, "No, no, no. I didn't do it. This is all wrong. No, no."

A red flush crossed Ron Applegate's face. He had

failed an innocent man, making this the single lowest moment of his legal career. Even worse was the knowledge that before the trial had started, Ben Bernard had been willing to plea-bargain the charges down to manslaughter in exchange for a guilty plea. Applegate had refused. If Dan was innocent, there could be no plea bargaining. Justice would be served only if he left the courtroom a free man.

He quickly gathered the paperwork in front of him and leaned toward Dan. "I'm sorry," he whispered. "We must continue to fight. You can't give up."

Meanwhile, Ben Bernard was whirling in the heady effects of what had become a stunning victory. A first degree murder conviction based purely on circumstantial evidence was virtually unheard of. As the jurors were excused, several of them stopped to shake the prosecutor's hand and congratulate him on his fine job.

When they had filed past, Brian Arnspiger grabbed Bernard's hand and shook it firmly. A broad grin covered the detective's normally stern face. In his mind he could hear the sound of yet another prison door slamming shut.

"Unbelievable," he said. "I mean it. Best darn job I ever saw, Bernard."

Bernard reached out and shook the detective's hand. "Listen, your investigation did it. I didn't have anything without you."

They looked across the room and saw that Dan was crying and complaining about not having had a fair trial. The bailiff said nothing as he handcuffed him and led him out.

"Can you believe they went for murder one?" Brian said as Dan disappeared from sight. "I never dreamed we'd get that kind of conviction."

Bernard scratched the top of his balding head. "I'd have been happy with manslaughter." He shrugged. "I guess they saw Dan for who he was."

"I can't wait till the sentencing."

"Are you coming back for it?"

Brian nodded. "Wouldn't miss it."

Dan's conviction on charges of first degree murder made the front pages of all the local newspapers. In many television and print accounts Ben Bernard was credited with having prosecuted the case perfectly. Overnight the phone in Bernard's office began ringing off the hook. Everyone wanted to know how a prosecutor who had been willing to plea-bargain a case down to manslaughter had achieved a murder one conviction based entirely on circumstantial evidence. Bernard was as surprised as anyone else. He had presented a good deal of evidence against Dan. But he believed that Dan would have come out better had he not represented himself.

Members of the press were not alone in recognizing the feat Ben Bernard had accomplished. In the days after the conviction his superiors discussed his being promoted to a more prestigious management position. He would be further removed from the courtroom, but after the Montecalvo case, Bernard was ready for that.

The sentencing of Dan Montecalvo came at 1:30 P.M. on Monday, December 3. First, the judge heard from Carol's father. Although the man had not been as close to his daughter as he would have liked, he blamed some of their later separation on Dan. Pointing an accusing finger at Dan, the white-haired man spoke angrily. "You betrayed us, you betrayed her. And if that wasn't enough you killed her." His eyes brimming with tears, the man asked Judge Tso to hand down the stiffest penalty possible.

Both attorneys were then given time to make final comments. Ben Bernard asked for a severe penalty to assure that no other well-meaning woman ever need fall victim to the dishonest ways of Dan Montecalvo. Applegate asked the judge for leniency, reminding him that Dan was virtually harmless and that he had not been convicted on any physical evidence. Judge Tso listened passively to the entire proceeding. When finally he spoke, he went over the evidence, assuring the defense that he was aware of Dan's disturbed childhood and the lack of physical evidence. For a moment Bernard wondered if Judge Tso was going to be easy on Dan. But then Tso told Dan that killing his trusting wife for financial gain was the epitome of evil and cowardice.

"And so," he continued, "after carefully considering all the evidence and the circumstances of this case, this court has decided to sentence you to the maximum prison time for your crime allowed by law. In this case, that means you will serve a sentence of twenty-seven years to life."

As the judge continued advising Dan of the specifics regarding his sentence, Applegate remained motionless in his chair. He felt as if he and Dan had just been banished to Siberia. The sentence was the ultimate defeat.

Several feet away, Brian Arnspiger jumped to his feet and began furiously pumping Ben Bernard's hand. "This calls for a celebration."

Bernard felt as if the world was turning in slow motion. The sentence was the toughest permissible by law. He smiled. "Yeah," he said. "Let's get out of here."

Before they left, Carol's father approached them.

"I know nothing's ever going to bring back our Carol," the man said, his voice choked with emotion. "But what you two did for her this past year . . ." His eyes filled with tears and he didn't finish his sentence. "I can only say thank you and take comfort in knowing Carol is at peace with God. If there was ever a person who took to heart the teachings of Christ, it was Carol. Somewhere, right now, my little girl is smiling. I really believe that."

Carmelo Tronconi shook hands with Bernard and Brian and then turned to leave. By then, Dan had been taken from the courtroom to a waiting transport bus which would take him to the county jail. He would stay there until he was assigned a cell in one of the state penitentiaries. As the bus pulled away from the courthouse that afternoon, Dan stared at the clear outline of the San Gabriel Mountains. "Why don't they believe me, Carol?" he asked out loud. "Why?"

Seventeen days later, on December 20, Dan did something that made even Ron Applegate wonder about him. He married Carol's longtime friend, Maree Flores. As had come out at the trial, Dan had proposed to her before it even began. Her sons, now nineteen and twenty-one, believed Dan innocent and had given their approval of the marriage. After all, Dan had shared their home for several months and they liked him.

"Look, Mom," her older son, Juan, had said after Dan had proposed. "Dan's been nice to me and Lino and he's been a friend to you. You two have been through a lot. If this makes you happy, I'll support you."

Before the trial Juan had spoken with Dan by telephone. "Dan, my mom's been in other situations where someone seemed nice and then later they let her down. She doesn't need that. Make sure you treat her good."

Dan was impressed with Juan's concern. "I promise you this much," Dan told the young man. "I will love your mother as long as we both are alive. You have my word."

After that the couple had sought approval to be married after the trial, and all parties had agreed on the December date just five days before Christmas. The ceremony took place in Judge Lawrence Tate's chambers and was over in minutes. After a chaste kiss, the first the couple had ever shared, Dan looked at his bride and took her chin in his hands.

"If anything ever happens to me, Maree, keep fighting. I don't care if I'm alive or dead. I want my name cleared. I want my marriage to Carol to be remembered for what it was. Do you understand?"

Maree nodded and brushed away the tears that slid down her cheeks. She loved Dan and was ready to fight to see that justice was served in his case. Just then, a bailiff interrupted the newlyweds and led Dan away in handcuffs. The honeymoon was over.

44

Three weeks had passed since Dan's sentencing, and Suzan Brown thought she was losing her mind. She had left the motel in Glendale and had moved to a run-down rented house in the city of Ontario, east of Los Angeles. She had read and reread articles about the verdict and sentencing and knew only that something had gone terribly wrong. The police had no guns, and still they convicted Dan for something she was convinced he didn't do.

Suzan had hidden herself away in her newly rented house agonizing over her next move. At times she gave in to her body's intense cravings for speed and for several days at a time she would exist in a hazy surrealistic world that bordered on drug overdose. Almost immediately she befriended a host of drug users, many of whom hung out in her depressed neighborhood. They soon began using Suzan's two-bedroom flat-roofed house as a crash pad. Now, rumpled clothing littered the floors and dirty dishes began piling up throughout the scantily furnished rooms. A week earlier Suzan had run into a former lover, a tank-shaped woman who promptly moved in with her. The lovers got a mixed-breed dog named Joanie and several mangy cats, all of which slept and ate in the house, giving it an odor some people said they could smell from the road.

Still, with all the people and animals around her to occupy her mind, Suzan often found herself sitting in her wheelchair, staring straight ahead at the stained walls of her house. She thought about Vietnam and realized she would rather be in the middle of a war than haunted by guilt. She would have been surprised if she'd slept a total of eight hours in the past three weeks.

Finally she could no longer stand it. Dan didn't kill Carol. Not for financial gain, or because he was angry with her, or for any other reason. Suzan knew that her sanity would not return until she told someone what had really happened that night.

She wheeled her chair to the refrigerator, opened it, and grabbed a shoe box from the second shelf. Sifting through loose change, used toothpicks, and crumpled pieces of paper, Suzan found what she was looking for —the phone number for Chuck Lefler and Gene Brisco. She stood up quickly, reached for the telephone, and began dialing. She had one digit left to dial when she suddenly hung up.

At that moment it occurred to her that she did not need to tell anyone the truth. What she needed was speed. Lots of it. Yes, speed would make everything okay. She hurried out the door and walked across the street to the check-cashing establishment on the corner.

With more than two hundred dollars in hand, she set out for the dealer's home, just two streets away. She walked up to the house and rang the doorbell. Someone new answered the door, but in San Bernardino County, everyone was new to Suzan. She handed over her money and asked for enough heroin-tainted speed to get her through the weekend. The man who had answered the door suddenly flipped out a police badge and snapped handcuffs on her wrists.

If Suzan thought the guilt was bad in her apartment, it was unbearable in San Bernardino County Jail. She constantly had to fight to keep the image of Dan in prison out of her mind. After two nights, she reached into her shorts pocket and pulled out the business card with the number for the investigators. After receiving permission to make a phone call, she began dialing. This time she did not hang up.

Gene and Chuck were in their office going over the details of various cases. Since learning about Dan's sentencing, a depression had fallen over the office. An innocent man had gone to prison, and with Dan's conviction, the court was no longer willing to finance an investigation into his innocence. For that reason, Chuck had decided to put the case behind him. Gene, however, constantly found himself thinking of new angles and by then had decided to continue working the case on his own time.

The detectives were in their office discussing a current investigation when the telephone rang.

"Give me Gene," the caller said gruffly. Chuck thought the voice sounded faintly familiar as he handed the phone to his partner.

"Hello?"

"Hey. It's Suzan Brown," she barked, and Gene immediately snapped to attention. "Need to talk with you a minute."

"I'm listening."

"About Carol"—Suzan coughed loudly into the phone—"well, you know. Gotta tell you Dan didn't do it. Dan didn't kill her."

"I know that, Suzan," Gene said, his Texas drawl slow and confident. "You ready to tell us who did?"

Suzan paused and for a moment it seemed as if the walls of the jail were closing in on her. "Yeah. Guess so."

"Where are you?" Gene needed to find out. They were on the verge of a breakthrough.

"County jail. San Bernardino. They caught me in a drug buy."

Gene wrote the address down on a piece of paper. "I'll meet you there tomorrow."

The next day, Gene, Chuck, and attorney Lorn Aiken arrived at the county jail in San Bernardino at 9 A.M. In light of Suzan's request to meet, Chuck and Lorn had immediately regained interest in the case. Suzan Brown had already been ushered into a conference room where the men joined her.

"See, I know Dan didn't do it," Suzan began, staring vacantly in front of her and speaking in a monotone. "I've got a conscience, and I'm tired of living with it."

Gene had been appointed to carry on the conversation with Suzan since he was the one she felt comfortable with. "Tell us about it, Suzan," he said.

"It wasn't planned out or nothing. Just a last-minute kind of deal. Me and the guys was sitting around the house, you know?"

Gene nodded. "We're listening."

"Well, we'd been doing a little speed, you know. Speed balls, that kind of thing. And, well, we ran out of drugs. No one had any money for more, you know."

Suzan took a deep breath and began coughing. The men waited patiently in silence.

"Well, what happened was I thought Carol and Dan had left for their vacation the day before. So we decided to raid their house and get a TV or something. Something we could sell and get some drugs with."

Gene realized that if this story were true, Suzan's entire testimony had been a lie. He said nothing, though, and Suzan continued. "Well, you know, we didn't want no attention or nothing like that. So me and one of the guys stayed out fronta my house arguing, like, you know. Trying to make a distraction for them. 'Bout the same time, the other two was sneaking into Carol and Dan's house."

Gene remembered that one of the neighbors had testified about hearing loud arguing just before the shots were fired. "You weren't in their house?" Gene didn't believe her.

"Nah. Never went inside," she snapped. "Anyways, next thing I know I sees Carol and Dan walk around the corner towards home. That's when I figured out that they was only on a walk and hadn't gone to Hawaii yet. Well, you know, me and the other guy who was arguing, we went back inside my house."

Suzan coughed again. "We went into my den and that's when we heard the gunshots. Two gunshots. And I turned to the guy with me and said, 'We're in damned trouble now.' That was about the time we heard this strange, muffled sound. Found out later it was the third gunshot."

Gene leaned forward. "Then what?"

"Well, you know, we were just waiting there to see what would happen and one of the other two guys came back to the house. He said, 'Damn. I got blood on my hands.' Then I think he went out back into the garage to wash his hands."

"Did you ask him what happened?"

Suzan nodded slowly. "Yeah, sure did. He told me Carol surprised him in the hallway and he shot her. You know, he told me it was an accident."

A strange laugh escaped from deep inside her throat. "Course, it wasn't no accident. You know, I sold him the gun just a few months before. A thirty-eight caliber."

"We need his name, Suzan," Gene said quietly.

"Okay. Ron Hardy. He never seemed to get in too much trouble before. Saw a different side of him that night, though." Next, Suzan told them about a second man who had been in the house and shot Dan with a .25.

For a few moments there was only silence as Chuck, Gene, and Lorn Aiken tried to digest this new version of what had happened to Carol Montecalvo. Gene broke the silence. "Why didn't you say anything before this?"

Suzan had prepared an answer for that question. " 'Fraid he'd kill me, too." She shrugged. "That's what Ron told me. Said if any of us talked to the police he'd take care of us."

"What about the other gun? The one Dan was shot with."

"Belonged to a friend of mine. Had it at the house."

"What happened to the guns?"

"Sold 'em. Right away. Sold 'em to Cathy, frienda mine."

Gene scribbled the name on a pad of paper. "The biggest question is, why tell us the truth now?" Gene knew there was no reason for her to come forward since Dan had already been convicted and sentenced. If Suzan's story was true, the men involved could have gotten away with murder.

Suzan sighed and stared blankly into space. After a few moments she hung her head and lit a cigarette. "I've been running for two years now. Left my house, stayed in the hospital. Moved from one apartment to the next, every few months. Even tried to kill myself. All that running gets a little tiring after a while." She waved an arm at Gene and Chuck. "And you guys wouldn't leave me alone."

"That's why you're talking?" Gene sounded doubtful.

"See, I know Dan didn't do it. And well, you know, the fact that an innocent man was convicted of something he didn't do is totally outrageous to me. My conscience couldn't take it anymore."

Gene waited. "Is that your story, then?"

Suzan raised her head up and took another drag from her cigarette. "I'm telling you guys what happened. I don't think too many people in their right mind would sit here and tell you guys that they were involved in a murder." Suzan paused and Chuck raised an eyebrow in Gene's direction. The partners were well aware that the woman they thought capable of murder was indeed mentally disturbed. It was a factor that would seriously hurt the credibility of her confession.

Suzan continued. "No reason to tell you now. Not after someone else has already taken the fall for it. We coulda gotten off scot-free."

Gene kept silent and after a few moments she continued. "Maybe I ought to get my head examined. But I guess it's better to tell you what happened and get this thing behind me."

For another two hours, Suzan rehashed this version of what she believed had happened to Carol Montecalvo. The story was both riveting and believable, even if it was being told by a mentally ill drug addict. There were parts where the detectives felt Suzan wasn't being completely honest. For instance, Gene's uncanny hunches told him that Suzan was probably inside the

Montecalvo house that night. But for the most part her story was the solution to their investigation.

They returned to the office just after one o'clock that afternoon and immediately Lorn Aiken put in telephone calls to the district attorney's office and the Burbank Police. The message was the same at both places. "We have information that will prove Dan Montecalvo did not kill his wife."

For the next several days, Chuck, Gene, and Lorn waited for Ben Bernard and Brian Arnspiger to contact them. They were concerned not only that Suzan might forget her story or change it, but also that she was about to be released from jail. She would then be free to go where she wished. They needed to tell the story to the authorities before that happened.

On the afternoon of Suzan's release from county jail, they still hadn't heard from Bernard or Arnspiger. Lorn Aiken convinced Chuck and Gene that it was time to demand the authorities' attention. He knew of one surefire way: to go public with the story.

Lorn picked up the telephone and dialed the *Los Angeles Times*. In five minutes he had set up an interview for that evening. At 5 P.M. Lorn and the private investigators would meet the *Times* reporter and photographer in Lorn Aiken's Los Angeles office.

The next morning, the story and a large photograph of Suzan Brown made the front page of the paper's Metro section along with this headline: "Tardy Confession: Woman Says Convicted Man Didn't Kill His Wife."

45

Prosecutor Ben Bernard had spoken with Lorn Aiken and knew what to expect when he opened the newspaper and saw Suzan Brown's story. What he didn't expect was the reaction the story would have on the public, and, in particular, on one of the jurors in the Montecalvo case.

Juror Martha Faylor, a retired Pasadena woman whose guilty verdict had been among those that convicted Dan, read the article in the *Los Angeles Times* with great interest. Since the trial, Martha had decided that perhaps she had made a mistake. She kept thinking back to the final day of deliberation and how several jurors had berated her for taking too long to decide Dan's guilt. One of them had even told her that if they didn't reach an agreement the judge would keep them locked up until after Christmas. Martha didn't actually believe that, but she was confused by the threat and felt pressured to agree with the others.

When Martha finally decided to cast a guilty vote against the defendant, her decision had little to do with the evidence presented. Instead, it was because of Maree Flores. When Maree had testified that she and Dan were in love, the thought occurred to Martha that if Dan wasn't put away, sweet Maree might be his next victim. Martha couldn't let that happen. So on the chance that Dan was responsible for Carol's murder, she agreed to hand down a guilty verdict. Anything to save Maree from such a terrible fate.

Not until after she was back home and following her regular routine did Martha realize that her decision was not very sound. After all, the defense had raised a good point. What had happened to the three footprints lifted from the Montecalvo kitchen floor? She had seen the document showing that they had been admitted as evidence after the murder. Yet none of the police or sheriff's personnel remembered having seen them or having collected them. Still, not until she read the article in the *Times* about Suzan Brown's confession was she absolutely certain of her mistake. Before wasting another moment, Martha sat down at her kitchen table, pulled out a piece of stationery, and began to write.

I, Martha Faylor, served as a juror in the Montecalvo trial during October and November, 1990, in the Superior Court in Pasadena, California. After thoughtfully considering the evidence presented in the court proceedings and after lengthy discussion with other members of the jury, it was—and continues to be—my opinion that the prosecution failed to convince me beyond a shadow of a doubt that Mr. Montecalvo is guilty as charged of the murder of his wife. I argued for acquittal for several days but failed to convince the other jurors of my opinion.

In the course of deliberations, the jury foreman and the other jurors became abusive and insisted that the judge would not tolerate a hung jury and would keep us there until Christmas if I refused to go along with the majority. Having had no previous experience with jury duty, I believed them and agreed, under duress, to vote with the other jury members. My position for acquittal was, and is, based on my belief that Mr. Montecalvo was treated unfairly by the court to the extent that I believe his constitutional rights were violated. The evidence presented was circumstantial and incomplete. Further I had the feeling that much important information was withheld and critical evidence seemed to have mysteriously disappeared. Sincerely, Martha Faylor.

Martha did not mention the fact that she had seen the newspaper article regarding Suzan Brown's confession. After all, she knew that her change of heart had arisen from her own doubts. The article had simply encouraged her to take action. She addressed the letter to Prosecutor Ben Bernard and once she had dropped the letter in the mail, Martha felt much better. She did not know what might be accomplished by writing such a letter, but she did not know how else to tell the authorities how she really felt about the case.

If Ben Bernard thought the Montecalvo case had taken a strange twist in light of Suzan Brown's confession, he was completely baffled after receiving Martha Faylor's letter. There was nothing he could do. Later in the week, when Martha contacted him, he told her as much.

"You were advised of the rules ahead of time and you made that decision," Ben Bernard explained to the angry and frustrated woman. "The system does not allow jurors to change their minds."

Not long after that discussion, Ben telephoned Brian Arnspiger. The two had shared several conversations since learning about Suzan Brown's story. In general, they agreed that Dan was still as guilty as he had been the night of Carol's murder. They also agreed that Suzan had confessed in order to gain publicity. In private moments, they both suspected the woman was not dealing with a full deck.

In addition, Ben Bernard and Brian Arnspiger believed that despite the local and national attention the story was getting since its latest development, the publicity would eventually die down and Dan would remain in prison. If one of the men might possibly have felt stronger about Dan's guilt, it was Brian Arnspiger. He would have bet his house that Dan had killed his wife. He had not spent more than a year investigating that murder only to have some lunatic off the street walk in and confess to details provided by the press.

While Bernard agreed with this assessment, there were still nights when he would lie awake wondering whether—by some monumental, terrible quirk of fate— Dan might actually have been innocent. But whenever those feelings would overcome him, he would mull over the basic evidence against Dan and in moments he would be sleeping like a baby.

In the following days and weeks Suzan Brown's confession did not easily disappear from public attention. Reporters found irresistible the story of a potentially innocent man sitting in prison while a crazy killer walked the streets. It ran in all the local newspapers and was picked up by the Associated Press wire service. A nationally televised news show did an entire segment on the story.

By then, of course, Ben Bernard had long since known what he must do to quiet the public uproar— and to pacify Martha Faylor. He called a meeting with two of the top investigators from the district attorney's office and explained the situation to them. Although the case had already been tried, a conviction decided upon, and a sentence handed down, he told them to spend as much time as necessary determining if there was any truth to Suzan Brown's confession.

"If Dan Montecalvo didn't do it, I will be the first one to ask that he go free," Bernard told a reporter from the *Los Angeles Times* as the investigation began. "But we have to have competent evidence that someone else did it. And (Suzan Brown) is an admitted perjurer."

When the reporter asked whether the investigators might be reluctant to pursue evidence that, if found, would place the district attorney's office in a bad light, Bernard flatly denied it. Of course, Dan would later complain that the district attorney's office could not possibly be unbiased during such an investigation. Dan's claim that he was being framed and treated unfairly went unheeded by Ben Bernard, if not by the press. By law, when a confession by another party is made after a conviction, the resulting investigation is always staged by the district attorney's office—the very office that would be most harmed if there was any truth to Suzan Brown's story.

46

Gene Brisco and Chuck Lefler kept busy in the weeks following Suzan Brown's confession doing the same undercover work that the district attorney's office was being paid to do. Like Dan they thought it unfair to have the district attorney's detectives investigating Suzan's confession. Therefore while the officials were checking Suzan's statements, Gene and Chuck spent several afternoons interviewing her. Gradually, she revealed many aspects of the case that she could not have known unless she had been inside the house. She knew what color the Montecalvo cash box was, she knew that eight hundred dollars had been taken from a white envelope, and she knew that several dollars in change had also been stolen. In addition, she knew the exact position of Carol's body after she was shot and the clothing she'd worn.

Next, the detectives checked with the newspaper morgues and reread every article written about the case. One month later, Gene and Chuck were satisfied that none of those details had ever been mentioned in the press. Finally, the men were convinced of two things. First, that Suzan Brown had not been telling the entire truth; and second, that she had definitely been involved in Carol's murder. They came to this conclusion after checking out the names of three men Suzan said were involved. Two of them, Gene and Chuck discovered, did not appear to have been anywhere near South Myers Street the night of Carol's murder. The third man—Ron Hardy—had no police record, but he had a reputation among his friends for being volatile.

According to their information, Ron Hardy had never been caught for what his friends said was a rash of home burglaries. Days after Carol's murder, Ron rented a one-room flat in Los Angeles. He promptly boarded the windows with plywood and began leading a very secluded life. Gene and Chuck wondered if the district attorney's office had found that information.

Then they did further research on Suzan Brown, who had by then admitted that the story of hearing people in her backyard was something she'd made up. They contacted her former roommates and asked if they thought she was capable of killing someone. Each thought she was.

"She's crazy," one woman told Gene. "She would do anything to save her own butt. If that meant killing someone, then so what. At least that's the Suzan I knew."

They also agreed that Suzan typically lied about nearly everything. She sometimes believed the lies herself. They thought that if Suzan had placed herself outside the murder scene, it was very likely a lie.

By the first week of 1991 Gene and Chuck had discovered what they thought to be several problems with Suzan's confession. They involved the number of people who had taken part in the crime and her location during the time of the murder. Gene and Chuck believed that only two people—including Suzan—had been involved and that Suzan herself had quite possibly shot Carol. That would explain Carol's last words, "What are you doing here?"

Another reason they thought that Suzan might have killed Carol was the way she was shot—once in the back of the neck and once on the right jawbone inches away from her spine. Medical examiners had been unable to determine which shot had been fired first. Gene and Chuck could picture Carol going into the house and walking down the hallway past the office before realizing someone was in her house. She would have looked over her shoulder and seen Suzan.

At that point, she would have said, "What are you doing here?" Carol did not know Suzan's friends, so it was reasonable to assume that she had said those words to Suzan. Suzan then would have pointed a gun at Carol just as Carol tried to turn away and escape into the kitchen. If that had been the scenario, the first bullet would have entered the jawbone and the second the back of the neck, and Carol would have died at the end of the hallway. Exactly where her body was found.

What concerned Chuck and Gene was that if the D.A.'s investigators caught Suzan lying about any details of the case, they might disregard her confession entirely. Finally, there was nothing they could do but wait for the official results.

The investigation came to a close January 14. The investigators notified Gene and Chuck of the results. In their opinion there was no truth whatsoever to Suzan's statements. They wanted to notify the press immediately.

Gene took a deep breath and tried to think quickly. Just as he had feared, the district attorney's investigators had discovered Suzan was lying about certain details so they had dismissed her confession entirely.

"Do me a favor first," Gene told the investigators. "Let's go to Suzan's house and you tell her your results in person."

Suzan was wearing a tank top and shorts when she let them into the run-down house. After they were seated, the investigators from the district attorney's office told her they thought her confession was a lie.

Suzan sighed and stared blankly out her apartment window. "Well, fine then," she said, looking up at them warily. "Wanna know what really happened?"

The prosecution investigators looked at each other and rolled their eyes. Gene and Chuck began taking notes. "Tell us," one of them said.

Suzan took a deep breath. "Those two guys, you know, the ones I said was with us?"

Suzan pulled a cigarette from her front shirt pocket and reached for a book of matches. After lighting it, she took a deep drag and continued. "Well, they wasn't with us. Not really. See, what happened was me and Ron was in the house when they came home and, well, you know, it wasn't me who did it to Carol."

Suzan looked defiantly at them. "Ron did it. He got scared and when Carol asked him what he was doing there he just shot her, you know."

Gene and Chuck exchanged a knowing glance. Since Carol's last words were not printed in the papers, how could she have known what was said? "You saw it happen?" Gene asked.

"You bet. Watched the whole thing."

"What happened next?"

"Well, you know, I was all scared and that's when Dan comes running in. So, I grabbed him and shot him."

At that point, one of the investigators interrupted.

"Why don't you stop right there, Suzan. I'm going to contact the office and see what they want us to do with this latest story."

Gene could hear the disgust in the investigator's voice and he had a bad feeling that the office would recommend that they stop wasting time and money on Suzan Brown.

"Enough is enough," Ben Bernard said when the investigators phoned him. "The woman has been lying since she took the stand for the defense. First we hear about the fallen woodpile and the cockamamy Reebok footprint. Then she tells us that's all a bunch of lies. Truth is Dan's an innocent man and she and three of her buddies are responsible for Carol's murder. Now that's a lie, too."

Bernard was unusually angry. In his opinion Suzan must have obtained privileged information from one of the police reports, all of which Chuck and Gene had copies of. By this time, he was tired of Suzan's lies.

"Listen. It took the jury seven weeks to reach a conviction. Now some crazy lady has us running circles trying to check out one lie after another. We have to draw the line somewhere. Call a press conference for tomorrow morning. Let's tell them the results."

On the morning of January 16 Ben Bernard walked into his office and found the front lobby littered with reporters excited about learning the results of the investigation. Ben Bernard felt confident about the findings. His detectives were very talented. If there had been any truth to Suzan Brown's story, they would have uncovered it. They had worked on the case for a month and even found a .25 caliber handgun Suzan said was used to shoot Dan. But test firing proved it had not been the gun, after all. Ben had taken the information and condensed it into an eight-page memorandum for his supervisor and the press. Ben looked at the reporters who awaited his statement. He cleared his throat.

"Thank you for coming here today. As you know, we are prepared to tell you the results of our lengthy investigation into the confession made last month by Suzan Brown. After carefully checking into each of Ms. Brown's statements, we have determined that she and her friends are not responsible for the murder of Carol Montecalvo. Whether she believes her statements or not is a question for psychiatrists, not prosecutors."

Ben watched as the reporters began scribbling notes furiously. He continued, reading from the report his investigators had given him.

"In summary, our investigation shows that a weapon Ms. Brown said was used in the commission of the Montecalvo murder was eliminated as a crime weapon after the gun was found and ballistics comparisons were done by the Los Angeles County Sheriff's Department ballistics experts. Also, our investigation shows that the persons Ms. Brown said burglarized the Montecalvo house that night, including the man she claimed shot and killed Carol Montecalvo, cooperated fully and voluntarily gave fingerprints when contacted by our investigators. The fingerprints were compared to unidentified latent prints found in the Montecalvo house. The fingerprints of the two men Ms. Brown claimed were in the house did not match."

Ben paused a moment, letting that detail sink in. "Our investigation also shows that all persons interviewed who have known Ms. Brown for a number of years have characterized her as a pathological liar, an ex-convict, and a former mental patient who will do anything for money. Also, the only person who has changed her story about the Montecalvo murder is Ms. Brown. So far she has related at least three separate versions of the events and now she states that most of those versions are untrue."

Ben continued, giving the reporters as many details as he could to convince them that his office had, indeed, been thorough. He also read them the statements that Suzan's former acquaintances had given about her.

The man whose home she was renting at the time of Carol's murder said this about her: "She's a very unstable person . . . there's nothing that comes out of her mouth that's fact."

Others called her a con-artist with no conscience. One woman Suzan had befriended in prison said that Suzan would drift off on tangents about her childhood. Many times those stories would include this new woman, when in fact she had only just met Suzan in prison. According to Bernard's official report a different former roommate said that she thought Suzan had a split personality. According to her, Suzan once beat her, telling her she was legally crazy and threatening that she could kill her and get away with it if she wanted to. Ben told the reporters this information even though it seemed to support Suzan's involvement in Carol's murder. He did not want to be accused of hiding details.

After several minutes, Ben finally concluded his report. "Based on the evidence and information we have gathered in an attempt to check out Ms. Brown's story, we find nothing in her statements that would lead us to believe they are anything other than a continuing series of lies."

Dan did not find out the results of the investigation until later that afternoon. Sometime after 3 P.M., he dialed Gene Brisco's number. Although he had often accused both the district attorney's office and the Burbank Police Department of being dishonest, Dan felt certain that Suzan Brown's confession would mean the end of his prison term.

Since his incarceration, he had told anyone who would listen that several members of the Burbank Police Department and the district attorney's office would owe him a big apology once they checked out Suzan Brown's story and found out he really was innocent after all. He even went as far as to suggest that various police personnel and the prosecutor might someday wind up in prison for manufacturing the case against him.

Gene answered the phone on the first ring.

"Tell me, Gene, what's the results?" Dan asked, unable to contain his excitement.

Gene sighed. "Dan, it didn't go the way we hoped."

For a moment, neither man said anything. When Dan broke the silence, his voice was barely audible.

"Gene, tell me you're kidding. Talk to me, Gene."

"It's no joke. They checked her out and decided she was a mentally ill liar. Nothing more. I'm sorry, Dan."

Gene could feel Dan's anger and disappointment. For several moments there was only silence and then Gene could hear Dan quietly crying. "Nobody will believe me, Gene," Dan said, his voice cracking as he tried to talk over the tears that were choking him. "I didn't kill her. I didn't do it, Gene. Why won't anybody believe me?"

"I believe you, Dan. Chuck and Lorn believe you. We're not giving up."

"But I'm still sitting here for something I didn't do. I was framed." Dan was shouting now. "I could never have killed Carol. Never."

Gene waited quietly until Dan stopped crying. He knew that in some ways the case was closed. Unless new grounds and evidence were discovered, Gene doubted that Dan would be granted an appeal. But Gene still had one glimmer of hope based on something no one but him knew about. If his suspicions were right, one day the authorities would have to issue a warrant for Suzan's arrest. When they did, it would not be for one count of murder.

It would be for two.

47

Throughout 1991 Gene Brisco kept his promise both to Dan and to himself. He continued to pursue the notion that Suzan Brown had actually held the gun that killed Carol. He also pursued a hunch about something else. By the fall of that year, Gene was convinced that Suzan Brown had not only killed Carol Montecalvo, but that she had also killed Sheriff's Deputy Charles Anderson. The off-duty deputy had been killed when he interrupted burglars in his home on January 24, 1987—a little more than a year before Carol's murder. Anderson lived just three blocks from the Montecalvo home. The murder remained unsolved through 1991.

From the beginning Gene believed the key to determining the truth was in spending time with Suzan Brown. By then she trusted Gene and never refused his requests to meet with him. Gene did not understand why Suzan allowed him to keep asking her questions. But then he did not pretend to understand the workings of Suzan's mind.

"Suzan, what do you know about the Anderson murder?" Gene asked her one afternoon.

Suzan's eyes grew perfectly round and Gene wondered if she was going to strike him. Instead she reached for a cigarette. After she had smoked it halfway to the filter, she suddenly put it out and stared at him.

"Nothing," she barked.

Gene changed the subject.

The next time, he approached the topic more subtly.

"I've come to a conclusion, Suzan," Gene said casually.

"Yeah, and what's that?" Suzan was flipping through a magazine, paying little attention to the detective.

"You didn't have anything to do with Carol's murder," he said, taunting her. "I bet you don't know a thing about it. Probably read it in the newspaper."

Suzan looked up from the magazine angrily. As she did, Gene was certain his plan was working.

"What's that supposed to mean?" she snapped.

"Just what I said. You lied about the whole thing."

Suzan's eyes narrowed; Gene had never seen her so angry. "Don't go telling me what I did and didn't do."

Gene shrugged, daring her to become even angrier. "Doesn't really matter what you say. You lie about everything. Anyway, it's just my personal conclusion."

Suzan's face grew several shades darker. "Listen, buddy. I was there, saw the whole thing."

"Lies." Gene said, pushing her.

"No!" she shouted. "The truth. I was there."

"Sure. The next thing I know, you're going to tell me you had a part in the Anderson murder, too."

Suzan exhaled slowly through her clenched teeth. Her brown eyes were blazing. "As a matter of fact, I know what happened to Anderson." She stopped for a moment, perhaps fearing she might have said too much. Then she shrugged, as if it were too late to turn back now. "I was there. Saw that one, too."

"Right."

"Listen here." Suzan spat out the words. "One of the

guys lost a jacket at the Anderson murder. A green jacket."

For a brief instant, the surprise must have shown in Gene's face because Suzan began to laugh. Then she stopped suddenly and pointed at Gene.

"Don't ever call me a liar again!"

Gene had taken the information and reviewed the police reports on the Anderson homicide. According to the initial investigation, an article of clothing had been recovered near the fence in the Andersons' backyard. It was described as a forest green windbreaker.

There were other details about the Anderson murder that emerged in his subsequent conversations with Suzan Brown. She knew about items taken from the home, the point of entry to the house, and the position and location of Anderson's body. None of the information had ever been mentioned in newspaper articles. Again, Gene could think of no way Suzan might have obtained the police reports.

Finally, by November, Gene was convinced that Suzan was responsible for both murders. This did not surprise him—what amazed him was that none of the agencies he took the information to seemed to show any interest in his findings. Burbank police laughed at the idea that Suzan Brown was responsible for Charles Anderson's murder. Brian was assigned to the case, and although it had been unsolved for nearly five years, he was still trying to crack it.

That fall, when a reporter asked Brian how the investigation into Anderson's murder was going, he said, "Fantastic." Although he told her he could not provide specifics, he said the department had new leads and might even be ready to make an arrest within the next year. He also flatly denied that Suzan Brown was the person or one of the persons being investigated.

Prosecutor Ben Bernard's comment was more to the point. "Those people don't ever give up, do they?" he told the reporter after learning that Gene Brisco believed Suzan Brown might be responsible for the Anderson murder also.

When Gene realized the wall of doubt he was up against, he began putting every bit of evidence in writing. Finally, by the end of November, he had constructed a case similar to the ones he had once put together while working as a detective for the sheriff's department. But there was a difference—this case was stronger than any he had ever prepared. He thought his information proved beyond a reasonable doubt that Suzan Brown was responsible for two murders.

On the morning of December 2 Gene Brisco took his findings to Los Angeles County Sheriff Sherman Block's office. The sheriff's department is responsible for crimes committed in unincorporated areas of Los Angeles County. Under normal circumstances, the Burbank Police Department would have been solely responsible for the Anderson murder, which took place inside Burbank city limits. However, because Anderson had been a sheriff's deputy, both departments had been involved in the investigation. Because Burbank police had originally thought Carol's murder resembled that of Anderson's, the sheriff's department had also been involved in the early stages of her murder case.

Block's assistants had promised they would give Gene's findings a fair look and if they were convinced, they would issue an arrest warrant for Suzan Brown. Gene could then relax. The case would no longer be in his hands. If the sheriff's department believed Suzan was responsible, they would take care of the matter and finally Dan would be released.

By early April 1992, the sheriff's department had determined that the case no longer belonged in their jurisdiction despite the fact that Anderson had been one of their men. At that time the department sent Gene's entire case to the Burbank police for further analysis. When Dan heard about this latest development, he had to agree with Gene that there was no longer any realistic chance of his receiving either a new trial or an early release from prison. "At this point I no longer know what else I can do," Gene said after hearing that Burbank police were now in charge of the case. "Burbank could have it for years, forever. It's not that I'm doing this for the attention or for any kind of financial gain," Gene told a reporter that week. "I don't really know why I'm so committed to this thing. But I've spent too long trying to catch bad guys. People like Suzan Brown, out there walking the streets. Meanwhile, an innocent guy sits in prison. I can't let something like that happen."

The reporter asked him what would happen if Suzan was arrested and Dan released from prison.

"I might just stand outside on my front lawn and scream at the top of my voice, 'Justice was served,'" Gene said.

Lorn Aiken was also interviewed. "I've said it before. I'll say it again," he said. "Dan's the first and only innocent man I've ever represented. Every day while he sits in prison I think about him and how the system failed him. It's insane to think of a lunatic woman running loose while an innocent man wastes away in prison."

* * *

By that time Dan actually *had* begun to waste away in prison. He had been moved that spring from the prison in Chino to the high-security facility in Vacaville because doctors at Chino had determined that he was suffering from depression and anxiety.

In Vacaville, an ominous northern California facility that housed some of the most desperate criminals in the state, doctors agreed that Dan's depression had grown even worse. They prescribed Valium so Dan could sleep at night and numerous medications to control his stomach ulcers and high blood pressure. Finally, prison doctors decided Dan could not take the stress of living in Vacaville so they sent him to the California Men's Colony in San Luis Obispo.

Among California criminals, there is no place more preferred than the California Men's Colony. The prison is sprawled at the base of the scenic Coastal Mountains just a few miles from the Pacific Ocean. It lies north of the Cuesta Grade and adjacent to the Seven Sisters, an area landmark made up of a seven-point mountain range.

But for the barbed wire and occasional watch tower, the prison might have been a resort. Inmates at the colony often remarked that the prison was cleaner than most hospitals they'd seen. The buildings almost always had a fresh coat of soft beige paint and the grounds were kept neatly mowed. No trash or graffiti marred the facility.

Still, cleanliness was not why the colony was preferred among prisoners. The inmates felt that they received better treatment here. California Men's Colony employees were generally happier and nicer than at any other prison in the state's system, perhaps because the facility was considered the country club of state prisons. One prison spokesman liked to tell visitors that the place was so well known for its shining example that it received nearly as many visitors as Disneyland and Universal Studios.

"This prison is absolutely nothing like the places you see in the movies," he would tell people. "The warden has had a standing bet that if any one of us ever finds any graffiti anywhere dinner's on him."

So far, the spokesman said, the warden has never had to buy dinner.

Dan Montecalvo experienced far less anxiety once he was moved to this prison in late August 1991. But even in this relatively calm setting, he continued to complain day and night about being framed by Burbank police and the district attorney's office for something he could never have done.

Finally, on September 25, Dan was eating his lunch when he felt a sharp pain in the left side of his body. The guards heard him cry out and quickly took him to the infirmary, where doctors confirmed that he was suffering a major heart attack.

"You're lucky to be alive," the doctor told Dan later that afternoon when Dan was resting in one of the infirmary beds. "You won't be so lucky next time."

The heart attack had taken its toll, deadening much of the organ's vital tissue and leaving Dan with a heart operating on just 42 percent of its original capacity. Doctors placed Dan on complete disability.

So while Gene worked to form the case against Suzan Brown that he would eventually take to the officials at the sheriff's department, Dan sat day after day in his prison cell. Dan's cell, which he shared with another man, was eight feet by ten feet and had no windows.

After his heart attack, Dan received most of his meals in this cell and was excused from participating in work duty and free time. Instead, he would sit on his cot all day long going over his case.

His constant companion was a black notebook which contained nearly 200 pages of documents used in his trial or obtained from police reports at the murder scene. After a year of studying those documents several hours a day, Dan had come to some conclusions. First, he had identified what he considered to be 235 lies that had taken place in the trial. Eighty of those, Dan determined, were either mistakes or what Dan claimed were blatant falsehoods made by Ben Bernard. For the most part, these came in the form of questions which Dan believed Bernard never should have been allowed to ask.

For instance, Ben Bernard might have begun a question to a certain witness like this: "Now, because you could never get an identifiable palm print from Dan Montecalvo . . ."

Dan would flip through his black notebook to the photocopy of a page of court transcripts that showed this question. Then he would flip to a document in which one of the evidence technicians had listed the prints found in the house and to whom they belonged. On this official document, one palm print found on the front door was clearly identified as Dan Montecalvo's. Therefore, that question became one of what Dan considered to be eighty falsehoods the prosecutor had concocted during the seven-week trial.

Bernard denied ever intentionally misleading his witnesses. If anything, he said, such a question might have been just a misunderstanding on his part.

"Don't you see," Dan would lament to whoever

would listen to him. "They framed me. Clear and simple."

Then Dan would cite precedent cases about the role of a prosecutor in criminal cases. For instance, in *Imbler* v. *Pachtman* (1976), it was decided that a prosecutor has a special obligation to assure that the rights of citizens, including the rights of criminal defendants, are afforded protection. He also cited *Berger* v. *U.S.* (1935), in which it was determined that a prosecutor's goal must not be to win a case but to make sure justice is done.

"According to those cases, (Bernard) broke the law," Dan would say.

When Ben Bernard—who by December had been promoted three times since the Montecalvo case—got wind of Dan's accusations, he chuckled softly.

"Dan thinks the way things are worded is all part of some elaborate plan to put him away for something he didn't do," he said gently. "Why in the world would we all be joining forces against someone like Dan Montecalvo?"

For that question, Dan had no answers.

"Right now he's the hero of this whole thing," Dan said of the prosecutor, his voice filled with bitterness. "But one day the truth will come out. And then I'd like to see him put away for the rest of his life. He should go to prison for the lies he's told about me."

When Dan wasn't complaining about Ben Bernard and the injustice done him, he spent his time thinking about Carol.

"The reason I married Maree is that she and I both love Carol," Dan said. "When she visits me, we talk about Carol. She understands and because of that, I love her very much."

Dan also admits to another, more practical reason for marrying Maree Flores. In case he dies in prison, Maree would legally be able to continue the fight to clear her husband's name.

"I don't want money, and I don't want a dismissal on some kind of technicality," Dan said quietly during a December interview in prison. "I want my name cleared. I want my marriage cleared.

"Carol must be in heaven somewhere shaking her head at what's happening down here. I loved that woman," he said. "She was the closest thing to God I've ever known. I could never, ever harm her. Don't you see? Doesn't anybody understand that? I didn't kill my wife. No matter what anyone says, I didn't kill her."

At that point, tears began to form in the eyes of the man who once called himself a chronic liar, the man who credited Carol Montecalvo with changing him and giving him a new lease on life, the man who authorities agree will most likely remain in prison until his twenty-seven-year term is up.

"I promised to love her as long as we both shall live. Well, I'm still alive and I still love her. I will always love her. Is anyone listening? I will always, always love her."